The Literary Symbol

The Literary Symbol

By WILLIAM YORK TINDALL

INDIANA UNIVERSITY PRESS · BLOOMINGTON

FOURTH PRINTING 1965

COPYRIGHT 1955 BY COLUMBIA UNIVERSITY PRESS

MANUFACTURED IN THE UNITED STATES OF AMERICA

LIBRARY OF CONGRESS CATALOG CARD NUMBER: 58-6957

Preface

*T*HIS DISCOURSE on what is not altogether beyond it begins with an approach to definition and proceeds with history. Analysis of parts, such as image, action, and structure, occupies the center and contemplation of form the end. Examples, following my interest, are commonly from our time. Since it is not my purpose to survey symbolic parts and wholes but to illustrate them, any adequate examples will do. Joyce and Yeats are more abundantly represented than others because they were handier. That some no less exemplary writers do not appear may be imputed by malice or charity to ignorance or taste; but the true reason of that, falling somewhere betwixt and between, is that I lacked time for making friends with some acquaintances, Goethe, for example, and Rilke, whose absence would trouble me were I out surveying.

Parts of this monograph have been presented before. During the Conference on the Novel at the University of Rochester under the direction of Kathrine Koller (February, 1951), I offered an early and briefer version of my chapter on the symbolist novel, of which a still briefer version appeared as an article in the magazine *A.D.* (Winter, 1952). My first chapter and parts of others composed a paper for the Symbolism Seminar of The Institute for Religious and Social Studies, held at The Jewish Theological Seminary of America, 1954; somewhat revised, this paper was offered at the fourteenth Conference on Science, Philosophy and Religion at Harvard University, 1954, and is published in *Symbols and Society* (Harper & Brothers, 1955). The present version has been expanded in places and contracted in others. A part of my sixth chapter appeared as "Dante and Mrs. Bloom" in *Accent* (Spring, 1951); and part of the second chapter appeared as "James Joyce and the Hermetic Tradition" in *Journal of the History of Ideas* (January, 1954). I thank the editors of these periodicals and the directors of these conferences for permission to use this material.

My ideas of the symbol were formed or improved not only in the Symbolism Seminar at The Jewish Theological Seminary, where Lyman Bryson, Kenneth Burke, Jessica Feingold, Louis Finkelstein, Albert Hofstadter, John LaFarge, S.J., R. M. MacIver, Margaret Mead, Ernest Nagel, I. I. Rabi, and others confronted puzzling things on Thursdays, but, before that, in my own seminar at Columbia, where I conducted my education in public for several years. To all members of this society, which pursued (and almost caught) the symbol, but to these in particular, I owe a debt: Leonard Albert, Chester Anderson, Avel Austin, Charles Burgess, Joseph Duncan, Saul Galin, Pierre Guiet, Sam Hynes, Hyman Kleinman, Allen Mandelbaum, Theodore Mischel, Barbara Seward, John Senior, Morton Seiden, Norman Silverstein, Grover Smith, Sol Stein, Philip Stern, Jean Sudrann, John Treacy, and John Unterecker. Susanne Langer, who attended this seminar twice, raised instructive questions. I am no less indebted for idea, fact, correction, or other aid to Dino Bigongiari, William Bridgwater, Christopher Herold, Saint Kevin of Glendalough, Joseph Mazzeo, F. L. Overcarsh, Daniel Weiss, Henry H. Wiggins, and all the explicators of my class in Contemporary Texts at Columbia.

I am grateful to Henry Allen Moe, the Trustees, and the Committee of the John Simon Guggenheim Memorial Foundation for the award of a fellowship which enabled me to complete this thing in peace or something like it; and I am grateful to my sponsors.

Passages from Virginia Woolf's *To the Lighthouse, Mrs. Dalloway,* and *Night and Day,* E. M. Forster's *Aspects of the Novel,* T. E. Hulme's *Speculations,* and T. S. Eliot's *Collected Poems* are quoted by permission of Harcourt, Brace and Company, Inc.; a passage from T. S. Eliot's "Ode" is quoted by permission of *The Harvard Advocate;* passages from *Collected Poems* by Wallace Stevens are quoted by permission of Alfred A. Knopf, Inc., passages from the *Essays* (copyright 1918) and the *Collected Poems* (copyright 1950) of W. B. Yeats are quoted by permission of The Macmillan Company; passages from the *Collected Poems* of Dylan Thomas, *Stephen Hero* by James Joyce, and Ezra Pound's *Selected Poems* are quoted by permission of New Directions; passages from Marcel Proust's *Remembrance of Things Past,* James Joyce's *Ulysses,* and William Faulkner's *Absalom, Absalom!* are quoted by permission of Mr. Saxe Commins and Random House, Inc.; a passage from *The Great Gatsby* by F. Scott Fitzgerald is quoted by permission of Charles Scribner's Sons; passages from James Joyce's *Portrait of the Artist* and Henry Green's *Party Going* are quoted by permission of Mr. B. W. Huebsch and The Viking Press, Inc. I heartily thank all these for their courtesy. By arrangement with J. M. Dent & Sons, Ltd. of London I quote an excerpt from Jean-Aubry's *Joseph Conrad, Life and Letters* and Joseph Conrad's *Secret Agent.*

W.Y.T.

Columbia University
January 6, 1955

Contents

The Literary Symbol

Excellent Dumb Discourse

*T*HAT symbols present thought and feeling while celebrating or constructing suitable worlds, though plain to Moses and other authors before the time of Blake, has been plainer since then. Melville, Baudelaire, and Ibsen come readily to mind, but the twentieth century brought with it an even thicker crowd of romantic symbolists, including the greatest writers of our period. Not only Yeats and Joyce, Valéry and Proust, Wallace Stevens and Faulkner, Mann, Kafka, and Conrad—all writers of the first order—but even more popular, though no less important, writers such as F. Scott Fitzgerald and T. S. Eliot, making symbolic worlds of symbolic elements, have shaped our vision of reality.

Consider Dr. T. J. Eckleburg's eyes in *The Great Gatsby:*

About half way between West Egg and New York the motor road hastily joins the railroad and runs beside it for a quarter of a mile, so as to shrink away from a certain desolate area of land. This is a valley of ashes— a fantastic farm where ashes grow like wheat into ridges and hills and grotesque gardens, where ashes take the forms of houses. . . . But above the gray land and the spasms of bleak dust which drift endlessly over it, you perceive, after a moment, the eyes of Doctor T. J. Eckleburg. The eyes of Doctor T. J. Eckleburg are blue and gigantic—their retinas are one yard high. They look out of no face, but, instead, from a pair of enormous yellow spectacles which pass over a non-existent nose. Evidently some wild wag of an oculist set them there to fatten his practice in the borough of Queens, and then sank down himself into eternal blindness, or forgot them and moved away. But his eyes, dimmed a little by many paintless days, under sun and rain, brood on over the solemn dumping ground.

Fitzgerald's desolating image, which recurs throughout the novel, is what most would call a symbol. If this vision of eyes is a functioning part of a larger structure, as the single eye on a signboard near the end of Faulkner's *The Sound and the Fury* or the eyes of Beatrice in Eliot's "The Hollow Men" are obscurely portentous but essential constituents of that novel and this poem, it becomes apparent that symbols may serve as elements of a work. That the work itself may be as symbolic as its elements is not unlikely.

The Cocktail Party seems a symbol composed of symbols, not there to be explained but to play their part in a conspiracy. Peripheral suggestions of gin and water, of making dishes out of nothing, and of single eyes may limit or deepen the total effect and excite the critic, but the audience, taking them as they come, enjoys the experience to which they contribute. As if referring to members of this audience, Eliot's Thomas Becket says: "They know and do not know."

The masters of those who know tell us that symbol-making is our natural activity and our condition. Catching up with artists or trying to account for them, recent philosophers provide an assurance that the value we place on symbols is not misplaced. Whitehead regards symbolism, if I understand him correctly, as a mode of perception and a cause of error, but, although he talks about literature

4

at times, he is too general and indifferent to help us with the literary symbol. Cassirer, who seems more to the point, says man is a symbolic animal whose languages, myths, religions, sciences, and arts are symbolic forms by which he projects his reality and comes to know it: "What reality is apart from these forms is irrelevant."

As these philosophers assure us, all perception, all our fanatical pursuits, and all our arts may be symbolic in some fundamental sense at all times, but at certain times symbolism has become conscious and deliberate. It is with one of these periods that I am concerned and with one of the arts. Before approaching the literary symbol as it is used in our time, I must accost symbol and tell the difference between symbol and sign or at least fix their usage. Webster says that a symbol is "that which stands for or suggests something else by reason of relationship, association, convention or accidental but not intentional resemblance; especially, a visible sign of something invisible, as an idea, a quality or a totality such as a state or a church." Something that stands for or suggests something else is an attractive account of the word as we use it in the market place but too general and maybe too clear for the closet. I prefer "a visible sign of something invisible," although this would seem to exclude unwritten music or music as we hear it. Webster's echo of the catechism or the prayer book might be intensified and the definition made more inclusive by saying that a symbol seems the outward sign of an inward state, if by inward state we refer to feeling or thought or a combination of the two. However, this gets us, as it got Webster, into trouble with the word sign.

The words symbol and sign are commonly interchangeable, yet at times some of us mean one thing by sign and another by symbol. That is a cause of trouble and this is another: sign, taken to mean an exact reference, may include symbol, and symbol, taken to mean a suggestive device, may include sign. Since Dr. T. J. Eckleburg's eyes occupy a signboard, they are plainly a sign, yet we agree or, I think, should agree that they are as plainly a symbol, which, in this case, must consist of a sign. If we define a sign as an exact reference, it must include symbol because a symbol is an exact reference too. The difference seems to be that a sign is an exact reference to something definite and a symbol an exact reference to something indefinite. Less of a paradox than they appear, exact and indefinite will get along more comfortably together if we consider the senses of exact, one of which is suitable. Dr. Eckleburg's eyes are a sign referring to Dr. Eckleburg and his business. As a symbol they suggest, to use Webster's word, more thoughts and feelings than we could state; for if we stated as many as we could—the wasteland, the suburb, the modern world, futility, or moral censure—some would be left over and some would remain unstatable.

As I shall use it, the word sign means a one-to-one correspondence. Example: the American flag is a sign of the United States, used to identify post offices, income tax bureaus, and ships. The flag may also suggest Iwo Jima, General Grant's cigar, and graduation day— as the sign TIMES SQUARE on that corner suggests as much as it indicates. The sign may have symbolic values; but ignoring connotations, overtones, and suggestions, I shall regard the sign as a pointer. Indifferent to the sign as symbol or as the container of a symbol, I prefer to look at the symbol as a container of a sign—upon the flag, for example, as a symbol which happens by proximity and custom to indicate a post office. Those eyes as suggesters of many things, some of them nameless, seem more entertaining than as references to an oculist.

If we receive sign as pointer and my variation upon Webster's second try as a provisional account of symbol, we may proceed to

6

art as symbol and symbol in the arts. According to Cassirer's *Essay on Man*, as we have seen, art is a symbolic form, parallel in respect of this to religion or science. Each of these forms builds up a universe that enables man to interpret and organize his experience; and each is a discovery, because a creation, of reality. Although similar in function, the forms differ in the kind of reality built. Whereas science builds it of facts, art builds it of feelings, intuitions of quality, and the other distractions of our inner life—and in their degrees so do myth and religion. What art, myth, and religion are, Cassirer confesses, cannot be expressed by a logical definition.

Nevertheless, let us see what Clive Bell says about art. He calls it "significant form," but what that is he is unable to say. Having no quarrel with art as form, we may, however, question its significance. By significant he cannot mean important in the sense of having import, nor can he mean having the function of a sign; for to him art, lacking reference to nature, is insignificant. Since, however, he tells us that a work of art "expresses" the emotion of its creator and "provokes" an emotion in its contemplator, he seems to imply that his significant means expressive and provocative. The emotion expressed and provoked is an "aesthetic emotion," contemplative, detached from all concerns of utility and from all reference.

Attempting to explain Bell's significant form, Roger Fry, equally devoted to Whistler and art for art's sake, says that Flaubert's "expression of the idea" is as near as he can get to it, but neither Flaubert nor Fry tells what is meant by idea. To "evoke" it, however, the artist creates an "expressive design" or "symbolic form," by which the spirit "communicates its most secret and indefinable impulses."

Susanne Langer, who occupies a place somewhere between Fry and Cassirer, though nearer the latter, once said in a seminar that a work of art is an "unassigned syntactical symbol." Since this defini-

7

tion does not appear in her latest book, she may have rejected it, but it seems far more precise than Fry's attempt. By unassigned she probably intends insignificant in the sense of lacking sign value or fixed reference; syntactical implies a form composed of parts in relationship to one another; and a symbol, according to *Feeling and Form,* is "any device whereby we are enabled to make an abstraction." Too austere for my taste, this account of symbol seems to need elaboration, which, to be sure, her book provides. For the present, however, taking symbol to mean an outward device for presenting an inward state, and taking unassigned and syntactical as I think she uses them, let us tentatively admire her definition of the work of art.

Parallel symbolic forms, says Mrs. Langer, the arts differ from one another in materials and in what is symbolized. As music uses sounds, painting colors, and sculpture stuff, so literature uses words to create an image of time, space, or dynamic patterns of feeling. Music attends to virtual time, painting to the semblance of space, and literature to vital patterns. However referential or discursive the materials and elements or constituent parts of painting or literature, these arts are as irrelevant and nondiscursive as music.

Words, which she finds trivial in themselves, seem more than materials of literature. Its elements may be character, action, and image; but words, more than the matter from which these elements that compose the form are made, also serve as elements in their own right as her metaphor of syntax should imply. The potency of the real thing, Cassirer says in *Language and Myth,* is contained in the word that creates it. If language, as he says elsewhere, is a symbolic form, literature uses elements of one symbolic form as those of another. Words are symbols, but like most symbols they are not without significance or sign value, as the grammarian's connotation and denotation imply. If words are elements as well as materials of litera-

8

ture, a poem, differing in this respect from a sonata or a plastic abstraction, is a symbolic whole composed in part of references. At once assigned and unassigned, literature troubles aesthetic philosophers and moralists alike.

My interest in literature is not that of the philosopher, still less that of the moralist. Cassirer talks about art in general as symbolic form, and Mrs. Langer about poems as symbols, whereas I have in mind not only that but the symbolic elements that compose the poem. My examination of the literary symbol will proceed from constituent images to whole works. Since the image seems an approximate epitome of the whole, we may acquire understanding of the literary symbol from a return to Dr. Eckleburg's eyes.

Taking that signboard as the image, we recognize it as a definite object, or at least as the semblance of an object, which, though nothing much in itself, has received import from experience and memory. We know that eyes, even virtual eyes, are for looking, watching, rebuking; and with them we associate many other activities and attitudes, which we can feel more easily than explain. If the signboard were alone in a kind of nothing, we might not know which of these implications to pick from memory or feeling and which to reject. Situated as it is, however, near a commuters' railroad between Wall Street and a suburb, near a highway for homing brokers, and in the middle of a waste of ashes and shacks, which is presented by charged, desolating words, that signboard or rather its meaning is at once enriched and limited by context. I agree that this would be no less true if the signboard found itself in a kind of nothing, for nothing as context becomes something. No constituent image is without context, and every image owes context part of what it bears. Since context owes as much to image, the roads and ashes and all the implied commuters acquire import from those eyes. By reciprocal limitation and expansion, image and context, two interacting components of what they create, carry feelings and thoughts at once definite and indefinite. This composite of image and context constitutes that symbol.

This image in context is an element of *The Great Gatsby*, but if it is an epitome of the symbolic whole in which it functions, it is no more than approximate; for although work and image alike are made up of elements which, working together, present a feeling and maybe an idea, the constituent image has immediate literary context and the work has not. Of course we may take the state of society, the literary tradition, what we know of the hand that wrote the book and what we feel of the hand that holds it, time, place, and the weather as a kind of context with which the work may interact; but such circumstance, of the sort that surrounds all our affairs, is too general and remote to serve as more than a parallel to the surroundings of Dr. Eckleburg's signboard. The work as symbol, therefore, differs from the image as symbol in lacking the limitation and enlargement provided by immediate context. Work and image may have similar syntactical structure and function, but without immediate context, the work, less narrowly directed, is harder to apprehend. This lack is more or less supplied by the greater richness and complexity of the internal relationships that, providing control and enhancement, compose the whole.

The literary symbol, whether a work or one of its parts, is clearly an embodiment. As the spirit or vital principal occupies our bodies and shines out, so thought and feeling occupy the form, shape, or body that we call symbol. With the symbol or something like it in mind, Shakespeare's Theseus in *A Midsummer-Night's Dream,* considering madmen and poets, speaks of "shaping fantasies, that apprehend more than cool reason ever comprehends."

10

> And, as imagination bodies forth
> The forms of things unknown, the poet's pen
> Turns them to shapes, and gives to airy nothing
> A local habitation and a name.

If we may take these verses as references to the literary symbol, it is a thing made by the shaping imagination to body forth an unknown airy nothing. Although made by the poet's pen and composed of words, these words, no longer in the service of cool or discursive reason, serve nondiscursive purposes; neither practical nor logical, the poet's speech is the builder of symbolic forms. Shakespeare again has the words for this kind of speech, no longer speech but shape, in *The Tempest,* where, speaking of shapes, gesture, and sound, one of his people calls nondiscursive though expressive form "a kind of excellent dumb discourse."

Unlike the sign, which interests us less for what it is than what it points to, this dumb discourse is interesting in itself. Unlike the sign, it cannot be separated from what it stands for; for it is what it stands for or else part of it by a kind of synecdoche. Not entirely translatable and without substitute, it resists what Wilbur Marshall Urban in *Language and Reality* calls "expansion." That transcendental philosopher, who believes that a symbol is a "condensation of meaning, of unexpressed reference," holds that it may be "expanded into expressed reference" or discourse. If that were so, there would be no need to employ symbols; for as the dancer said, "If I could say what it means, I should not have to dance it." Justly rebuked for those notions, Urban has retired to the arms of New Critics. But the symbol remains, calling for explanation and resisting it. Though definite in itself and generally containing a sign that may be identified, the symbol carries something indeterminate and, however we try, there is a residual mystery that escapes our intellects.

11

As Carlyle said, and what he said is true to our impression, the symbol at once reveals and conceals.

The symbol conceals what it carries and resists total explanation because it is founded upon analogy, which, philosophers say, is primitive, childish, and irrational. Cassirer has told how primitive man confused analogy with fact, and Whitehead, seeking things as they are, has found in analogy a cause of modern error; but men of letters, recovering an ancient illusion, have made of it a device for presenting apprehensions, counteracting the world of fact, and creating something more suitable. If symbol is analogy, it is related to metaphor, but the account of that relationship can wait awhile. For the present it is enough to say that the symbol seems a metaphor one half of which remains unstated and indefinite. As in metaphor, the halves of the equation may be related by partial similarity, which is qualitative at times and structural or functional at others but hardly ever imitative or representative. Dr. Eckleburg's eyes and their environment are an analogy for an unexpressed feeling and thought about our condition, not an imitation of it.

The creator of such a symbol is not unlike Henry James's antique dealer, who, taking the golden bowl from its box, "left the important object—for as 'important' it did somehow present itself—to produce its certain effect." Certain from one point of view, this effect is uncertain from another, and the producer of the effect or the symbol itself is definite enough to call for definition—to call in vain maybe; for, if we may judge by the definitions I have reviewed and by my own approaches and withdrawals, the enterprise is difficult. Here, nevertheless, is my attempt to establish the important object:

The literary symbol, an analogy for something unstated, consists of an articulation of verbal elements that, going beyond reference and the limits of discourse, embodies and offers a complex of feeling and

12

thought. Not necessarily an image, this analogical embodiment may also be a rhythm, a juxtaposition, an action, a proposition, a structure, or a poem. One half of this peculiar analogy embodies the other, and the symbol is what it symbolizes.

I am afraid that this approach to a working definition, hopelessly general, might fit all literature at all times, but there are differences in degree between *Tom Jones,* let us say, and *Moby Dick.* What I have in mind is less literature in general than symbolist literature, my term for writing deliberately symbolic and for writing in symbolist periods which, though not necessarily deliberate, takes its method from current practice. Most of the writers I shall consider are conscious symbolists—not that it matters whether they are or not; for what matters is the kind of thing they made. I think we can recognize the difference in degree that separates their work, if symbolist, from *Tom Jones,* which, like all literature, is symbolic. The mark of distinction is embodied or immanent analogy.

Returning to the conscious or unconscious use of analogy, let us consider the statements of four symbolists. In a letter to Mrs. Hawthorne about *Moby Dick,* Melville said:

Your allusion for example to the "Spirit Spout" first showed to me that there was a subtle significance in that thing—but I did not, in that case, *mean* it. I had some vague idea while writing it, that the whole book was susceptible of an allegoric construction, & also that *parts* of it were—but the speciality of many of the particular subordinate allegories, were first revealed to me, after reading Mr. Hawthorne's letter, which, without citing any particular examples, yet intimated the part-&-parcel allegoricalness of the whole.

By allegory he meant, I think, what we mean by symbol. Happy to discover what he had made and tolerantly aware that what his creation carries is an affair between the reader and a book, no longer the creator's but an object for creating feelings and ideas in others, Melville appears to have been no more than partly conscious of what he was creating. In his Preface to *Paludes,* an early work, André Gide says:

Before explaining my book to others, I wait for them to explain it to me. To explain it first is to limit its sense; for if we know what we wished to say, we do not know if we have said only that.—One always says more than that.—And my interest is what I have put into the work without knowing it,—the unconscious part that I like to call God's.—A book is always a collaboration, and the greater its value, the smaller the part of the scribe. As we expect all things in nature to reveal themselves, so let us expect our books to be revealed by readers.

Speaking in a letter of the symbolic character of all art and of unconscious and conscious symbolism, D. H. Lawrence said that while much of his own symbolism was intentional, some of it escaped his notice until later. In an interview William Faulkner, speaking of how critics take his images, said: "I'm just a writer. Not a literary man. . . . Maybe all sorts of symbols and images get in. I don't know. When a good carpenter builds something, he puts the nails where they belong. Maybe they make a fancy pattern when he's through, but that's not why he put them in that way." Although Faulkner's statements to his public not uncommonly reveal tongue in cheek, maybe those nails are an analogy for analogies.

Whether consciously, unconsciously, or with a profession of this or that, authors make symbols and readers receive them. We must discover, if we can, the function of symbols and for whom they are designed. As for the second of these, a symbol in a novel may serve a character, the author, the reader, or the critic.

Some symbols, plainly for a character in the book, are there to carry something to him and by his reaction to enlighten us about him. If like the green-eyed man in Joyce's "An Encounter," the character responds to hair and whips, we understand his nature a little better. To find how the symbol serves the author we must consult psychology and history (which I do not propose to do here); for time and fixation may determine usage. Beyond these he may use symbols to embody what he cannot think, to discover what he feels or to express it, or, if he is an artist like Faulkner, to function as elements in a design. Convinced of the inadequacy of discourse for all that lies outside the rational and the prosaic or persuaded that things as they are are not entirely explicable, he may resort to analogical embodiment, which is useful too for supplementing a discursive meaning with overtones, qualities, and implications beyond logical handling. "Where there is an obscurity too deep for our Reason," says Sir Thomas Browne, " 'tis good to sit down with [an] . . . adumbration." Dissatisfied with what is, the author may use the symbol to create something better. For the philosopher, the psychologist, or the historian it is all right to inquire into the relation of author to symbol, but not for the critic, lest he commit the "intentional fallacy."

To a point the reader may share the author's concerns and find in the symbol a reminder of his own; but for him the principal function of symbol is organizing his experience and enlarging it. This supposes apprehension of the symbol, but even if careless of it, the reader may respond beneath the level of awareness and find himself surprised by an enrichment he cannot account for. Perhaps this is the commonest and best way to take symbolist writing. For critics, however, unawareness is a fault. Their response to symbolism, far keener than that of most authors and readers, is of two kinds: exercising ingenuity as over a puzzle, they may explain meaning and reduce embodiment to discourse; or, if aesthetic, they may try to fix the function of parts in the whole.

For author and reader the symbol is unitive. By its roots, as the dictionary tells us, the word symbol implies throwing or putting together. Taken from one realm of experience, vegetable nature for example, to serve in another, let us say the moral, the symbol joins those realms. By uniting the separate it can organize experience into a kind of order and, revealing the complex relationships among seemingly divided things, confer peace. Men of God praise the symbol's mediatory power. Whether verbal or iconographic, the religious symbol, and the political too, can unite man with man and man with something greater than he, society or God. Jung, speaking of the symbol as reconciler, finds it uniting the unconscious with the conscious, and Whitehead finds it connecting modes of experience. In a world as scattered as our own this ability is not without value. More important or at least more immediate for us is the power of the symbol to put parts of a literary work together in the service of the whole.

The symbol may put things together, but we must find if it puts author and reader together by establishing communication between them. The trouble with the symbol as communicator is that, although definite in being the semblance of an articulated object, it is indefinite in what it presents. In the first place the symbol is an analogy for something undefined and in the second our apprehension of the analogy is commonly incomplete. Moreover, the terms of the analogy are confused. Since one is embodied in the other, our search for a meaning apart from the embodiment must return to it and we are left with a form, at once definite and indefinite, and significant perhaps only by seeming so.

16

For communication there must be reference to actuality or to something accepted. The symbol may communicate by incorporating a sign or a traditional association. In so far as it has significance in the sense of containing a sign, it may unite author, reader, and fact, but significance is the symbol's lesser part. The greater part, remaining mysterious, carries no guarantee of communicating. As we have seen, the author's community with his symbol is often incomplete; therefore what passes between him and the reader through intermediary embodiment must be less nearly complete. When we pass beyond significance, communication is uncertain or partial at best. What the reader gets from a symbol depends not only upon what the author has put into it but upon the reader's sensitivity and his consequent apprehension of what is there. The feeling of profundity that accompanies it comes from a gradual but never final penetration of the form. T. S. Eliot's remarks about the poem seem relevant here: an independent object, the poem (or symbol) stands between author and reader, related in some fashion to each, but the relationship between author and object is not necessarily similar to that between object and reader. It may express the author and suggest to the reader, but expression and suggestion need not coincide. I. A. Richards, Eliot's opposite, who finds poetry the highest form of communication, finds it so by reducing symbol to sign. If the symbol, apart from incorporated sign, has little value as communicator between author and reader, its value may lie in communication between itself and the reader. What it submits to him and what he receives, however, may be different things. Nevertheless the value of the symbol to readers must be sought in this imperfect relationship.

Maybe the symbol has value as a way of knowing; but the meaning of knowing depends upon one's school. If one belongs to the scientific school, knowledge means acquaintance with fact, the sign becomes

17

the instrument of knowing, and, as Ernest Nagel has pointed out, the symbol of science, a fiction ancillary to sign, is only a means of arriving at it. In the sense of direct reference to fact, the literary symbol, like that of science but worse, is so far from cognitive that even the sign it incorporates seems useless or vague. If we take knowledge to mean acquaintance with truth, the literary symbol, equally uncertain, may seem a more suitable instrument. However, Yeats, an old man at the time, said: "Man can embody truth but he cannot know it." By "know" in this place he seems, like a rationalist, to mean apprehend by discursive reason, though we should expect a romantic poet to find the symbol a way to another kind of knowledge—intuitive (immediate apprehension without logical interference) or else emotional. For him, the symbol, embodying intuitive truth and feeling, might present something which, although imperfectly received, feels like knowledge. As a character puts it in a novel by Charles Williams: "I sometimes think the nearest we can get to meaning is to feel as if there was meaning." Virtual knowledge, addressed to our feelings, might be what the symbol carries. But "virtual" implies that true knowledge is scientific and so does the quotation from Yeats.

Before we accept that meaning of knowledge we should consult Cassirer, an enemy of "naive realism," to whom scientific knowledge is one of many kinds, each a symbolic form for showing what reality is like. The literary symbol, which presents knowledge of its own reality, may not communicate this knowledge, but by its form, which corresponds in quality to a nature of things, creates it. In so far as we apprehend the form we too are informed. The value of the symbol, if we accept this account of it, lies therefore in creating a vision of reality and submitting it to our apprehension. Not only creative but heuristic, it serves to discover the reality it shapes. Perhaps in

18

view of the narrow sense of "knowledge" it would be better to speak of the literary symbol not as a way of knowing but of embodying awareness or of conceiving in the sense of becoming filled with or pregnant.

If feeling is part of conceiving, we must consider feeling, which may be of several kinds. Aside from that experienced and embodied by the author, feeling may be our reaction to the stimulus afforded by the embodiment, a sign for us, if we are sensitive and experienced, that something of value is there. But those who find fallacies congenial tell us that this is subjective and, except for indication of possible value, unreliable. In the second place, the feeling may be that embodied in the symbol and offered to us. This, as T. S. Eliot says in "Tradition and the Individual Talent," is objective, impersonal, and "significant." In the third place, the feeling may be what the embodiment creates. Equivalent to an apprehension of the feeling in the symbol, this is not so much a feeling of our own as an awareness, at once distant and sympathetic, of immanence—by a kind of empathy. If that is the case, contemplation of feeling rather than feeling itself marks our happiest encounter with these fictions.

As the feeling in the symbol is more important than our emotional response, so the symbol is more important than what it suggests. Lacking embodiment and the semblance of actuality, what it suggests turns back to its source to recapture a body and enlarge it. The symbol is not there like a sign to point to something else, to take the place of something else, or even to stand for it, but to display itself with all it has created and welcomed home. The trouble with Whitehead in this connection is that he thinks a symbol may be exchanged with what it symbolizes, as if the halves of the peculiar equation were of equal importance. This may be true of certain signs or of symbols that only convenience recommends, but it is far from

19

true of literary symbols. Our concern, less with disembodied souls than with embodied ones, keeps our metaphysics warm—or, to call upon a more classical poem, the symbol haunts us with its body on.

Since his region is on the other side of logic, the critic of such embodiments has no rational way of proceeding from analysis of part and function to a judgment of the whole. If he feels that symbols offer something that analysis fails to guarantee, he must call upon intuition and feeling for help, not only the sudden intuition and feeling that accompany discovery of the object but the feeling that accompanies the apprehension of feeling in it. Analysis, justified by these feelings, may help to account for them: "I no sooner felt," says Coleridge in *Biographia Literaria,* "than I sought to understand." However impersonal the critic or the work itself, the criticism of literature is a transaction between an impersonal object and a person. However cold-blooded and objective the "exegetical inquirer" may pretend to be, he is a feeler; for we feel more than we think. If he is sensitive, feeling must attend and direct his analysis and assist his apprehension of feeling in the object. Maybe such feeling is another word for taste or for what Eliot calls sensibility. If, ignoring his commendation, we fear the subjective with all its horrors of irrelevance and eccentricity, we must try to endure our condition; and if, in this doubtful region, fearing the danger of obscurantism, we long for Euclid, we must recall that the symbol, occupying another region, does what discourse cannot do. The best equipment for a critic of symbolist literature may be what Keats called Negative Capability: "being in uncertainties, mysteries, doubts, without any irritable reaching after fact and reason," and "remaining content with half-knowledge."

The principal justification of the analyses which constitute the greater part of this essay is displaying the text and calling those parts

20

to notice that might be missed by a more casual approach. Partly intended, moreover, to illustrate the kinds of symbol, my analyses are exemplary in that sense alone. Far from exhausting the texts or preventing further interpretation, they invite the reader's rivalry, and if his response is better than mine, pleased by having helped, I applaud. If, however, the reader protests that since texts embody the indefinite, his interpretations may be infinite, I reply that indefinite does not mean infinite and hasten to add that all interpretation, his or mine, is limited by what is there before us—by the symbol in its context, both immediate and more generally circumstantial. For the attempt, however vain, to find exactly what the text presents, analysis, which keeps it before us, seems as good a way as any, though not so all-sufficient as the austere prefer.

For vain attempts, whether austere or warmly moral, upon a haunting body, let us turn to critics of Moby Dick, that great yet exemplary symbol. In *The Enchafed Flood,* an investigation of "romantic iconography," W. H. Auden says: "A symbol is felt to be such before any possible meaning is consciously recognized; i.e., an object or event which is felt to be more important than reason can immediately explain." This seems almost unobjectionable, but, he continues: "A symbolic correspondence is never one to one but always multiple, and different persons perceive different meanings." He illustrates this point by stating what Moby Dick means to Starbuck, Ishmael, Ahab, and the captains of other ships. Since each interpretation differs from the others and each is thoroughly explicit, we must conclude that the meaning of the whale is both multiple and definite. This seems Auden's own position; for although he allows multiplicity of meaning, he inclines to allegory and sign, and we are left with a series of clear equations. Not multiplicity of definite meanings, however, but indefiniteness is the mark of the symbol, a conclusion too obscurantist perhaps for Auden's brilliant mind, a reasoning engine which, making signs of symbols, provides a fitting introduction to commentators who, like Auden's mariners, are devoted to significance.

During the course of *Studies in Classic American Literature* D. H. Lawrence comes to Moby Dick: "Of course he is a symbol. Of what? I doubt if even Melville knew exactly. That's the best of it." Later on, however, reproving Melville for a transcendentalism unlike his own, and refusing to accept the story as "a voyage of the soul," Lawrence prefers to take it literally as a "sea yarn." That is a good beginning: the whale is a whale—but he also seems more than whale, and Lawrence, unable to resist, leaves the literal story he has been enjoying for a definite interpretation in the light of his philosophy: "What then is Moby Dick?—he is the deepest blood-being of the white race. . . . And he is hunted . . . by the maniacal fanaticism of our white mental consciousness." If we contemplate the image of the whale, we must admit that it embodies sexual suggestions. That it presents the phallic being endangered by the mind is possible, but it seems illiberal to exclude possibilities which are as plainly embodied. Each of us, carrying his own baggage to the symbol, admires what he has brought without care for what the pile obscures. The symbol seems to invite this undertaking; and our excuse must be that we find it hard to endure the indefinite.

The mediaeval bestiary includes the whale. In the first part of the verses devoted to that "fish," he is described, and in the second his significance is defined. This emblematic habit of mind, persisting to our day, limits or disembodies Moby Dick, who, becoming a mirror for critics, "represents" or "signifies" their anthropological, political, sociological, or psychological concerns. Almost as if he had such critics in mind, Melville includes the following quotation in his prefatory extracts: " 'My God! Mr. Chace, what is the matter?' I answered, 'We have been stove by a whale.' "

Although William Ellery Sedgwick calls the whale an "emblem" of the mystery of creation, he refuses to make definite equations of symbols: "No statement as to their meaning can convey how vital, how meaningful these symbols are. Separately and in relation to each other [the whale, Ahab, and the sea] will not be held to any final definition or any fixed subject-object relationship." Interrelated yet unlimited, he continues, they baffle the intellect. Charles Feidelson, who agrees that the symbol is supralogical, finds *Moby Dick* a philosophical quest. Seeking vision through images of whale and sea, the voyaging mind approaches Emersonian knowledge of reality. Although Newton Arvin confuses Melville with himself at times and parodies Dante at others, the literal, Freudian, moral, and mythical meanings of his whale fail, as he says, to exhaust it. For other men other whales.

Not entirely aware, perhaps, of what he was composing, Melville was conscious enough to include passages which serve not only as elements of his book but apparently as clues to how we are to take it and how not. At the Spouter Inn, for example, Ishmael confronts a painting "so thoroughly besmoked, and every way defaced, that in the unequal cross-lights by which you viewed it, it was only by diligent study and a series of systematic visits to it, and careful inquiry of the neighbors, that you could any way arrive at an understanding" of "such unaccountable masses of shades and shadows." Contemplating this obscure and marvelous object, he is puzzled yet compelled by its "indefinite sublimity" to try to find what it is. "Ever and anon a bright, but, alas, deceptive idea would dart you through. —It's the Black Sea in a midnight gale.—It's a blasted heath.—It's a Hyperborean winter scene.—It's the breaking-up of the ice-bound

23

stream of time. But at last all these fancies yielded to that one portentous something in the picture's midst." His "theory," tentative and based in part upon the opinions of many aged persons, is that the portentous something in the middle is a whale. This painting is plainly an analogy for the book. Ishmael's compulsive attempt at explanation corresponds to the predicament and endeavor of reader, critic, and maybe the author. It is worth noting that Ishmael, content at last with discovering the image, stops short of its significance—though his preliminary speculations about it are better than those of most critics.

A little later Father Mapple finds a definite lesson in the story of Jonah and the whale. That this, however, is not how to take the story of Ahab and the whale is suggested by the Ecuadorian doubloon, nailed by Ahab to the mast as an incentive to the discovery of Moby Dick. This golden coin from the center of the earth, richly stamped with a design of three mountains, a tower, a flame, a cock, and half the zodiac, revered by the mariners as the White Whale's talisman, invites interpretation. In "some monomaniac way" Ahab finds these strange figures significant; for as they say in Emersonian Concord, "some certain significance lurks in all things, else all things are little worth, and the round world itself but an empty cipher, except to sell by the cartload, as they do hills about Boston, to fill up some morass in the Milky Way." Not only monomaniac but egocentric, Ahab sees the coin as an image of himself and the world, which "to each and every man in turn but mirrors back his own mysterious self." Healthier but allegorical, Starbuck sees the sun as God, the valleys as our life, and the three mountains, "in some faint earthly symbol," as the Trinity. Stubb, fixing upon the zodiac, thinks of Bowditch and the cycle of life. Flask sees the coin as money for cigars: "There's another rendering now; but still one text." Only feeble-minded Pip, a critic of critics, makes an admirable comment: "I look, you look, he looks; we look, ye look, they look." We are left with the object and lookers at it; but whether monomaniac, eccentric, or practical, these lookers are mistaken. Far from being a clue to the interpretation of the book, as some critics have taken it, this episode of the doubloon shows how not to interpret *Moby Dick* or any other symbolic form.

The chapter on the whiteness of the whale seems more exemplary. "What the White Whale was to Ahab, has been hinted," says Ishmael. "What, at times, he was to me, as yet remains unsaid." Taking a quality for the whole, he finds whiteness ambivalent, full of warring contraries, and universal. A "vague, nameless horror" on the one hand, it serves on the other to "symbolize whatever grand or gracious thing." Few are "entirely conscious" of the effect of whiteness in either of its aspects. Even Ishmael, who is conscious enough, finds the meaning of whiteness so "well nigh ineffable" that he almost despairs of putting it into "a comprehensible form"; and "to analyse it would seem impossible." By analogy and example, calling upon white towers, white mountains, and white seas, he suggests "the nameless things of which the mystic sign gives forth such hints." Is it "a dumb blankness, full of meaning?" he asks. "Is it that by its indefiniteness it shadows forth the heartless voids and immensities of the universe?" After such questions, analogies, examples, and contradictions, which build up the feeling and idea of indefiniteness, he concludes: "And of all these things the Albino Whale was the symbol."

Let us see how that symbol is composed. By description Melville presents the whale's indifference, its ferocity, and its "uncommon bulk." By the action and the nature of the sea, the ship, and the quest he improves the whale's solidity and complicates his import. "The

25

overwhelming idea of the great whale himself" is further qualified by the thoughts of those in quest of him: Ahab's idea of him as the "incarnation" of all evil and Ishmael's idea of him as a thing of the "wonder-world," a "grand hooded phantom" which, midmost in the "endless processions of the whale" that floated through his soul, seemed "a snow hill in the air." From discursive chapters on the whale's anatomy, the history of whaling, the process of trying whales out, and the like, the image acquires greater body and depth—as Somerset Maugham, omitting these elements from his edition, failed to see. "Taken with context," however, as Father Mapple observes, "this is full of meaning." His observation, which refers to an incident of Jonah's life, may be taken as a reference to Melville's whale; for the monster, like Dr. Eckleburg's eyes, is made by an interaction of image and context.

Melville's success in shaping them to embody his vision of reality is proved by the variety of critical interpretation. Working within the limits of his fixation or his gift, each critic takes an aspect or two of Melville's vision as the whole, and each is more or less justified by parts of image or context. Those who are fitted to find sociological or political significance are encouraged by the emblematic ending of the book. Those who are devoted to Freud find evidence in Ahab's missing leg. Those who prefer the metaphysical find ample corroboration everywhere. But that whale in context is more than a thing to a man. All things in heaven and earth, unassigned and indefinite, he embodies our feeling and thought when face to face with ourselves and with what surrounds us.

To every dog his patch; but what of the undogmatic critic? If, preferring the whale to the part, he finds the image a general vision of reality, inexpressible save by itself, he incurs the danger of monotony; for the same thing might be said of *Ulysses, The Trial,* or

"Bateau ivre." But, however general, each symbol is particular in feeling and quality, and the critic, without trying to define the indefinable, may suggest its singularity. By analysis of image and context he may reveal the shape of the image, the relation of part to part and to the whole, and the function of each part. For aid he may consult the author's intention, if he can, and the circumstances of time and place. Anything goes as long as, decently skeptical of all else, we remember that the text is the thing and that the symbol, an apparent object, is the object. Contemplating that appearance, we may find it becoming what Wallace Stevens calls a "transparence," but if, like Ahab and his critics, we find it becoming a mirror, we must look again.

Roses and Calipers

*T*HERE IS difference in nature and function between the roses of Dante and Yeats, or, to take less florid examples, there is an even more apparent difference between Donne's compasses and Wallace Stevens's caliper or between Donne's flea and Kafka's cockroach. Philosophy, psychology, and the explication of texts may help us to approach these symbols, but here our immediate problem or its greater part is time. To find how and why the romantic symbol differs from those of the Middle Ages and the Renaissance we must supplement analysis by history. "For the analysis of every symbolic form," says Cassirer, "we are dependent on historical data."

At the beginning of his *Comedy* Dante finds himself in a dark wood. Quitting that intolerable place and about to commence the ascent of a hill toward the sun, he meets a spotted leopard, a lion, and a she-wolf. Their demeanor is bestial, and he retreats to await the support of Vergil, who understands these matters. At the end of his *Comedy* Dante, guided now by Saint Bernard, contemplates an enormous rose, bathed in radiance and attended by angelic bees.

This white flower with yellow center seems a garden of concentric petals within which Beatrice, the Virgin, and all the redeemed occupy suitable chairs. Penultimate, that rose is the most impressive and the most efficacious of "shadowy prefaces," as Dante calls them, to his ultimate vision of circles and light.

As Dante's rose is his preface to illumination so, for many of us today, T. S. Eliot is the preface to Dante and to such illumination as we enjoy. We may be less familiar with the Florentine's leopard and rose than with the three white leopards that devour the more or less American poet under a juniper tree in *Ash Wednesday* or with his roses and gardens. Such images, he says in his essay on Dante, need not worry us, for "It is really better, at the start, not to know or care what they do mean." All we need know is that allegory means "clear, visual images." They may gain intensity by having a meaning but, before we discover it, it is enough to be "aware that the meaning is there" while the brilliant images work upon our sensibilities.

Dante and other men of the Middle Ages, not content with images, thought it well to have meanings in mind. Of that we can find assurance not only in the first question of the first part of Saint Thomas's *Summa Theologica* but also in Dante's letter to Can Grande, which serves as a kind of preface to the *Paradiso,* or in the *Convivio,* an explanation of his odes. None can understand their "true meaning," he says, unless he relates it—"because it is hidden under the figure of allegory." Of the four meanings to be found in every work, he continues, one is literal and three are allegorical. The literal surface, which is most important, carries the other meanings.

By the dark wood Dante seems to have intended the moral, political, and theological quandary in which he found himself at the middle of his life, and, beyond that, the confusion and perplexity of his time. The beasts, probably from Jeremiah, seem to signify sin,

Rome, and empire. By its light, heat, and shape the sun stands for God in His three aspects and, below that in their degrees, the emperor, perhaps, and virtue. The rose, a figure of heaven, the body of Christ, and the Virgin, suggests by quality and shape a vision of order and beatitude. In this figure Dante found appeasement for his religious, moral, and political troubles, and, seeing it as an artist, made it the unifying center of his narrative. What he calls his "polysemous" method, unlike the ambiguity and paradox dear to romantics, offers many meanings without contradiction or uncertainty. Interrelated, these meanings support each other to create a harmonious world; and the polysemous rose, though "figuring Paradise," as he says, is also the image of that harmony.

Multiple meanings are not the sign of symbol. Moreover, the limitation placed by Dante upon his meanings seems to forbid interpreting his images as symbols. But in *Symbolism in Medieval Thought and its Consummation in the Divine Comedy* Helen Flanders Dunbar, working under the auspices of Jung, finds Dante's allegory not unlike other less definite devices. Her symbol, defined as "an expression of meaningful experience" having a basis in association, includes emblem, metaphor, and allegory. Depending upon the kind of association, symbols are of three kinds: the extrinsic, an arbitrary association not to be distinguished from our sign; the intrinsic, the more descriptive association of metaphor; and the true symbol of insight, the most important and Dante's favorite. A way of knowing, discovering, and expressing, the insight symbol allows author and reader to apprehend the infinite. Ignoring dialectics, Dr. Dunbar holds that insight symbols, such as Dante's rose, offered men of his time their only way of knowing the nature of things and expressing it. When in the late Middle Ages the symbol became more important than the transcendental reality it disclosed, the method fell into decay, and we are left without it. Whatever her confusion of romantic with mediaeval method, Dr. Dunbar makes us wonder if Dante's rose, more than a sign with four definite meanings, is also an embodiment of vision and the only way of presenting it. Perhaps there is less difference between allegory and symbol than we had thought.

Before deciding that, we should look at *The Romance of the Rose* and at a commentary on its method by C. S. Lewis. The first part of *The Romance of the Rose,* by Guillaume de Lorris, agrees better than Dante's rose with what we commonly mean by allegory; for Guillaume uses personification, and his images, intellectually conceived before they are fitted to the idea, are separable from what they represent. In symbolism, however, conception and embodiment are not only simultaneous but so involved that one cannot be parted from the other. The symbol is the only possible embodiment of what it presents, whereas an allegorical image, one of several possibilities, is a substitute for what it represents. To project his analysis of courtly love, Guillaume personified each aspect of his lady. A rose on a bush surrounded by a hedge and by a walled garden, her love invites the lover's hands while her other aspects, presented as persons, help those hands along or prevent them. His fumbling, her courtly scruples, and the intricacies of convention could be returned to the discourse whence they came without loss of sense. The loss would be one of color, concreteness, and charm. Lacking the resources of the analytic novel, Guillaume chose for his tale of sentiment the most entertaining method afforded by custom. In *The Allegory of Love* Lewis treats Guillaume's method as convenient personification. Associating symbolism with "sacramentalism" on the one hand and with romantic aspiration on the other, he derides those of our day who, preferring symbol to allegory, try to make Dante a romantic symbolist. To Lewis symbol and allegory are opposites. Starting with

31

an abstraction, the allegorist produces a concrete fiction. Starting with a concrete fiction, the symbolist proceeds to spiritual reality. Not a mode of thought like symbolism or a way to mystical knowledge, allegory is a mode of expression. But Lewis avoids Dante's rose as Dr. Dunbar his personification.

Their disagreement, of words in part and in part of position, is not serious; for those scholars are talking in different terms of different aspects of a thing that manifests itself along a scale from sign to symbol. Lewis limits himself to one extreme and Dr. Dunbar to the other. Historically minded, he sees his signs as they were intended; from her position as psychologist, she sees her symbols as romantics must.

However various in origin and function, both allegory and symbol are analogies. Occupying one end of our scale, allegory, an extended simile, as Lewis says, is limited in meaning; but even the most definite personifications of *The Romance of the Rose* carry something beyond intention or significance; for if the artist is good, he must embody more than he thinks. Dante's beasts, more signs than symbols perhaps, are not without symbolic value. His rose, at the other end of the scale, may have four definite meanings, but what it is and what it suggests are more important—or seem so to us—than what it signifies. Every symbol, we recall, contains a sign or signs as every sign may serve as symbol.

The word allegory, sometimes the mediaeval term for what we would call symbol and sometimes a term for sign, appears to be a principal trouble. If Lewis, forgetting his adherence to allegory, calls his images and personifications symbols at times, he has ample precedent for his confusion. Dr. Johnson and Baudelaire, as well as Melville and many others, used allegory and symbol as interchangeable words; but most men of our time are as prejudiced against the word allegory as against the thing it has come to stand for. Yeats, for example, in his essay on "William Blake and His Illustrations to *The Divine Comedy,*" separates "symbolic imagination" from allegory, "one of many possible representations of an embodied thing." A product of fancy and memory, allegory is no better than an amusement; whereas symbol, a product of "wizard frenzy," is a revelation. "I tore up hundreds of pages," says Yeats, "in my endeavour to escape from allegory."

His distaste for "sterile" allegory was natural; for allegory in its present sense of limited analogy with high significance is an unfashionable art. Since *Pilgrim's Progress,* in point of fact, there have been few examples. Swift used it in *A Tale of a Tub* and George Orwell in *Animal Farm,* but on the whole, lacking certainty, we prefer indefinite analogies. Definite analogies, such as the allegory and metaphor of the Middle Ages and the Renaissance, were designed to present not abstractions alone but the nature of things. If we are to distinguish these limited instruments more plainly from the romantic symbol that we prefer, we must consider two worlds. The first of these, which R. G. Collingwood in his *Idea of Nature* calls "organic," lasted from the time of Pythagoras to the late seventeenth century. The second, which replaced it, is mechanical in one of its aspects and developmental in another. What we call the romantic movement is the endeavor to make the world organic again.

The organic or harmonious world of the Middle Ages and the Renaissance, excellently described in E. M. W. Tillyard's *Elizabethan World Picture,* took the form of a hierarchy of being. Commonly conceived as a chain or ladder, this great order accommodated the lowest, the highest, and the intermediate. In its comfortable coherence, angels, men, and vegetables accepted their place without quarreling about it. Above man, who occupied the center of this chain, the links

33

were crowded, as the pseudo-Dionysius affirms, by angels in their degrees, archangels near the bottom, cherubs and seraphs at the top, and above that God Himself. Below central man came animals, vegetables, and minerals, each of which, like angels above, composed a hierarchy below. The lion or sometimes the eagle occupied top place among animals and the oyster the indubitable bottom. Below him, beans and cabbages, gold and lead found appropriate places. A parallel chain of four elements, with fire at the top, and lateral extensions to include the body politic, the planets, and all other things completed what Sir Thomas Browne calls "the ladder and scale of creatures," of which each deserved its place by proportion of matter and spirit. A seraph may have been impaired by one percent of matter, an oyster improved by one percent of spirit—or less—but man enjoyed about fifty percent of each, though even he composed an order, according to capacity, from king to knave. Within man the faculties (such as reason), the virtues (such as justice and fortitude), and the organs formed additional hierarchies which imitated the structure of all things; for man was the microcosm.

Hierarchy was linked to hierarchy by affinities or analogies by which the noblest occupant of each order corresponded to the noblest of the others. The king, for example, found himself on a footing of congeniality with the lion, the sun, fire, gold, and the subtlest among vegetables—maybe the rose. Dante's lion, sun, rose, and all his other analogies, celebrating things as they were, commended God, the emperor, justice, and reason. As definite as the logic of Saint Thomas, allegory was a proper instrument for revealing this definite world; yet the overtones and suggestions embodied in the most definite analogies expressed the wonder and, in spite of logical assurance, the mystery of things.

Renaissance analogies, while similar to the cool equations of the

Middle Ages, says Tillyard, were less exact. As identity declined into resemblance, allegory was generally replaced by metaphor, and, although remaining the king, the sun became something like him as well. This gradual development, interrupted by allegorical Spenser and Bunyan, may be ascribed in part to the effect of Copernicus and Galileo and in part to humanism. While celebrating the old relationship of things on one hand, metaphor expresses a shadow of doubt on the other. To Dr. Johnson, who inhabited the mechanical world, Donne's metaphor, seeming not only alien but ambivalent, was a *"discordia concors,"* a concordant discord. *Discordia,* the noun to be qualified, occupies the center. Whatever his misunderstanding of an obsolete world and its ways, Dr. Johnson was right in placing discord above harmony in some of the metaphors of Donne; for that poet, who knew his Copernicus, was less certain of the order he sometimes sang than some of his successors, Sir Thomas Browne, for example, or Andrew Marvell, whose metaphors affirm the chain of being as faithfully as Dante's allegory.

Metaphor, an analogy in which the elements compared are at once similar and dissimilar, may take the form of an equation of stated elements or an image by which one term is presented while the other remains implicit. Unlike allegory, the metaphysical metaphor generally consists of a complete equation. It may range from convenient expression, like Guillaume's allegory, to essential embodiment, like that of Dante at his most sublime, uniting regions of reality and presenting their connections. It may range from an innocent and somewhat primitive acceptance of identity to an awareness of analogy as analogy. It may include decoration, in the case of John Cleveland, or substance as in the poems of Donne. Before we proceed with the metaphysicals, however, it is fitting to consult authority on metaphor.

35

"Every metaphor," says C. S. Lewis, "is an allegory in little." W. B. Yeats in his edition of Blake's prophetic works says: "All poetic metaphors are symbols." But Aristotle—and Dante calls him the master of those that know—says in his *Poetics* that metaphor "consists in giving the thing a name that belongs to something else; the transference being either from genus to species, or from species to genus, or from species to species, or on grounds of analogy." To descend a little, however, and provide an easy transition back to the metaphysicals: Caroline Spurgeon, defining metaphor as a "likeness between dissimilar things," finds that it "holds within itself the very secret of the universe." In the Renaissance at least—and she is speaking of Shakespeare—it did that.

When Richard Crashaw compared the eyes of his weeper to "portable and compendious oceans" or a sort of bathtub, he had no sense of incongruity; for as Sir Thomas Browne observes: "There are no grotesques in nature." Crashaw's portable ocean may be less compendious than Marvell's Platonic ocean, an analogy for mind, "where each kind does straight its own resemblance find," but it is from the same geography. Comparing a drop of dew to the soul, the one a little globe reflecting its native element, the other a thing whose "circling thoughts express the greater heaven in an heaven less," Marvell fixed the relationship of microcosm to macrocosm. ("Are we struck with admiration," asks Coleridge in *The Statesman's Manual*, "at beholding the cope of heaven imaged in a dewdrop?") When Marvell defined desperate love by analogies of poles, planisphere, parallels that never meet, and planetary opposition, he not only recreated the structure of reality but created a structure suggestive of feeling to which each unlikely metaphor contributes. Wit, the power of perceiving and using the analogies that nature affords, may be more than what romantics were to call fancy.

Metaphor and symbol are plainly of a family. When Yeats in his "Symbolism of Poetry" said that metaphors are not "profound" enough to be moving unless they are symbols, he implied that metaphor can serve as symbol, though what he meant by "profound" is not entirely plain. Maybe a metaphor seems profound when comparatively unlimited by equation, when only one term is given, or when the terms evade reason by incongruity. Marvell's "Definition of Love" proves that metaphor can act as an element in a composite symbol. It is possible, moreover, to regard one term of a metaphorical equation as the symbol of the other or their interaction as creative. In the metaphysical metaphor, however, the usual equation of the terms limits meaning more than romantics would think suitable; for to them a metaphor, though of the same kind as symbol, would seem too narrowly assigned to be one. The early seventeenth century, a time when the old world was still more vital than the new, found the generous assignment of metaphor appropriate.

That old world was not to endure. The uncertainty that qualifies many metaphysical equations and the growing consciousness of resemblance rather than actuality in the most definite equations are signs of a world's death. The dissociation of sensibility that T. S. Eliot laments is another sign of this death and not, as he once thought, the unfortunate consequence of Milton's verse. To be sure, Milton, who could confuse seraphs with archangels, shows the uncertainty that attended the breaking of an order, but the effect that Eliot ascribed to him could be ascribed with greater reason to the advancement of science, the incursion of classical ideals, and the rise of puritanism. The old world died, and with it, as Marjorie Nicolson points out in her *Breaking of the Circle,* went the system of analogies that had composed it. Metaphor, no longer a method appropriate to the nature of things, became detachable and decorative simile. The chain of being was broken in the middle, the upper half, fallen away, was lost to mind, and men retired with relief to the lower half, where they remained contented for a hundred years. Whatever the virtues of the enlightenment, it was bad for analogy. Reason proved adequate for exploring or expressing what remained, and not enough of the ineffable was left around to urge recourse to symbol.

Symbol, as we know it today, emerged during the romantic movement, which is best understood perhaps as an attempt to recover the upper half of the broken chain and, uniting it with the lower, to create something like the lost world of the Middle Ages and the Renaissance. The upper half of this restoration, however, acquired new meanings. Not only the place of spirit, it came to mean the imaginative, the subjective, the unconscious, or sensibility, separated by that famous dissociation from fact and reason, which continued to occupy the lower half of the chain. An enemy of Newton, Locke, and dark satanic mills, Blake commended what he called "vision" or imagination.

Coleridge, the principal authority on imagination, defines it in *Biographia Literaria,* the ode to Dejection, and elsewhere. Taking issue with his friend Wordsworth, who confused imagination with fancy in the Preface to the 1815 edition of his poems, Coleridge, as everybody knows, distinguished sharply between fancy, "the aggregative and associative power," and imagination, the "shaping spirit." This "vital" faculty dissolves and dissipates in order to re-create, whereas fancy is a mode of memory that finds its materials by the law of association. Fancy accounts for allegory and metaphor, imagination for symbol, at once its "educt" and its instrument. This "reconciling and mediatory power . . . gives birth to a system of symbols, harmonious in themselves, and consubstantial with the truths of which they are the conductors." In *The Statesman's Manual* he says:

38

"by a symbol I mean, not a metaphor or allegory or any other figure of speech or form of fancy, but an actual and essential part of that, the whole of which it represents."

Now an allegory is but a translation of abstract notions into a picture-language, which is itself nothing but an abstraction from objects of the senses; the principal being more worthless even than its phantom proxy, both alike unsubstantial, and the former shapeless to boot. On the other hand a symbol . . . is characterized by a translucence of the special in the individual, or of the general in the special, or of the universal in the general; above all by the translucence of the eternal through and in the temporal. It always partakes of the reality which it renders intelligible; and while it enunciates the whole, abides itself as a living part in that unity of which it is the representation.

His hostility to metaphorical association did not include analogy. Metaphor, he said in *Aids to Reflection,* expresses difference by resemblance; analogy or symbol, on the other hand, finding sameness essential, presents the thing in itself. Maybe it was the limitation of metaphor and the deliberateness of eighteenth-century simile that turned him away from these comparisons.

It is plain that Coleridge valued the symbol for helping him pass from matter to spirit or giving him the feeling of that passage. His "translucence," different from Wallace Stevens's "transparence," is that of a frosted window opening upon the infinite and the eternal, matters that the age of cool reason chose to neglect. Maybe the frosting discouraged Voltaire; but Coleridge, valuing the lower half of the chain for its power to accost a possible upper and surprise it into approximate revelation, is not unlike Carlyle or Emerson, who found symbols equally useful.

In *Sartor Resartus* Carlyle attends to the "high transcendental aspects of the matter." Nowhere, he says, was his Professor more "impalpable" than in his remarks on man, who, like Cassirer's symbol-making animal, lives and works consciously or unconsciously in and through and by symbols. Though based upon "the small Visible," the Professor's man "does nevertheless extend down into the infinite deeps of the Invisible, of which Invisible, indeed, his Life is properly the bodying forth." In this context, deeps, equivalent to altitudes, are no less transcendental, though more interior perhaps. Finding mechanism and logic inadequate and imagination irrelevant unless it maintains at least a toe upon fact, the Professor finds symbols a way of joining "mystic wonderment" with "the small prose domain of Sense."

Remarking "the benignant efficacies of Concealment," and of Silence as well, he continues: "Of kin to the so incalculable influences of Concealment, and connected with still greater things, is the wondrous agency of *Symbols*. In a Symbol there is concealment and yet revelation: here therefore by Silence and by Speech acting together, comes a double significance." That the bearing of this nondiscursive agency is less secular than transcendental is almost immediately apparent: "In the Symbol proper . . . there is ever, more or less distinctly and directly, some embodiment and revelation of the Infinite; the Infinite is made to blend itself with the Finite, to stand visible, and as it were, attainable there." Whether extrinsic (arbitrary or conventional), intrinsic (artistic) or divine, the symbol reveals "Eternity looking through Time" and affords "some dimmer or clearer revelation of the God-like." Not uncommonly that revelation, concealing more than it revealed, was dimmer than clearer during a period of unsatisfied search and cosmic reconstruction that produced *Moby Dick* and the essays of Emerson.

Detecting no "accurate adjustment" between matter and spirit, Emerson in essays on the poet and on nature turns away from nature as the field of science to nature as the symbol of spirit. However inaccurate, such natural symbolism provides a kind of adjustment between the regions and, what may be of more interest to us, between the objective and the subjective. Not only "the dial plate" of the supernatural, nature is "a metaphor of the human mind," but what dials indicate or metaphors connect remains uncertain: "For all symbols are fluxional." Emerson reproves those who, enamored of definiteness, try to make what symbols bear "too stark and solid," since what they bear may be less impressive than what they are. "I find that the fascination resides in the symbol." He also rests content with the imagination, which by making things "translucid," enables him to make analogies and to guess their meaning.

Unlike Dante or Marvell, these transcendentalists used the symbol not to express or to explore the upper half of the chain but to assure themselves of its possibility. Dante and Marvell had a good idea of what their images embodied, but the transcendentalists of the early nineteenth century, lacking news of translunary things, and honest about their ignorance, could expect intimations alone. However concrete their symbolic instrument, it revealed the indefinite or the unknowable; and to our own romantic but less transcendental day the symbol has retained something of the character they gave it. At once prevented and teased by their instrument, they made the symbol a way to what feels like knowledge and its only expression; for, like mystics coming home, these feelers could not translate their feelings into prose.

To apprehend the romantic symbol a little better, let us consult example—with Emerson's verses from the essay "Nature" as a suitable prelude:

> A subtle chain of countless rings
> The next unto the farthest brings;

>The eye reads omens where it goes,
>And speaks all languages the rose.

Speaking Tuscan, Dante's rose offers four definite meanings or, by his own account at least, was cultivated for that purpose. Beyond these references, which footnotes help us understand, the rose embodies his feelings and by the aid of context presents feelings which may or may not be the same as his. But this indefinite meaning, although affirming the rose as more than allegorical and comprising after the decay of his convention almost the only meaning that persists, is secondary. With Yeats's English-speaking rose, the proportions of definite and indefinite are reversed. A difference not only of garden but of season and climate is the reason of that.

When in the 1890s Yeats wrote poems of the rose, the definite meanings, less important than the indefinite, were multiple. Devoting poems to aspects, he bestowed, as he tells us by context or in notes, these meanings on his fading rose: political in part by local tradition, she is Dark Rosaleen or Ireland herself; philosophically, she is all but Shelley's intellectual beauty on one hand and on the other the flower of Rosicrucians or spirit nailed by time upon the cross of matter; alchemically—for Yeats was an alchemist too—she signifies the great work of transmuting matter into spirit or, by increasing its spiritual content, of promoting it a little along the chain; aesthetically, she represents that organization of elements, even of opposites, that provides catharsis and peace; and, as my pronoun should make plain, she is woman. By embracing nation, love, and the occult, this rose, at once fleshly and ideal, contains his three central interests, the conflicts among them, and his hope of reconciliation. In "The Rose of Battle," the flower, though made of matter from flux and time, is eternal. In "The Rose Upon the Rood of Time," she embodies the more pneumatic of two conflicting opposites

42

and presides over a dangerous compromise between them. Including fear and desire, quarrel and peace, the many-petaled form expresses his quandary. However clear to Yeats, these meanings, dependent upon private association and upon traditions more or less obscure or so familiar as to seem obvious, become no more than possible to us and, because rather than in spite of multiplicity, indefinite. In a note to one of his poems in the 1899 volume Yeats said: "This poem has always meant a great deal to me, though as is the way with symbolic poems, it has not always meant quite the same thing." To depend upon privacy or even upon traditions in an age without them is no way to fix your meanings. But even assuming an awareness of these multiple meanings and calling them definite, we must agree that the greater part of that flower remains unlimited.

"The Secret Rose" is a poem invoking a flower not only most secret but far-off and inviolate. Describing the rose by a passing reference to great enfolding leaves, and defining it in the loosest fashion, Yeats tries to support the idea of a flower with circumstances that should limit or expand it. Men have sought his rose, he tells us, in the Holy Sepulchre, the wine vat, beauty, and beyond defeated dreams. Seeking rather than sought, his rose has enfolded the three Magi, who may be magicians as well as kings, and Irish heroes such as Cuchulain, Conchubar, and Fergus. Such support proving inadequate, he decides to "await" something, maybe a revelation such as came to Magus or hero. Ending the poem with a question mark makes it plain that although he desires a rose and feels it deeply, he does not know for sure with what manner of plant he has to do or what it symbolizes; and in his title the word "Secret" may mean hidden, remote, unknowable, ineffable, or indefinable. At this period of his development he was a seeker like Emerson and equally transcendental, but what was "translucid" to Emerson was all but opaque to

43

Yeats. His rose, beyond all multiple reference, is a device not only for straining the radiance of eternity but for expressing his obsessive uncertainties and, like other romantic symbols, for suggesting what discourse cannot handle. It may be, as Yeats said, that man, unable to know truth, can embody it, but the trouble with his "symbolic rose" is that, although named and vaguely circumscribed, it lacks body, whereas Dante's rose, palpable and heavenly although assigned, has body enough to please the imagination.

In Dante's world of certainties, for which allegory was suitable, imagination and fact were one. In Donne's world, although falling apart, they maintained some connection. But Yeats, in his romantic time, found himself engaged in a war between imagination and fact that had persisted inconclusively for years. Making a stand, however insecure, in the upper half of their divided reality, the more romantic of two ignorant armies, spurned the lower half of matter and fact, which was occupied securely by scientists, rationalists, and men of affairs. That these practical men were no less belligerent is proved by the opening scene of *Hard Times*. " 'Now, what I want is, Facts. Teach these boys and girls nothing but Facts. . . . We hope to have, before long, a board of fact, composed of commissioners of fact, who will force the people to be a people of fact, and of nothing but fact. You must discard the word Fancy altogether.' " Thomas Gradgrind, who says this, is a retired wholesaler of hardware, who "proceeds upon the principle that two and two are four, and nothing over." "He seemed a galvanizing apparatus, too, charged with a grim mechanical substitute for the tender young imaginations that were to be swept away." As we might suppose, his children, like rational young John Stuart Mill, suffer from "starved imagination." Leaving victims by the way, partisans of either side illustrate the dissociation of sensibility from thought and fact that Eliot made us aware of.

The symbol, though drawing substance from the lower half of reality, was used at first by partisans of imagination to affirm the upper half or at least to call it to mind. Yeats's rose upon the rood of time seems an example of that usage; but however hostile to science and reason in his youth, Yeats was unable to forget their claims upon him, and even in this poem he asks the invited rose not to come too near lest, filling him entirely, it end his concern with the world of nature, nation, and love. Whatever their delicacy and seeming confusion, the petals of the rose spring from a common center, and although once used to separate the areas of reality, the symbol is better adapted to joining them. It is not surprising that writers of the later romantic movement, trying to unite the halves of reality, found symbols the agents or celebrants of union. About ten years after Yeats wrote his poems of the rose, he called for "unity of being," and, directing poems to that end, began to use symbols to join his worlds and acclaim their identity. "By the help of an image," he said, "I call to my own opposite."

The most famous of such images is the circling moon, which, passing in the course of a month from darkness to light through phases of partial illumination and back to darkness, embodies all warring opposites and reconciles their disagreements. The fortnight of greater light, equivalent to the upper half of our chain, is the residence of imagination, spirit, Platonic ideas, sensibility, and subjective life. In the darker half of the circle, equivalent to the lower half of the chain, reside matter, fact, and all mechanical crude things. But pure only when disembodied, spirit and matter cooperate in the other twenty-six phases, where they are proportionately embodied.

45

The man of greater imagination, incarnated in the upper half, must find expression or mask in the lower. Including psychology, religion, history, and aesthetics, the wheeling moon unites again all sublunary with all translunary things, and the circle, broken in the seventeenth century, as Marjorie Nicolson tells us, resumes something of its ancient shape. But the old circle was public, and Yeats's restoration was for himself alone. What is more, less circle than gyre when looked at from the side, his symbolic figure carries modern suggestions of development, not those of static perfection which used to surround the image.

Wallace Stevens, making imagination and fact his theme, employs symbol not only to display those conflicting opposites but to unite them and present their synthesis. To be sure his antitheses of moon and sun, blue and green, north and south are closer to sign than symbol, but he uses symbol within this significant frame. When in "The Comedian as the Letter C" imaginative Crispin goes to sea, his "barber's eye" attributes mustachios to "silentious porpoises" in vain; for sea is fact and, despite imaginative evasion, Crispin is all at sea. The jungle of Yucatan to which he voyages is also "quintessential fact," but Carolina, midway between north and south, blue and green, is more suitable. Here like a florist "asking aid from cabbages," he makes "prose" or fact "wear a poem's guise at last." *Daughters with Curls* are his solution and his final symbol. A daughter is a natural thing, a matter of fact in fact. Add curls and she becomes to one like Crispin, who has a barber's eye, a triumph of imagination and art. A daughter with curls embodies and presents the parts of reality in agreeable synthesis or what Stevens calls "blissful liaison"; and fact and fiction, whatever their quarrel, become one again.

The French symbolists, standing behind Stevens if not Yeats, mark the second stage of the romantic movement. These poets used symbol not so much to unite worlds as to create them, but their origin in transcendentalism is plain. In "The Purloined Letter," Edgar A. Poe, to whom they confessed a debt, says: "The material world abounds with very strict analogies to the immaterial." Starting there, they proceeded by a process beyond Poe's capacity. "Une fois, par un minuit lugubre, tandis que je m'appesantissais, faible et fatigué, sur maint curieux et bizarre volume de savoir oublié. . . ." When Poe's raven, transformed utterly by Mallarmé, says "Jamais plus," a terrible beauty is born.

Transforming Poe's essay on the raven, Baudelaire renders the poet's intention of making the bird "emblematical of *Mournful and Never-ending Remembrance*" as "l'intention de faire du *Corbeau* le symbole du souvenir funèbre et éternel." But when in "Correspondances," his sonnet on the symbol, Baudelaire says:

> La Nature est un temple où de vivants piliers
> Laissent parfois sortir de confuses paroles:
> L'homme y passe à travers des forêts de symboles
> Qui l'observent avec des regards familiers,

he does not differ in substance or image from Emerson, who in his essay on the poet calls nature "a temple whose walls are covered with emblems . . . and the distinctions which we make in events . . . disappear when nature is used as a symbol." Baudelaire's symbol, however, differs from Emerson's by uniting not only nature and spirit with confused words but, confusing the senses with one another, by uniting parts of this world. Neither Baudelaire nor his *semblables* drew fine distinctions between symbol, emblem, allegory, sign, and image, all of which meant symbol. Sometimes he used parallel metaphors, sometimes traditional symbols, and sometimes

47

those images of city life, rag pickers, dead horses, or garbage, that T. S. Eliot was to find congenial and useful as embodiments of our social, subjective, or spiritual condition. Principally, however, the poem itself, a structure of image, rhythm, and tone, served Baudelaire as symbol.

That he is a transitional figure, standing midway between Emerson and Mallarmé, is apparent from his prose. Accepting Coleridge's creative and unifying imagination, Baudelaire finds this "queen of the faculties" of service in a double capacity. In the first place she can detect and arrange materials offered by memory or by nature, that great dictionary of analogies. "The visible universe," he says in his "Salon de 1859," "is only a store of images and signs to which imagination gives place and relative value; it is a kind of fodder that the imagination must digest and transform." In the second place, moving beyond existing analogies, the queenly faculty has power to create new ones, "la plus haute *fiction*," for example, or what Wallace Stevens, one of Baudelaire's most distinguished followers, came to call a "supreme fiction." Since art is not copying nature, imagination must create a world to replace the uncomfortable and divided world in which the poet finds himself. This private world, aesthetically organized, is self-subsistent like Poe's work of art; and imagination in her second capacity also unites Baudelaire with Mallarmé and later makers. In his survey of Baudelaire's tradition, Marcel Raymond, dividing poets into two kinds, those who followed Baudelaire the seer and those who followed Baudelaire the artist, supports the idea of his transitional duality. As seer the great poet belongs with the earlier transcendentalists and as artist with those who, finding aesthetic construction a substitute for cosmic reconstruction, made something like autonomous worlds.

Such worlds served Mallarmé as symbols. Without intended reference to external reality, his worlds or poems are "inclosed." Fictions or virtual realities, they exist as a piece of music does, by symmetry, interaction of parts, and what he called "reciprocal reflections." A poem, he observed, is "a geometry of phrases" which, not logically but symphonically arranged, is as far as possible from discourse—and so is his discourse. Unfortunately words, the elements of poems, have reference; and to purify the language of the tribe, he transformed habitual and faded significance by syntactical dislocation until words, remade in this manner, make a "total word," new, strange, and incantatory. That this "marvelous organization" is a world cannot astonish us; for the transition from word to world is familiar. That his world or poem is a symbol may be harder to accept; for what it symbolizes is a question. His assurance that what it "suggests" or "evokes"—he uses both words—is at once precise and indefinable seems not enough; but during an interview, or what the French call an inquest, he said that symbolism consists in evoking an object little by little in order to reveal a state of mind or, inversely, choosing an object and from it disengaging a state of mind. The "total arabesque" or the "pure harmony" is there not only as evidence of itself but as creator of a state of mind, soul, or feeling. This state, far from being a reminder of anything we have known, is a fresh creation; and this creation is the effect of an analogy, not from nature's store but made by the poet. What it is an analogy for must be guessed by the reader as the poem creates his state of mind. Putting this excellently in his essay "The Symbolism of Poetry," Yeats, who knew of Mallarmé at second hand through Arthur Symons, says that a poem evokes an emotion "which cannot be evoked by any other arrangement of colours and sounds and forms." All such arrangements, he continues, "evoke indefinable and yet precise emotions," and when the elements of a poem are "in a musical relation" to one

49

another, they become one form and "evoke an emotion that is made out of their distinct evocations and yet is one emotion."

Like many of Baudelaire's followers, Mallarmé had spiritual inclinations and interests. In one of his letters, he says that he lives habitually in Eternity, but, he continues, it is an Eternity that he carries around within himself. This portable Eternity, hardly to be distinguished from that which is embodied in a work of art, is not the Oversoul of common transcendentalists, but private, like his poems. As a follower of Baudelaire the artist, Mallarmé is on firmer but no less private ground. Accepting Poe's idea of pure art without metaphysical or ethical significance, he held the poem to be impersonal, objective, and uncommunicative. It may correspond, to be sure, in some way to his "interior climate" and create something comparable in a reader, if any, but the charm of his self-subsistent world is "indecisiveness" of meaning. What he says in a letter about "Ses purs ongles très haut dédiant leur onyx," one of his best and most enigmatic sonnets, is relevant: "the sense, if there is one, is evoked by an internal mirage of the words themselves." Save that it is a universe which may suggest our own, he prefers not to attempt to fix its meaning since a poem like this celebration of sumptuous emptiness and splendid absence is an enchanting compound of the rich and the vague in which, he says, one cannot put a brutal finger on anything.

Discouraged critics, C. M. Bowra (in *The Heritage of Symbolism*) among them, have complained that such poems are too remote from life and society to have moral value or human interest. The trouble with the French variety of symbolism, they say, is the musical autonomy that Mallarmé prized. From those with moral or sociological concerns this objection is understandable, but in making worlds with indefinite suggestion, Mallarmé and his followers were doing no

50

more than artists have always done, though more conspicuously perhaps and in some ways better than some.

Before we proceed with the nature of these romantic worlds, it is fitting to recall the way in which symbols as constructs were preserved through the age of reason and handed to our time by the Hermetic tradition. Hermes Trismegistus is the Egyptian god Thoth, somewhat Hellenized. Associated at first with the moon and the ibis, dog-headed Thoth became secretary to Osiris, in which capacity he invented speech and writing, not to mention the signs of the zodiac and alchemy. Since magic depends upon words, he became magus-in-chief and, under Greek auspices, the Logos or creator of things. This god of words and original secretary was destined to become the patron of Renaissance writers. Reappearing in the romantic period, but separated now from the idea of nature it had affirmed, Hermetism once more gave men of letters method. Emerson, Baudelaire, Mallarmé, Yeats, and Joyce himself are among these denatured Hermetics.

The works of Hermes, known as the *Corpus Hermeticum* or the *Pimander,* though basically Platonic, are confused by additions from Zoroaster, the great magus. Peculiar in no way, as Festugière, the principal authority, affirms, Hermetism is one of many almost identical doctrines that pleased those in Alexandria or at the Mareotic Lake who, tiring of Greek dialectic, preferred to lose themselves in a mystery. The revelation of Hermes, which dates from a century or two before Christ to a century or two after, may have survived the rival claims of the magi and the oracles because of Plato's ghost, but it is more likely to have survived because it has a convenient and suggestive name, which came to mean all the more useful wisdom of the past, whether astrological, alchemical, magical, or philosophical and whether strictly Hermetic or not.

51

To Hermes-Thoth the cosmos was a unity of interdependent parts, connected by sympathies or antipathies and arranged in curious paradigm. The heart of it was the chain of being with which we are familiar, but what was to fascinate men of letters was the idea of correspondences or analogical connections. In the *Asclepius,* one of his dialogues, Hermes finds "a reciprocal relation" governing reality: "All things are connected one to another by mutual correspondences in a chain which extends from the lowest to the highest." It was not until Marsilio Ficino translated the *Corpus* in 1463 that the philosophy of Hermes became generally available. But whether or not their wisdom came directly from Hermes, alchemists and alchemical divines of the Renaissance, such as Agrippa and Boehme, were labeled Hermetic. *Tabula Smaragdina* (1541) or *The Emerald Tablet,* another work attributed to Hermes, expressed the essence of Hermetism with unforgettable neatness: "As above, so below," a phrase that for many in later times became all that need be known of Hermes and, indeed, all that was known.

Although the Renaissance idea of nature, with its correspondences between macrocosm and microcosm and among all things, was not altogether Hermetic, it was so much like the idea of Hermes that not uncommonly his name, linked with that of Plato, was invoked to support it. Sir Thomas Browne, who saw man in a kind of spherical vivarium as "that great and true *Amphibium,* whose nature is disposed to live not only like other creatures in divers elements, but in divided and distinguished worlds . . . the one visible, the other invisible," reveals authority for his vision a few pages away: "The severe Schools shall never laugh me out of the Philosophy of *Hermes* that this visible World is but a Picture of the invisible" nor out of understanding a mystery "without a rigid definition, in an easie and Platonick description." Meanwhile in some high lonely tower Milton's thinker was watching out the Bear "with thrice great *Hermes*" and "the spirit of *Plato*" by his side. Whether Platonic or Hermetic or more general than either, the doctrine of correspondences provided a poetic century with method.

As we have seen, however, this organically interconnected world in which Andrew Marvell's garden of analogies could flourish, gave way to another in which part was connected with part by a kind of engineering. Analogy seemed—as indeed it is—irrational; and Hermetic correspondence, both cosmic and metaphorical, went underground for a hundred years. To be sure the eighteenth century was not altogether rational, still less altogether mechanical. It produced Methodists, an edition of Boehme, and Emanuel Swedenborg. Not Methodists, but Boehme and Swedenborg, both Hermetics, preserved and helped bring back not the world of Hermes but his correspondences as literary method. The world of Hermes was dead, and no degree of nostalgia could bring it back. Although analogy became method again, it was no longer a picture of fact. The servant of a new reality, it became a way of discovering, uniting, and even creating not a world perhaps but worlds.

Blake, whose Tiger is half a metaphor the other half of which is left unstated, found hints of method in Paracelsus, Boehme, Swedenborg, and, if we may draw conclusions from *The Song of Los,* in Pythagoras, Plato, and Trismegistus himself. It is not surprising, therefore, that Blake could "see a World in a grain of sand, and a Heaven in a wild flower," or that, announcing his "fourfold vision," he prayed "God us to keep from single vision, and Newton's sleep!" Coleridge was familiar with Boehme, and Emerson found authority in Swedenborg, the alchemists, and all the Platonists, both neo and original. Romantic poets were ready for the revelation from Hermes and his disciples that commenced about the middle of the nineteenth century and continued well into our own. This revelation came from the occult, which, having stored the doctrine of correspondences away during an alien period, gave it to poets waiting to receive it.

In his essays, which are among the most important documents of our period, Baudelaire attributes his doctrine of correspondences to Swedenborg, who taught that "comparisons, metaphors, and epithets are drawn from the inexhaustible depths of universal analogy." That this archaic yet romantic notion has a source more authentic than Swedenborg is suggested by the address to the hypocritical reader with which Baudelaire introduces his poems. Here he refers to the Satanic enchantments of "Trismégiste . . . ce savant chimiste." It seems not unlikely from this that the images of swan, city, voyage, and the like, with which his poems abound, are Hermetic correspondences. In his hands, however, "as above, so below" increasingly became *as here, so there* or *as in, so out*.

His poems appeared in 1857. Two years earlier Eliphas Lévi, the most eminent magus of the nineteenth century, had published his *Dogme de la Haute Magie,* the work above all others that disclosed Hermes to poets. Enlightened by the "lamp of Trismegistus," he says, the magus can proceed up and down the scale of being to discover by "analogical correspondence between the sign and the thing signified" the secrets of reality. "To pronounce a name is to create or evoke a being or a thought." It is by no means odd that poets, substituting poet for magus or leaving it as it stood, adopted Lévi's Hermetism as symbolic method and took evoke, their favorite word, from magic.

After reading Lévi, Rimbaud called himself "voyant" or seer and re-created or maybe created visions in his *Illuminations*. These poems, composed of symbols, are symbols or correspondences for feeling and idea. It is not without Hermetic significance that the important part

54

of his *Season in Hell* is called "Alchemy of the Word." Here, when he says of his poems, "I put down the inexpressible" and "I reserved the rights of translation," he is noting the nondiscursive nature of the symbol and the folly of explicators.

Villiers de l'Isle Adam, a Rosicrucian, wrote Mallarmé a letter warmly commending *Le Dogme de la Haute Magie*. That he read it seems probable from references to "grimoires" in his poems. After attending a meeting of Rosicrucians, he wrote the essay on magic, in which, after discussing alchemy and black magic, he says: "There is a secret connection between poetry and the ancient methods of magic. To evoke the hidden object by allusive words, never direct," is the way of both arts. But by the time of Mallarmé, the work of Lévi had inspired many similar works. Societies of Rosicrucians, Cabalists, and Theosophists, flourishing in both France and England, enchanted many men of letters. The world of Hermes may have been dead in fact and forgotten by society, but to these poets, exiles from society and enemies of matter and machine, the world of Hermes was a symbol of their rebellion. That they desired this world is plain, but it is hard to determine the degree of their belief in it. There can be no doubt, however, about their belief in the theory of knowledge and the literary method belonging to a cosmic system less actual perhaps than convenient. Nor can we doubt that Hermes provided plans for replacing the incomplete world of science by complete aesthetic worlds. As organic as the Hermetic universe, the work of art need not hold a mirror to nature, but may replace it by something more like a world. It was no accident that Virginia Woolf called the work of art "a globed compacted thing."

Yeats, who spent his days in occult pursuits, called himself a Hermetist. Madame Blavatsky, a second but more copious Lévi, became his spiritual guide in the 1880s; and he joined a Rosicrucian order, which in his *Autobiography* he calls the Hermetic Students. He edited the prophetic books of Blake and read not only Lévi but all occult, Cabalistic, and Platonic literature he could lay his hands on, and there was a lot of it around. Like Mallarmé, he wrote an essay on magic and the power of correspondences; like Valéry, he wrote an essay on Swedenborg. His early poems, filled with correspondences, reflect these interests; but even in one of the "Supernatural Songs," written late in life, he says: "things below are copies, the Great Smaragdine Tablet said."

Yeats is the conspicuous Hermetist of our time, but several others belong in their degree to the tradition. Lawrence, for example, found the key to analogy in the works of Madame Blavatsky. Mann, another of those who applied the method of analogy to the novel, made Settembrini, the champion of liberal humanism in *The Magic Mountain,* commend Hermes. Defending the word, he speaks of "the Egyptian god Thoth, identical with the thrice renowned Hermes of Hellenism; who was honoured as the inventor of writing, protector of libraries, and inciter to all literary efforts." Naphta, his absolutist opponent, seeing only the occult side of Hermes-Thoth, condemns him as an ape and moon god "of whom late antiquity made an arch-enchanter, and the cabalistic Middle Ages the Father of hermetic alchemy." In view of the functional character of Mann's materials, this debate on Hermes seems there in part as clue to literary method.

Even Joyce, whose humor would seem to forbid such interests, was on a familiar footing with Hermes. This is not as surprising as it seems, for Joyce used analogy even more consistently than most writers of a time when important literature is symbolist; and if it is true that Hermes, whether directly or indirectly, is partly responsible for symbolic method during the romantic period, a connection

56

between Joyce and Hermes becomes the most natural thing in the world. Joyce, who knew his Baudelaire, Rimbaud, and Mallarmé, regarded Yeats with not-always-respectful awe. We know that young Joyce attended Theosophical meetings in Dawson Street or at the home of A.E., and that around the turn of the century, although poor, he bought several Theosophical books, in one of which Hermes is conspicuous.

References to Madame Blavatsky and the Theosophists in *Ulysses* are invariably cynical; for by the time Joyce composed that book he had long abandoned the occult as a possible way to divinity. It is notable, however, that in two of these references the Theosophists are called Hermetic, as if under that label their teaching could be subsumed—as indeed it can. In the Aeolus chapter of *Ulysses*, Stephen Dedalus, a projection of the young Joyce of 1904, mentions "that hermetic crowd, the opal hush poets: A.E. the master mystic? That Blavatsky woman started it." Thinking of her *Isis Unveiled* in the library scene, Stephen remarks: "The faithful hermetists await the light." That Joyce, like other amateurs in this attenuated Hermetism, also investigated some of Madame Blavatsky's sources is made plain by this passage from *A Portrait of the Artist:* "A phrase of Cornelius Agrippa flew through his mind . . . shapeless thoughts from Swedenborg on the correspondence of birds with things of the intellect. . . ." At the commencement of this rumination Stephen is thinking of augury and at the end of symbol. At the beginning of the third chapter of *Ulysses*, the Proteus or Egyptian episode, the phrase "Signatures of all things" implies Stephen's acquaintance with Jacob Boehme.

However ironic about Theosophy, Stephen is plainly impressed if not with the metaphysics of Hermes at least with his applicability to literature. Since there is nothing in Joyce that is casual, nothing

57

that serves no purpose in the total structure, and since a principal theme of his books is his development as an artist, it is likely that the following passages on Hermes-Thoth as the god of writers, put into the mind of a hero who is an incipient artist and surrogate of Joyce himself, have the profoundest significance as a clue to the nature of Stephen's future method, when, as Joyce, he composed *A Portrait of the Artist* and *Ulysses.* As Stephen in the *Portrait,* standing suitably on the steps of the National Library, thinks of Agrippa, Swedenborg, and symbols, he thinks "of Thoth, the god of writers, writing with a reed upon a tablet and bearing on his narrow ibis head the cusped moon." In this description, which shows considerable acquaintance with the person and habits of Hermes, bird and moon appear to function as traditional signs of the imagination, in the service of which Stephen has declared himself a priest; the reed seems to indicate music and poetry; and the tablet, of course, is green. Inside the same library, in *Ulysses,* Stephen ruminates: "Coffined thoughts around me, in mummycases, embalmed in spice of words. Thoth, god of libraries, a birdgod, moony-crowned. And I heard the voice of that Egyptian highpriest. *In painted chambers loaded with tilebooks.*" That Stephen, going beyond the emerald tilebook, had some knowledge of the *Corpus Hermeticum* is suggested by that passage from the Circe episode in which A.E., the Theosophist, appearing in the guise of Mananaan Maclir, speaks of the "Occult pimander of Hermes Trismegistos."

For Yeats and a few other transcendentalists who believed or wanted to believe in a macrocosm they did not know but which correspondences might reveal, such analogies are sometimes vertical, as Hermes recommended. For writers like Joyce, who had lost belief in the upper half of Hermetic reality, except in so far as it could be equated with the poetic imagination or the unconscious, correspondences were generally horizontal, and *The Emerald Tablet* was modified, as we have noticed, to mean *as here, so there* or *as in, so out.* The method of Hermes, separated from his world and adapted to what was left, still seemed a way of exploring, unifying, or revealing the relationship of part with part. Joyce used correspondences to show the connection between man and man, man and society, man and nature, and, as if to prove himself a romantic, between past and present. The sublunary reality so revealed seemed, as a result perhaps of nineteenth-century biology, an organic and changing whole. To provide an image of this world, to present the feeling of it, and, if we may change the metaphor, to note the harmony of parts the modified correspondence seemed eminently suitable. Since, moreover, the correspondence puts things together, it might connect the individual more closely with what surrounds him by making him aware of it and serve, however indirectly, a moral purpose—such as the commendation of charity. But Hermes was most useful to Joyce in showing him not how to represent a world but how to create one.

The circle, that image of the closed and unified world of the past, is one of Joyce's principal symbols. Not a gyre, as in the system of Yeats, but a "Wheel of Fortune," as it is called in *Finnegans Wake,* Joyce's Viconian circle is an image of time and destiny, which impartially distributes "the seim anew." But what appeared to men of the Renaissance an image of perfection now seems the image of temporal recurrence, to be made the best of with gaiety and sympathy. That the image of the compass, once associated with the perfect circle, should recur in *Finnegans Wake* is not surprising. "The Goat and Compasses" is not only the name of a pub but an image of the family that creates the circle in which it revolves. The Goat is both God and H. C. Earwicker; the compasses he wields are his twin sons, who describe themselves in the manner of Donne as "a daintical pair of accomplasses." "A daintical" means identical, and the twins are confused with the two dainty lasses whom the Goat also uses to circumscribe his destiny.

Analogy is not only the method of *Ulysses* but its substance. Out of a maze of correspondences Joyce created a world, complete and self-subsistent, but not without reference to external things nor without power to organize our feeling about them. Unable or unwilling to revive the world that died in the seventeenth century, he made another world in its image. That this world is an aesthetic rather than a cosmic structure is what we might expect; for poets today seeking unity, find it in art alone.

But they have this advantage over their predecessors who inherited a world already made. As creators, they can enjoy the sensations of God and like Him they can retire into what they have made or sit upon it. Stephen concludes his discussion of art in the *Portrait* with these words: "The mystery of esthetic like that of material creation is accomplished. The artist, like the God of creation, remains within or behind or beyond or above his handiwork, invisible, refined out of existence, indifferent, paring his fingernails." His aesthetic substitute for the actual world, Stephen has just observed, must have wholeness, harmony, and radiance. In other words this world, unlike our own, must resemble the complete, harmonious, and significant world of Hermes, whom Stephen discusses a few pages later. It is not unlikely that Hermes, the "god of writers" and the creative Logos, gave Joyce not only hints of method but lessons in composition which proved useful when, as he expresses it in *Finnegans Wake* he "made mundballs of the ephemerids."

The Hermetic revival, which resulted in these private or semi-private worlds, was accompanied by a revival of metaphysical

60

metaphor. Once better adapted than symbol to the affairs of above and below, this limited analogy of the Renaissance pleased romantic symbolists, who found in it another way of connecting parts of whatever worlds they had or wanted. Whether as element of a symbolic structure or as a supplement, metaphor proved congenial and not without symbolic possibilities. It was particularly convenient for transcendentalists trying to match an above to their below. In his essay on nature, for example, Emerson quotes George Herbert's "Man," a poem of macrocosm and micrososm: " 'He is in little all the sphere.' " Nothing could be more Hermetic or more metaphysical.

The characteristic of metaphysical metaphor is apparent incongruity in the service of harmony. Hopkins was no Hermetic but he too searched Herbert and possibly others of the seventeenth century for incongruous comparisons. "The Blessed Virgin Compared to the Air We Breathe," an extended comparison of the commonplace with the celestial, is witty in the sense that Donne understood the word; for wit in his sense, as we have noticed, is the analogical faculty, a means of exploring and affirming both realities, not of decorating this one. Such logical elaboration of the conceit or apparently incongruous comparison as Hopkins uses, while not necessary for metaphysical poetry, is typical of it. The earthly term of Hopkins's analogy, though limited by equation and less indefinite for that reason than the romantic symbol, is not without symbolic effect; for it embodies vision, and the two terms, working together, create between them another vision, as any two elements of a poem may do.

Browning read the metaphysicals; Emily Dickinson must have read them; and Arthur Symons in the 1890s imitated Donne as well as Baudelaire; but the full revival of Donne followed Gosse's biography of the poet in 1899 and Grierson's edition in 1912. T. S. Eliot,

61

who made the revival known to the common reader, had learned of Donne at Harvard and of the symbolists from Arthur Symons. Finding both symbolists and metaphysicals agreeable, he proceeded to confuse them with one another; for although devoted to tradition, he was never strong in history. It is true that both schools have analogy in common, but symbolist analogies differ in kind and function from those of Donne. The metaphysical analogy, logically developed and comparatively definite, serves an orderly, public universe; the symbolist analogy, remote from logic, serves worlds that are either indefinite or private. The appearance of incongruity in metaphysical verse that attracted young Eliot serves to discover the harmony of all things; the metaphorical incongruities of Mallarmé establish aesthetic harmony alone.

Twentieth-century symbolists who were still transcendentally inclined used the conceit at times to commend the connection of above with below. Yeats, who was imitating Donne's conversational style around 1905, says in his *Autobiography* that Donne "could be as metaphysical as he pleased" without seeming inhuman and hysterical as Shelley often does, "because he could be as physical as he pleased." In "Supernatural Songs," which Yeats called poems "of a passionate metaphysical sort," the "sexual spasm" of Godhead upon Godhead is a conceit combining the regions—though somewhat less spectacularly than Eliot's lyric of the "wounded surgeon," which, logically constructed upon Sir Thomas Browne's analogy of world as hospital, is the most elaborate imitation of Donne in recent times. These metaphorical poems by Yeats and Eliot are functional parts of symbolic structures, which, like their originals, are dedicated to a desire for the harmony of above and below, Irish and Indian on the one hand and decently Anglican on the other.

Sometimes, however, twentieth-century symbolists called upon the conceit for those possibilities of disharmony, inherent in the form, that Donne exploited in his more doubtful moments. Eliot's patient etherized upon his table, the opening of "Prufrock," is typical of analogical custom before and after the first World War. Wallace Stevens's conceit of the caliper is hardly more agreeable.

The difference between a seventeenth-century conceit and a contemporary one is shown by my promised comparison of Donne's famous compasses with that caliper. The soft souls of Donne's lovers go away and come together like the legs of stiff twin compasses:

> Thy soule the fixt foot, makes no show
> To move, but doth, if the other doe.

It was wit's business to find the similar in the dissimilar; and the seeming incompatibility of mechanical drawing and love at a time when each thing was involved with all other things was nothing. Stevens in "Last Looks at the Lilacs" calls one of his lovers a caliper, a device that by usage, character, and shape suggests intellect, measurement, science, and industry. That mechanical lover, the man of course, tells his companion, a "divine ingénue" among the flowers, that bloom is the bloom of "vegetal," a lilac preparation once advertised in subways by Ed. Pinaud. In this case, the caliper, far from uniting those lovers, marks their difference; for today calipers belong to one region, girls and love to another, and what once seemed incompatible is incompatible indeed. That the girl can confuse a caliper with "gold Don John" is strange but no stranger than girls choosing professors or engineers and by Kantian projection enjoying them. Donne's conceit is a hymn to the conjunction of parts whereas Stevens's is an ironic acknowledgment of their separation.

The difference between Donne's flea and Kafka's insect—maybe a cockroach—is no less exemplary. Having sucked him, then her,

Donne's flea their "mariage bed, and mariage temple is." Whatever their seeming inconsistency, fleas and marriage beds are part of a system; but, since flea is lower than lover in the hierarchy of being and distinguished among creatures by toughness, agility, and rapacity, Donne's pleasing conceit, the favorite of a conceited century, may imply an attitude toward marriage—whether dim, ironic, cynical, wise, comic, or neutral it is difficult to say. Suggesting almost as much as it says, the metaphor approaches symbol; but, however indefinite in tone, attitude, and feeling, this comparison seems limited when compared with the central analogy of Kafka's *Metamorphosis*. Poor Gregor Samsa, waking in the morning, finds himself transformed in bed to an enormous insect. Less assigned than unassigned, this symbol implies the attitude of Samsa's family toward Samsa, his opinion of himself, and, in addition to these, ideas and feelings about our society, our time, and the miserable condition of humanity. Donne's flea and Kafka's significantly nameless bug are well adapted to their environments and their times. The difference between that metaphor and this symbol is less of kind or analogical habit than of worlds.

Kafka's disgusting bug is a fair sample of the twentieth-century symbol. His hero's quandary is like something out of nightmare by Freud; for even the most transcendental symbols of our time, differing in this respect from earlier romantic images, owe part at least of content and quality to the revelations of that Viennese, who announced our century and marked its difference from others with his *Interpretation of Dreams*. Revealing the unconscious, he provided symbolists with new territory for romantic exploration and a new store of images from the depths of night. Not that exploring poets had avoided this territory and these images, but, making poets aware of what some had been doing, he confirmed a growing interest and established a new dimension. The vertical, by his aid, became more nearly horizontal. *As above, so below,* though surviving here and there, commonly yielded to *as in, so out.* Reason, at last dethroned, was replaced, for men of sensibility at least, by imagination and the unconscious, which, although within man, came to occupy the place that he used to think above him in the upper half of the chain. Designed for exploring and for handling more than reason can manage or discourse define, the symbol, improved by Freud's brilliant mind and given a more suitable climate, flourished as never before.

Although to the best of my knowledge Freud never quite defined symbol, he calls it a product of the "unconscious imagination." The dream-work of his censor, designed to conceal rather than to reveal, makes use of images. Wondering for a time whether these recurrent images, which he calls symbols, have fixed and permanent meanings like the signs of shorthand, Freud finally concluded that although they are significant, what they carry at each appearance is determined by context and by the associations of the dreamer. To interpret such symbols, then, requires not only a knowledge of typical signs but analysis of changing circumstance or context. Despite such qualification and such warnings against arbitrary and facile interpretation, Freud tended to regard his images as nearer sign than symbol. He uses the words signify and represent and seems convinced that he can "translate" his symbols as an Egyptologist his hieroglyphics. Freud was a medical man, of course, and that his interest was symbol as symptom is not surprising; but for his readers what he revealed of the symbol-making power of the unconscious imagination was not limited by his scientific interests. Ignoring his diagnoses, poets and Carl Jung made his revelation more general and more romantic.

To Freud symbols were not only unconscious but primitive, like images of folklore and myth: "The symbolic relationship seems to

65

be a residue and reminder of a former identity." When Jung broke with Freud, he took this idea of symbol along with him; and his archetypes, which lie behind all symbols, are vestiges of man's experience. Dismissing Freud's symbols as signs, romantic Jung saw the symbol as the best possible way to express something for which no verbal concept exists. Although its rational component can be made comprehensible, he said, the symbol's irrational component, never to be fully explained or interpreted, can be grasped by feelings alone. Ambiguous, filled with contradictions and intimations, Jung's "true" symbols are inexhaustible. But by these devices, at once expressive and impressive, the unconscious and the conscious, together with all opposites, are fused and reconciled. That his mediating symbols are not unlike those once used by alchemists confirms their place in the Hermetic tradition and explains their appeal to romantic men of letters.

Freud and Jung were anticipated and abetted by Frazer and other anthropologists, who, revealing images from man's past more fully, added still another dimension to symbolic relationship. *As above, so below* and *as in, so out* were joined and supplemented by *as then, so now,* a return to vertical correspondence perhaps, but vertical in time. Frazer's revelations about Vergil's golden bough were used by Yeats, who had already consulted the works of the solar mythologists. Even Eliot's symbolic wasteland comes from one of Frazer's disciples, and the eating of god in *Finnegans Wake* recalls Frazer no less than the practice of Christians, whether literal, symbolic, or betwixt and between.

But what of autonomy? If art in our time is autonomous, as many critics affirm, we must ask how the symbol can derive substance, reference, and quality from disciplines which connect it with man's unconscious and his past. But Mallarmé, the most nearly autonomous

66

of poets, never realized his ideal; for literature, after all, is not music nor can it be as free from reference as that art, whatever our desire. Words, the elements of literature, have reference, and a literary work is but the semblance of a world. The aesthetic worlds created by Mallarmé and Joyce are forms which, suggesting man's condition, are symbols of living. That is part of their value. "To construct something on which to rejoice," as Eliot puts it in *Ash Wednesday,* is to construct something at once aesthetically autonomous and, by reference or suggestion, moral and human. Once at a party in Paris when someone proposed a toast to immorality, Joyce put his glass of white wine down and said: "I will not drink to that."

Supreme Fictions

*A*S TIGHT and reflexive as poems, symbolist novels insinuate their meanings by a concert of elements. Images, allusions, hints, changes of rhythm, and tone—in short, all the devices of suggestion—support and sometimes carry the principal burden. "Whatever is felt upon the page without being specifically named there—that, one might say," says Willa Cather, "is created." Presenting themselves, such creations offer a vision of reality.

Since symbolism is the necessary condition of literature, all novels are symbolic. By the poetic or symbolist novel I mean a kind distinguished by the deliberate or unconscious exploitation of symbolic possibilities. Authors of such novels, which have abounded in the later romantic period, try to present something beyond narrative and discourse or even to do without them. Almost a hundred years ago, in his essay on Théophile Gautier, Baudelaire commended "la nouvelle poétique," which he imagined rather than observed. Devoted less to description of external realities than to "vision," this kind of novel or story must borrow from poems not meter and rhyme, he said, but "concise energy" of language. Melville and Flaubert had written novels of this sort; Lewis Carroll and Dostoyevsky were about to make their contributions; and many uncommonly thought of as symbolists were making use of incidental images. A gradual development culminating in the twentieth century realized Baudelaire's ideal, which Henry James may have had in mind when he said: "Don't state—render."

The twentieth-century novel, having taken lessons from poetry, all but supplanted it. To be sure, poets continued to appear—Yeats and Valéry, Rilke, Stevens, and Thomas—but few read their works. Eliot alone, rivaling the easier triumph of Tennyson, almost made poetry popular again; and even he, in an interview published in 1953, confessed himself disappointed with those poets who twenty years earlier had seemed to promise so much. "I sometimes lean toward the view," he said, "that creative advance in our age is in prose fiction." What he had in mind, as he made this announcement in that office overlooking Russell Square and adorned with pictures of Valéry, Yeats, and Virginia Woolf, was the work of Henry Green. But Blake's "Fair Nine, forsaking Poetry" preside over that of other novelists as well.

Whatever the cause, interest in verse declined; but readers of prose who could ignore the general indifference to letters in our society seem to have retained some capacity for poetic suggestion. Serving that vestigial interest and combining the virtues of two forms, novelists, whose narratives and characters were still inviting, took over the function once exercised by poets and did what they had done for the fathers of this meager audience. The better novel became a kind of poem. In "Notes on an Elizabethan Play," an essay in *The Common Reader,* Virginia Woolf complains that the novel is not entirely poetic yet: "The play is poetry, we say, and the novel

69

prose," but, taking example from the Elizabethan play, the novel may avoid descriptive particulars and "reveal by illumination." We await impatiently, she continues, "what may yet be devised to liberate us of the enormous burden of the unexpressed." She herself was busy devising that; and as she worked, Forster, Lawrence, Joyce, Eliot, and Conrad seemed encouraging signs—though Conrad was little better than a foreigner and Eliot expressed himself in verse, however free. Like Dostoyevsky and Flaubert, these writers made her think not only of what is present on the page but of vaster, suggested things. The greater part of *Mr. Bennett and Mrs. Brown,* the pamphlet where these reflections appear, is devoted, however, to Arnold Bennett, the bad reigning novelist, who, avoiding imagination, accumulated facts.

The Old Wives' Tale may be one of the best novels of the naturalistic tradition, in which details and actions, limited and thoroughly understood, are supposed to imply little or nothing beyond time, space, cause and effect, and the other categories of science; but Bennett's novel is far from destitute of suggestion—as the great letter from Constance to Sophia proves. We must agree that Virginia Woolf was a little unfair to Bennett and the tradition in which he worked; for most naturalists, however external and partial to causes, made use of symbols. Zola's manifestoes are so much closer to his intention than to his practice that if we consult them alone, we are deceived. In *L'Assommoir,* the great machine is as symbolic as Mrs. Woolf's lighthouse, and so is the coal mine of *Germinal.* Seemingly there for their own sake or to make a scientific or sociological point, the concrete details of Zola's novels serve other purposes as well. But impatient with such signs of grace, symbolists reacted violently against naturalism; and the poetic novel, which they devised, owes part of its character to this reaction.

There have been enough studies of symbolist poets and of symbolist poetry to make another unnecessary, but although the symbolist novel is one of the outstanding forms of our time, it has received comparatively little notice. It is true that Melville, Kafka, Faulkner, Woolf, Joyce, and Mann have been applauded in book, essay, and lecture, in most of which, however, symbols, if not ignored, have been treated in passing. Recent French critics such as Dandieu and Fiser have found Proust a symbolist; E. M. Forster and E. K. Brown have inspected aspects of the symbolist novel; but I have found little acknowledgment of the form nor am I aware of any general treatment.

When we read a symbolist novel for the first time or even the second or third, we may find it slight or even naturalistic. When we read it again, however, we find that the concrete particulars and arrangement which gave us that impression are there to carry meanings beyond immediate significance; and as we proceed, a greater meaning gradually emerges. Each rereading adds fresh discoveries, changing our idea of the whole until we despair of reaching the end of that suggestive complexity. Reading in groups—where each member, stimulated by the others and rebuking their occasional irrelevance or excess, contributes his understanding of the text—seems the best approach. Still, of such works the last word will not be spoken, for since the effect of any symbolic structure is indefinite, works of this kind cannot yield entirely to analysis. If, however, as some maintain, literature is increasingly private, reading it in company seems a good way to make it almost public again and all but sociable.

To convey the experience of reading such works, we commonly have recourse to the metaphor of levels. The work seems many-leveled like a cake, which, if eaten from the top down, reveals layer after layer of agreeable substance. Maybe, however, the metaphor owes no more to cake than to Dante's seven-story mountain or else

71

to Freud's dream, in which the manifest content seems to occupy a level above the latent. Whether it owes its origin to cake, Freud, or Purgatory, the overworked metaphor is inexact; for everything a book contains is present or implicit on the printed page. There are no levels. The surface may be so difficult that we do not find at once what is there, but surface is all. Both Saint Thomas and Dante, considering the senses of a text, placed emphasis upon the literal, which must contain the others. Yet level, suggesting at least a third dimension, may do for our experience of deeper and deeper penetration if not for the work itself. As for that, we may change the metaphor for that of the symphony, which implies time, or for those of labyrinth or world, which imply surface, organization, and development. Whatever the trope, it means that, entering the work by degrees, we discover parts at first and, if we can, the whole; or else that, having felt the whole, we discover parts.

Though none of these tropes fits the great Victorian novels, some of them, displaying symbols, distantly anticipate the poetic novel of our day. The "London particular" that fills the first chapters of *Bleak House* is a case in point. Fixing the atmosphere through which the narrative gropes, this fog suggests Jarndyce and Jarndyce, a trial as incomprehensible and monstrous as something from Kafka; and when reappearing as "a dense particular" in the third chapter of *Finnegans Wake,* it suggests by allusion the kind of evidence, gossip, and slander that plagues H. C. Earwicker's trial. Mr. Krook's warehouse of rags, paper, bottles, and bones in *Bleak House* not only supports and expands the image of fog but, like the junk shops of Dickens's other novels, the heaps of "dust" that fill the back yard in *Our Mutual Friend,* and the dark, cobwebby room in *Great Expectations,* embodies feeling and thought about middle-class society. In *Richard Feverel* the burning rick presents the theme while connect-

72

ing its parts, and although E. M. Forster dismisses Clara's double-blossomed cherry tree in *The Egoist* as a sign, that tree, the enclosed estate, and all those mirrors break through their limitation. The desolate moor and the lonely man that open *The Return of the Native* are an epitome of the book. Not only setting, the moor, like the fungoid forest of *The Woodlanders,* becomes symbol, ambivalently presenting nature in both her aspects: vestigial, Wordsworthian, and benign on the one hand, casual, Darwinian, and frightening on the other. Although the scenery and action of *Alice in Wonderland* may be unconscious and almost embarrassingly Freudian, their organization, which William Empson has explored, places the book farther along the road to recent symbolism than most of its less clerical contemporaries.

In *Madame Bovary* the agricultural fair, which consists of alternate, incompatible layers, may bring the structure of cake to mind, but it struck Flaubert as "symphonic." In his symphony, he observed in a letter, "one hears at once the bellowing of bulls, the sighs of love, and the phrases of administrators." Dissonant unions of inner and outer, past and present, strange combinations of manure and love, of oratory, both intimate and public, and a kind of resolution in damp fireworks at the end reveal a reality he called "bottomless, infinite, multiple." Of such disharmonies, he proudly said, he had made a harmonious, serene, and incomprehensible form for presenting vision. "Exactitude et mystère!" he exclaimed; and he was pleased when Baudelaire found *Madame Bovary* "suggestive." Under its simple appearance, said Flaubert, changing his metaphor, his novel is a complicated machine. To read such books, he added, changing the metaphor again, you need "initiation."

Ignorant of what Melville had done a few years earlier, Flaubert reinvented the symbolist novel. Some have confused him with realists and sociologists, but he detested realism and loathed photography with Baudelairian passion. The objects of which his novel is composed serve the purposes of poetry, which, he said in another letter, "is a way of perceiving external things, a special organ which sifts matter and which, without changing it, transfigures it." He sought a style "as rhythmic as verse, as precise as the language of science, and with the undulations and modulations of a violoncello," yet the commonplace was the matter of this poetry; for, as Baudelaire observed, "In certain almost supernatural states of soul, the depth of life is revealed in ordinary everyday happenings. Ordinary life then becomes the Symbol." The facts and trivial dialogue of *Madame Bovary* are not there to celebrate scientific observation but to suggest what they embody. Discarding analysis and commentary, the traditional resources of novelists, Flaubert made concrete, evocative, or what he called "intrinsic," details assume the load. By relationship with one another and with the theme they create the "form"—and "all must speak in forms"—through which alone reality is apparent. Carried away by the desire for pure art that was to tease Mallarmé, Flaubert dreamt of a novel about nothing, without exterior connections, held together by the internal force of style, expressive by shape alone. *Madame Bovary* is not that novel, but, a step in the direction, it helped make the novel a creative relationship of images, rhythms, and tones.

Madame Bovary's arrival in her husband's house is typical of Flaubert's method. Although the details of that establishment are given at some length, her impression receives neither analysis nor comment; but at the end of the suggestive catalogue she acts: going upstairs, she notes her predecessor's bridal bouquet and stares from a window between two pots of geraniums. In this act all her trouble and her future are revealed; and equally revealing, the veil through which,

74

when on horseback, she contemplates bourgeois reality conceals it with blue, romantic haze. The ball at the château, the cigar case (at once remote, male, and aristocratic), the gradual disintegration of the plaster curé in the garden, and countless other images work together to enrich and deepen the narrative.

Such details, however functional, are less impressive than the great images of lathe, carriage, and beggar. Emma's emotional crises are commonly attended by the sound of Binet's lathe, which, going round and round, turns out useless objects. It attracts Emma as it does us because, working below the threshold of awareness, its motion, hum, and pointlessness are somehow analogous to hers. This desolating analogy is supplemented later in the book by the closed carriage in which Léon and Emma tour Rouen. Round and round they go, almost like a napkin ring on Binet's lathe, blinded by blinds, in no directions, making love and passing pink mounds left in gutters by makers of jam. The blind beggar who accosts Emma through the window of another conveyance is a symbol that reveals another aspect of her character and anticipates her goal. Singing of love, this miserable creature, who appears at the beginning of her affair with Léon and at its end, is love's victim. It is suitable that her last words concern this analogous embodiment of love and death. The performance of *Lucia* that she attends in Rouen not only advances the plot but projects for her and reader alike her romantic illusion. Like the rest, these interconnected images, also serve what Flaubert called "the precision of the grouping, the perfection of the parts . . . the total harmony." It is not for nothing that Mallarmé, who hated realism, praised Flaubert for composing a kind of poetry.

The symbolists of the early twentieth century, Conrad, for example, and Joyce, owe a considerable debt to *Madame Bovary*. Referring to it several times in his letters, Conrad praises "the sheer sincerity of its method" and the marvelous "rendering of concrete things." What Flaubert did for him, he continues, was open his eyes and arouse his emulation. He did not read *Madame Bovary* until he had finished *Almayer's Folly,* but it was between that work and *Lord Jim* that Conrad developed his imagistic method. As for Joyce, who wrote the stories of *Dubliners* shortly after the appearance of Conrad's great symbolist work, he knew pages of Flaubert by heart. What he learned from him is expressed in *Stephen Hero* where Stephen, after rejecting naturalistic "portrayal of externals," says that the artist must free "the image from its mesh of defining circumstances . . . and re-embody it in artistic circumstances chosen as the most exact for it in its new office." In that office the details of observed reality, so precise that they have caused critics to confuse Joyce with the naturalists, are "transmuted," as he puts it in *A Portrait of the Artist,* into radiant images. Not only Flaubert, to be sure, but symbolist poets and the Hermetic tradition led Joyce to his method; and it is fitting that *Chamber Music,* the sketch from which his poetic novel developed, is verse; but that Flaubert remained central in Joyce's mind is suggested not only by his concern with the observed image but with the *mot juste* and expressive rhythm. Many passages in Flaubert's letters, with which Joyce must have been familiar, anticipate and maybe helped to shape the aesthetics of Stephen Dedalus. Speaking as Stephen was to speak of the need for impersonality, Flaubert says in one of his letters that the artist must "be in his work like God in creation, present everywhere and visible nowhere. Since art is a second world, its creator must act by analogous methods."

A Portrait of the Artist, at once the residence and the creation of Stephen's nail-paring God, differs from most other novels of adolescence in detachment and method. At first glance, however, Joyce's improvement upon the *Bildungsroman* seems simple enough because the main burden is carried, as in ordinary novels of this sort, by character and action. We have plainly before us the story of a sensitive, gifted boy who is disappointed in his hope of communion with parents, country, and religion. Refusing the actual world at last, as in the role of the Count of Monte Cristo he refuses the muscatel grapes that Mercedes proffers, he constructs a better world to replace it. "If you have form'd a circle to go into," says cynical Blake, "go into it yourself, and see how you would do."

The theme of *A Portrait of the Artist* is normal enough. Joyce differs from most of his predecessors, as Flaubert from his, in greater dependence upon image, rhythm, juxtaposition, and tone to supplement the narrative and in giving attitudes and feelings body to support them. What Joyce in his notes for *Exiles* called "attendant images" could be omitted without destroying the outline of his book, but some of its quality and depth must be attributed to this accompaniment. At times, moreover, forgetting their capacity of attendants, images and other devices become essential and assume the principal burden as they were to do in *Ulysses*. Yielding place to other things at such times, the narrative grows "obscure," a word which means that narrative has given way to suggestion and discourse to nondiscursive elements having more effect on feeling than on mind. While still attendant, however, images may be too familiar or obvious to attract notice. Even Tolstoi used them.

When Vronsky in *Anna Karenina* rides his mare to death at the races, breaking her back by his awkwardness or zeal, his action, unnecessary to the plot and far from realistic, embodies his relationship with Anna. But Tolstoi's image of the mare is so narrowly assigned and painfully deliberate that it does little more than discourse could. Joyce's images, though partly assigned, however deliberate, are suggestive, indefinite, and not altogether explicable. Ambivalent, they reveal not only the quality of experience but its complexity. Without attendant or essential images, *A Portrait of the Artist* would be so much less immediate and less moving that few would pick it up again.

Images play other parts in the great design. Embodying Stephen's experience before he is entirely aware of it, and doing the same service for us, they prepare for moments of realization, which could not occur without them. Operating below conscious notice, the images, rhythms, and other forms project an unconscious process that comes to light at last. This function is no more important, however, than that of relating part to part and, composing a structure which, with the dominant narrative it supplements and complicates, creates what Stephen calls radiance or the meaning of the composite form.

The first two pages of *A Portrait of the Artist* present the images that, when elaborated, are to compose the supplementary structure and take their place in the form. We are confronted here with a moocow coming down the road, with a rose (maybe green), with wetting the bed, with a girl, and with an eagle that plucks out eyes—not to mention a number of other things such as dancing to another's tune. Without much context as yet, these images, acquiring fresh meanings from recurrence and relationship with others, carry aspects of Stephen and his trouble. Never was opening so dense as this or more important.

Take that road, long, narrow, and strictly bounded, along which comes a moocow to meet the passive boy. Diction, rhythm, and the opening phrase (the traditional beginning of an Irish "story") suggest the condition of childhood and its helplessness. Confined to the road, the child cannot escape encounter with a creature traditionally associated with Irish legend and with everything maternal. Later,

78

Stephen delights to accompany the milkman in his round of neighboring roads, although a little discouraged by the foul green puddles of the cowyard. Cows, which have seemed so beautiful in the country on sunny days, now revolt him and he can look no longer at their milk. Yet as he pursues "the Rock Road," he thinks a milkman's life pleasant enough, and looks forward with equanimity to adopting it as his own. Innumerable connotations of word and phrase make it almost plain at last that the road suggests tradition, that the cow suggests church, country, and all maternal things, and that the milkman suggests the priest. The little episode, far from being a sign of these meanings, is no more than the embodiment of possibilities. What it implies awaits corroboration from later episodes, Stephen's rejection of the priesthood, for example, or his aesthetic query about the man hacking a cow by accident from a block of wood. It is certain that none of these connected images is casual. As for the road itself, it develops into the circular track round which Mike Flynn, the old trainer, makes Stephen run; into the track at Clongowes where Stephen, breaking his glasses, is almost blinded; into the dark road alongside which Davin meets his peasant woman; and, after many reappearances, all of which confirm and enlarge the initial idea and feeling of tradition, into its opposite, the road that promises freedom on the final page.

The images of rose, water, girl, and bird are so intricately involved with one another that it seems all but impossible to separate them for analysis. Take the rose, however, a symbol which, carrying traditional significance, becomes, after much recurrence, Stephen's image of woman and creativity. Lacking sufficient context at its first appearance to have certain meaning, the rose, made green by Stephen, is not altogether without possibilities. Green is the color of Ireland, of immaturity, and of vegetable creation; yet a green rose is un-

79

natural. Art is unnatural too. Could the green rose anticipate Stephen's immature desire for Irish art? We cannot tell for sure. At school Stephen is champion of the white rose that loses to the red in an academic war of roses; and during his period of "resolute piety" his prayers ascend to heaven "like perfume streaming upwards from a heart of white rose." It is the red rose, however, that attends his creative ecstasies near the Bull Wall, after he resolves to follow mortal beauty, and in bed, after composing a poem. His soul, "swooning into some new world," shares Dante's penultimate vision: "A world, a glimmer, or a flower? Glimmering and trembling, trembling and unfolding, a breaking light, an opening flower, it spread in endless succession to itself, breaking in full crimson and unfolding and fading to palest rose, leaf by leaf and wave of light by wave of light, flooding all the heavens with its soft flushes, every flush deeper than other." This heavenly vision, which follows the hell of the sermons and the purgatory of his repentance, anticipates his ultimate vision of Mrs. Bloom, the heavenly yet earthly rose of *Ulysses*.

Woman, associated with rose, embodies Stephen's aspiration and, increasingly, his creative power. Eileen, the girl who appears at the beginning of the book, unattainable because Protestant, is soon identified with sex and the Tower of Ivory, symbol of the Blessed Virgin. Mercedes, a dream who inhabits a garden of roses along the milkman's road, suggests the Virgin by her name while adding overtones of remoteness, exile, and revenge. At Cork, however, Stephen's "monstrous" adolescent thoughts injure her purity by desire. When Emma, a teaser, replaces Mercedes as object of desire and becomes in addition an image of his mother country and his church, Stephen transfers his devotion to the Virgin herself, over whose sodality he presides, and whose "office" becomes his formula. The wading girl near the Bull Wall, who embodies mortal beauty, unites all previous suggestions. Associating her with Emma, the Virgin, the rose, and the womb of the imagination, whose priest he becomes, he finds her an image of his own capacity: "Heavenly God!" his soul exclaims, its eye no doubt upon himself. His repeated "Yes" anticipates Mrs. Bloom's as the girl, stirring the waters "hither and thither," anticipates the hither and thithering waters of Anna Livia Plurabelle: "He would create."

Other women take their place in the great design. There is the common girl, persisting in memory, who stops Stephen on the street to offer flowers for which he cannot pay. Connected in his mind with a kitchen girl who sings Irish songs over the dishes, she develops near the end into the servant maid, who, singing "Rosie O'Grady" in her kitchen, proffers the suggestion at least of Irish flowers, green roses perhaps. Cranly's *"Mulier cantat"* unites her in Stephen's mind with "the figure of woman as she appears in the liturgy of the Church" and with all his symbolic women. Unprepared as yet to receive what she proffers in her song or unable to pay the price of acceptance, Stephen says, "I want to see Rosie first."

That Rosie, another anticipation of Mrs. Bloom, sings in a kitchen is not unimportant. After each of his ecstasies, Stephen comes back to the kitchen, which serves not only as an ironic device for deflating him but as an image of the reality to which, if he is to be an artist, he must return. It is notable that his acceptance of Mr. Bloom and the communion with mankind that precedes the vision of Mrs. Bloom takes place in a kitchen. Rosie in her kitchen, the last great image of woman in *A Portrait of the Artist,* unites the ideal with the actual. Neither the wading girl nor Mercedes, both ethereal, can present to Stephen the idea and feeling of a union which someday he will understand. Far from seeing Rosie first, he sees her last, but by her aid, of which he is not fully aware as yet, he comes nearer his vision of above and below, of heavenly roses to be sure but of roses in kitchens.

Woman is not only rose but bird and sometimes bat. The bird, which makes its first appearance as the eagle who is to punish Stephen's guilt by making him blind as a bat, makes its next appearance as Heron, who, looking and acting like a bird of prey, tries to make Stephen conform. Bad at first, birds become good as Stephen approaches mortal beauty at the beach. He thinks of Daedalus, "a hawk-like man flying sunward," and wants to utter cries of hawk or eagle, images no longer of oppression but, retaining authority, of creation. The wading girl is "a strange and beautiful seabird." "Her bosom was as a bird's, soft and slight, slight and soft as the breast of some dark-plumaged dove." As Stephen observes their flight, birds also become what he calls a "symbol of departure or loneliness." When, becoming birdlike Daedalus, he takes flight across the sea to exile, he unites all these meanings and confirms their association with water. Bats are anticipated by images of blinding, not only those of the eye-plucking eagle, of glasses broken on the track, and of dull red blinds that keep light from boys of Belvedere during their retreat but that of the woman into whose eye Mr. Casey spits: " 'Phth! says I to her.' 'O Jesus, Mary and Joseph!' says she . . . 'I'm blinded and drownded . . . I'm blinded entirely.' " When they appear at last, bats gather up these anticipatory associations with woman, custom, and country. Davin's peasant woman at her door along the dark lonely road seems to Stephen "a type of her race and of his own, a batlike soul waking to the consciousness of itself in darkness and secrecy and loneliness." Seeming almost a bird for a moment, Emma, revisited, becomes another bat, but its darkness, secrecy, and loneliness connect it with himself as artist about to try silence, exile, and cunning. Blind to reality as yet, he may improve. Like the images of

82

bird and flower, the bat is ambivalent, not only bad but good. If bat suggests things as they are, and bird things as they ought to be, it is the artist's job to reconcile them. If all these women are aspects of woman, and if woman is an aspect of himself, the creative part, he too is presented by images of bird, bat, and, besides these, water.

Ambivalent from the first, water is either warm or cold, agreeable or frightening. The making of water at the beginning of the *Portrait* seems an image of creation that includes the artist's two realities. At school Stephen is shouldered into the "square ditch," square not because of shape but because it receives the flow of the urinal or "square." Plainly maternal by context, this image warns Stephen of the perils of regression, to which like one of those rats who enjoy the ditch, he is tempted by the discomforts of external reality. The "warm turf-coloured bogwater" of the bath adds something peculiarly Irish to his complex. Dirty water down the drain at the Wicklow Hotel and the watery sound of cricket bats (connected in his mind with pandybats and bats) confirm his fears. The concluding image of the first chapter, assigned only by previous associations, embodies his infantile career: "Pick, pack, pock, puck," go the cricket bats, "like drops of water in a fountain falling softly in the brimming bowl." If Stephen himself is suggested by this bowl and his development by an ablaut series, water is not altogether bad. This possibility is established toward the middle of the book, where, changing character, water becomes good on the whole and unmistakably a symbol of creation. On his way to the beach, Stephen still finds the sea cold and "infra-human." The bathing boys repel him, but the sight of the wading girl gives water another aspect. Rolling up his trousers like J. Alfred Prufrock, he himself goes wading. From that moment of baptism and rebirth inaudible music and the sound of waters attend his creative ecstasies. It is true that, relapsing a little,

Stephen fears water again in *Ulysses,* but Mr. Bloom, with whom he finally unites, is a water lover, and Anna Livia Plurabelle is the river Liffey.

These families of developing images that, supplementing the narrative, give it texture, immediacy, and more body are not the only symbolic devices Joyce commands. As we have noticed, large parallels, rhythms, shifts of tone, juxtaposition, and all else that Flaubert commended complicate the "significant form." But deferring these, I shall confine myself in this place to some of the relatively unassigned and unattached images that concentrate feeling at important points.

Consider, for example, the opening of the second chapter. Uncle Charles, who is addicted to black twist, is deported to the outhouse, whence rising smoke and the brim of his tall hat appear as he sings old songs in tranquillity. Position gives this image an importance that import cannot justify. Hints of exile, creation, and piety, all relevant to the theme, may divert our understanding without satisfying it entirely. Few of Joyce's images are so mysterious as this and, while occupying our feelings, so resistant to discourse. The scenery at Cork appeals more readily to the understanding. While in that town with his father, Stephen finds in the word "Foetus," carved in the wood of a desk, what Eliot would call an objective correlative of the "den of monstrous images" within him. After this corroboration of inner disorder, he emerges from schoolroom into the sunny street where he sees cricketers and a maid watering plants; hears a German band and scale after scale from a girl's piano. In another book this urban noise and scenery might serve as setting alone. Here, more functional than that, it presents a vision of the normal, the orderly, and the quotidian from which the discovery of his monstrous interior has separated him.

Characters are no less symbolic. The two dwarfish eccentrics that Stephen encounters, one on the street and the other in the library, seem caricatures of Stephen's possible future and of the soul of Ireland, but aside from that, they evade significance. By action, speech, and context, on the other hand, the figure of Cranly becomes more nearly definite. That last interview which drives Stephen to exile concentrates in Cranly the forces of admission, submission, confession, and retreat, and he becomes the embodiment of all that has plagued the imperfect hero. Cranly's preoccupation with a book called *Diseases of the Ox* adds to the picture. Since Stephen as "Bous Stephanoumenos" has been identified with the ox, Cranly's devotion to his book reveals him as Stephen's most reactionary critic, not, as we had supposed, his friend.

When Stephen turns seaward toward his great experience with the wading girl, an image which might escape casual notice not only suggests the finality of his action but adds to our understanding of his complexity: he crosses the bridge from Dollymount to the Bull. Readers of *Dubliners* may recall that crossing bridges in that work is as portentous as Caesar's crossing of the Rubicon; in *Ulysses* Stephen, a frustrated exile back from Paris, is "a disappointed bridge." In the *Portrait,* on the bridge which marks his passage from old custom to freedom and the waters of life, he meets a squad of uncouth, tall-hatted Christian Brothers, marching two by two, going the other way. Their direction, their appearance, and their regimentation are important, but what reveals Stephen's character is the contempt with which he regards those who are socially and intellectually inferior to Jesuits. The episode, therefore, includes both his escape from one tyranny and his submission to another, the greater tyranny of pride, which, until he understands the Blooms, will keep him from uniting the regions of reality by art. Stephen may think of charity or

Joyce talk of pride, but this revealing episode contributes more than all that talk or thought to the portrait of an autist.

The writer of this kind of novel, says E. M. Forster, "is not necessarily going to 'say' anything about the universe; he proposes to sing." His song—and Forster has both Melville and Lawrence in mind—must "combine with the furniture of common sense." In *Aspects of the Novel,* where this reflection appears, Forster excludes Joyce from the great company to which he himself belongs. Rejecting symbolist as a term for it, he prefers prophetical. "A prophet does not reflect," he says. "That is why we exclude Joyce. Joyce has many qualities akin to prophecy and he has shown (especially in the *Portrait of the Artist*) an imaginative grasp of evil. But he undermines the universe in too workmanlike a manner, looking around for this tool or that: in spite of all his internal looseness he is too tight, he is never vague except after due deliberation; it is talk, talk, never song." As for *Ulysses,* it is "a dogged attempt to cover the universe with mud," an "epic of grubbiness and disillusion," and "a simplification of the human character in the interests of Hell." It seems a pity that one great symbolist cannot comprehend another, but the Irish Sea is wider than it looks and considerably deeper.

As an example of another kind of symbolic structure I might take *A Passage to India,* but, reserving that for later examination, I prefer to consider *Heart of Darkness* here. Conrad regarded his fiction "as the outward sign of inward feelings." To create a story, he says in one of his letters, "you must cultivate your poetic faculty. . . . You must search the darkest corners of your heart . . . for the image." As for the naturalist school of Zola and Bennett: *"Tout ça, c'est très vieux jeu";* for "realism in art will never approach reality." He himself tries to pierce "the veil of details" to arrive at "the essence of life." "I am but a novelist," he says in another letter, "I must speak in images." Consequently his work does not "lend itself to exact definition," and his "inexplicable" stories "expand far beyond their frame." In short, as these remarkable letters prove, he saw himself as symbolist:

A work of art is very seldom limited to one exclusive meaning and not necessarily tending to a definite conclusion. And this for the reason that the nearer it approaches art, the more it acquires a symbolic character. This statement may surprise you, who may imagine that I am alluding to the Symbolist School of poets or prose writers. Theirs, however, is only a literary proceeding against which I have nothing to say. I am concerned here with something much larger. . . . So I will only call your attention to the fact that the symbolic conception of a work of art has this advantage, that it makes a triple appeal covering the whole field of life. All the great creations of literature have been symbolic, and in that way have gained in complexity, in power, in depth and in beauty. . . . As to precision of images and analysis my artistic conscience is at rest. I have given there all the truth that is in me. . . . But as to 'final effect' my conscience has nothing to do with that. It is the critic's affair to bring to its contemplation his own honesty, his sensibility and intelligence.

To the common reader *Heart of Darkness* is a simple tale of adventure; for it was Conrad's purpose to maintain a surface "trivial enough . . . to have some charm for the man in the street." Distracted by that, the reader may pass lightly over what Conrad calls in a letter the "obscure beginning" and the "unfathomable dénouement" of his story. On the surface we have a simple journey up the Congo to find Kurtz, an ivory trader. Marlow, compelled by fortune to become a fresh-water sailor, undertakes this quest and reports its result to the trader's fiancée. But the narrative may be read in several ways—as an economic or political commentary, as a moral discourse, or as a psychological investigation. Marlow's contempt for the Belgian imperialists, with their indifference to British ideals of duty, is the most obvious theme of the book. His concern with empire, however, is surpassed by his desire to satisfy his curiosity about Kurtz, a gifted, eloquent man, who seems destined to become manager of the trading company. As we know from *Lord Jim,* Marlow is obsessed with preconceptions about the integrity of white men under difficulties in alien surroundings, and if Kurtz had not seemed to bear within him the seeds of morality, Marlow would not have been interested. The discovery of Kurtz's collapse and, in that famous exclamation, of his recovery constitutes the moral theme.

Throughout this moral quest, however, Marlow is less concerned with Kurtz than with self-realization: exploring Africa's interior becomes the exploring of man's interior, and in finding Kurtz he finds himself. The most you can hope from life, he observes, is some knowledge of yourself. When he sees natives howling and capering on the bank of the river, he is dismayed, but the worst thing about it is that they are not altogether inhuman. In fact he feels within himself a faint response to their primitive ritual. Jungle and savages have disclosed to him the primitive and unconscious depths of his mind which, because of his preference for the civilized, seem so "ugly" and untidy that he has to take refuge in navigation, a way of celebrating order. But Kurtz's loss of integrity is even more frightening. However responsible he once seemed, he has yielded to the primitive, the unconscious, and the natural. Not even his belated assertion of awareness— although a moral victory—is enough to appease Marlow, who gloomily confronts his horror. Even the Thames, that river of British light, seems at the end of his story, to "lead into the heart of an immense darkness."

His multiple quest, which includes the action, is symbolic in itself. Its function, however, is not only to present and organize meanings but to lead to further meanings, which are disclosed by the image around which the work is organized. Once the narrative has led us to the great forest, the rest falls into place around that center, and even the narrative becomes subsidiary. More than the place and goal of the quest, the forest is the symbol that, attracting additional body from supporting elements, embodies all. Contemplating the forest, Marlow is struck by "its mystery, its greatness, the amazing reality of its concealed life." It seems an "implacable force brooding over an inscrutable intention." Statements of this kind, uniting with description and action, help to establish the symbol.

Its meaning is qualified by a system of supplementary actions and images, ranging in kind from significant episodes to metaphors and all but disembodied hints. At the beginning the primitive darkness of the Thames and the reaction of the civilized Roman to its swampy edges provide a parallel to Marlow on the tropical river. In the city which, though probably Brussels, suggests both Kafka and Chirico, the company maintains an office where Marlow discovers two women knitting black wool. This fatal suggestion is followed by that of the gunboat, anchored off the African coast, shelling the forest. "In the empty immensity of earth, sky, and water, there she was, incomprehensible, firing into a continent." When he reaches the trading post, Marlow is depressed by heaps of dead machinery: a boiler in the grass, rusty rails, and a truck lying on its back with three wheels in the air. That Eliot was on the point of taking his epigraph for *The Waste Land* from *Heart of Darkness* is not surprising.

Conrad's desolating images demand and find suitable relief in the figure of the dandy, who like Baudelaire among citizens, keeps the alien and the natural at one remove by elegance. Marlow's discovery of a tattered book on navigation in the deserted hut also affirms the ideal of discipline, but such imagistic affirmations of man's hope are rare. Even the similes and metaphors reiterate the burden

89

of horror: the river is a snake, the city and the forest are graves, filled with nameless corruption, and the dying natives occupy an Inferno.

The atmosphere of the forest and its accompaniments is that of dream. Recounting his "weary pilgrimage amongst hints for nightmares," Marlow says: "It seems to me I am trying to tell you a dream —making a vain attempt because no relation of a dream can convey the dream-sensation." He is far too modest; for his images, his manner of speaking, all those "hints for nightmares," convey the authentic sensation. Like Kafka's *Trial, Heart of Darkness* may be read as dream; but the images of dream have significance, and we must ask the meaning of the forest, the heart of Conrad's darkness. It would be tempting to conclude that this symbol means the natural, the primitive, and the unconscious. As sign, it conveys these meanings, but as symbol it carries feelings and ideas that are at once expanded and limited by these meanings and the context. No statement is adequate for a vision of reality whose only equivalent is the book, an elaborate analogy for a conception. The "idea" of *Heart of Darkness,* Conrad said in one of his letters, "is so wrapped up in secondary notions that you . . . may miss it. And also you must remember that I don't start with an abstract notion. I start with definite images and as their rendering is true some effect is produced."

Telling of his "inconclusive" experience, Marlow calls the forest "incomprehensible," and his journey, he confesses, was "not very clear. And yet it seemed to throw a kind of light." For Marlow, says Conrad, the meaning of an episode was not inside but "outside, enveloping the tale which brought it out only as a glow brings out a haze." This luminous halo consists of all kinds of suggestions. The Russian's story of Kurtz, for example, seems to Marlow "an amazing tale that was not so much told as suggested to me in desolate exclamations, completed by shrugs, in interrupted phrases, in hints ending in deep sighs." The words of Marlow and Kurtz at night in the forest are the ordinary words of waking life, but behind them is the "terrific suggestiveness of words heard in dreams." Marlow's attempt to be discursive about his nightmare reveals not only the inadequacy of statement for explaining symbols but its possible suggestiveness.

It should be plain that Conrad's vision, though no less symbolist than *A Portrait of the Artist,* differs from it in structure. In Joyce's book, narrative, attended by images that enlarge it, is central; in Conrad's book, narrative and subordinate details are centered in image. Tied to narrative, Joyce's images develop thematically in time, whereas Conrad's organization, more nearly static, is spatial in effect. If metaphors of other arts can help, Joyce's arrangement is musical and Conrad's sculptural. T. S. Eliot once said that the sense of a poem is there to keep the reader's mind occupied while the rest of the poem does its work. Conrad's narrative assumes the function of Eliot's sense; and Joyce's narrative, however important, seems, after contemplation, central by a kind of displacement. Maybe it, too, is there to distract us while it organizes images that, although beneath notice, do more to create the general effect.

Of *Nostromo,* which is organized like *Heart of Darkness,* Conrad said in a letter: "Silver is the pivot of the moral and material events, affecting the lives of everybody in the tale. . . . The word 'silver' occurs almost at the very beginning of the story proper, and I took care to introduce it in the very last paragraph, which would perhaps have been better without the phrase which contains the key-word." Like that of *Heart of Darkness,* the principal image of *Nostromo* is surrounded and abetted by others, which improve it: the island, for example, and the ship proceeding without captain or helmsman at night without lights. Also lacking the density and richness of *Heart of Darkness, The Secret Agent* is nevertheless more nearly parallel, and like its predecessor, as Conrad said in a letter, "does not lend itself to exact definition." In place of the forest he used for his tale of the Greenwich observatory, as he tells us in the "Author's Note," the image of a great city. The idea of the book came to him, he says, as a "vision of an enormous town . . . a monstrous town" from which in "darkness enough" to suit him "endless vistas opened up." No longer a center of light, London with its anarchists, idiots, and a mean little shop in its heart, proves blacker than the Congo. Each night on going to bed, Mrs. Verloc asks " 'Shall I put out the light?' " " 'Put it out,' " replies Mr. Verloc, and London "with its maze of streets . . . was sunk in a hopeless night," which seems fit setting for the falterings of a decrepit cab and all those anarchists. Not there to establish a political, social, or economic point, the anarchists and their activities, which thrive on night, are elements in this vision of chaos, and the attempt on the Greenwich observatory, which marks our time, becomes an attempt on time, space, and navigation. Mrs. Verloc's tragedy is accepting this darkness and confusion, as Kurtz accepts his, without looking too deeply into it.

A third kind of symbolist novel is represented by the work of Henry Green, whom Eliot, praising the poetic novel, praised. At first reading, *Party Going* may seem centered in the symbol of the railroad station as *Heart of Darkness* in the forest or *The Secret Agent* in the city, but after exploring a little we find a less federal order. What seemed centralized now seems a system of almost equal elements, cohering not by subordination to a great image or a narrative but by glancing reflections. Maybe refraction would be a more accurate metaphor for the exchange between part and part and part and whole, but prisms are too physical for an effect at once indefinite and social. Finding adequate words, Green called his work a "conspiracy of insinuations." In "The Symbolism of Poetry" Yeats, finding a word for the same effect, admires the way a poem "flickers with the light of many symbols . . . as a sword-blade may flicker with the light of burning towers." He too may call upon the metaphor of reflection, but "flicker" is as good a word as Green's "conspiracy." Too subtle for the intellect to follow, Yeats continues, reflexive flickering escapes analysis. If he is right, all we can do is point to parts or open them up; but we must try, while responding to their "exquisite" relationships, as Joyce puts it in *Stephen Hero,* to contemplate the whole until from the "organized composite structure" the "whatness" leaps out. Maybe all we can do while attending that great emergence is ask questions.

Party Going concerns a temporarily frustrated but finally successful departure for the south of France. Max invites a number of his loves and parasites to go along, but it is London, and a black fog maroons them in the station with thirty thousand ordinary people. Max's wealth enables his party to retire to the station hotel, whence, while making a sort of love, they look down on the crowd below. The steel shutters that keep that crowd out keep Max's party in. Will the shutters hold, will the fog ever lift, is the luggage safe with the servants in the awful station, which of his girls will Max choose, and what of Miss Fellowes, indisposed, maybe drunk, with her dead pigeon in the next room? Such anxieties occupy them until the fog lifts, and with the exception of poor Miss Fellowes and her pigeon, they are off.

"This journey is being so long isn't it?" says Angela. And Alex, addressing a perfect stranger, says: "I'm afraid everything must seem very odd to you. I mean there seems to be so much going on, but you see we are all going on a party together abroad, and now here we are stuck in this hotel on account of fog." Their predicament, the station, and the fog imply many things. It is difficult, however, to say whether Green intends a study of men and women, of rich and poor, of modern society, or of the miserable condition of humanity— or all of these and more.

The meaning of the fog-bound station is complicated by recurrent images of birds and artichokes that seem somehow related to the larger symbols. As for birds, one occurs in the first sentence: "Fog was so dense, bird that had been disturbed went flat into a balustrade and slowly fell, dead, at her feet." Miss Fellowes, who is there to see the voyagers off, picks it up, washes it in the ladies' room, and, observed by two nannies, wraps it in brown paper. She has no idea why she does this. As she lies in bed, ill or drunk, watched over by those nannies, the others ask what it means: "She never belonged to any societies for animals did she? She never kept pigeons herself I mean?" Why did she pick her pigeon up somewhere and then get so ill? She can't have bought it off a barrow—they don't sell them. "What did she want it for, it was so dirty? I'm sure that's what's been worrying us, but when you come to think of it, darling, there's nothing in it is there? What is it after all? Now if it had been a goose, or some other bird. . . ." Those two nannies, as odd as Kafka's assistants, are no less mysterious. But the birds that Julia sees flying under the arch in the fog are easier to follow. Signs of sex and flight, as the dead pigeon seems almost a sign of frustration, they change meaning with their contexts as they recur together with other images: the childhood memory of a thicket of bamboos or maybe artichokes and the curious individual who may or may not be the hotel detective. Reappearing at the end, these puzzling images somehow relieve our anxieties.

As in *Living,* an earlier novel of men and birds, Green uses the idiom used by his characters. His prose, therefore, presents what he is talking about; and his ambiguous tone is a comment on it. The spoken English of the most idle class agrees with tone, symbol, sign, and metaphor to compose his great conspiracy. What it insinuates, through his offhand manner, is a frightening vision of our oppressive world, but even this statement seems too definite and far too crude to do justice to all that flickering.

These remarks about *Party Going,* written in approximately this form a number of years ago, represent a second reading. I allow them to stand as they are without attempting deeper descent under later lights, for here I am more inclined to demonstrate an early, and I think normal, response to such novels than to achieve a record for depth. Another reading might almost fix the relationship of artichoke, station, and bird that baffles and delights me, but "almost" is the important word. In enterprises of this kind we confront the penultimate at last, and if, avoiding it by some dodge, we could attain our goal and comprehend the incomprehensible, what else could we do? After all, we are but romantics, eager to lose ourselves in a mystery, in spite of our nostalgia for Lancelot Andrewes.

Of *Loving,* which seems no less indefinable, I can speak with greater assurance because, no doubt, I have read it more often than *Party Going* and more recently. *Loving* has hardly any plot at all. We find ourselves among English landlords and servants of an Irish house in time of war. The master is away, fighting Germans (it is the second war), and the mistresses, now here and now away, leave management to servants. Of these, Raunce, the butler, is chief, but there are maids as well, and also a solitary Irishman who keeps the peacocks. Neutral, alien Ireland surrounds them, anxieties trouble their erotic fumblings, until Raunce decides to marry Edith, a maid, and, returning to England, to confront reality. This plot, if it deserves the name, conveys little. Almost all is done by images, their relationships, and tone. From their emanations and ghostly exchanges comes something that, striking mind as well as feelings, may be talked about.

Furnished with gilt milk pails and chinoiseries, the house itself is meaningful: "For this house that had yet to be burned down, and in particular the greater part of it which remained closed, was a shadowless castle of treasures." That it contains the furniture of Marie Antoinette and that it is called a castle, an enclosure of refuge and defense in hostile surroundings, imply its isolation. The servants, forbidden to talk to natives, never leave the grounds. The younger mistress, when not in England, entertains none but an Anglo-Irishman—and him in bed. Mistresses and servants alike are separated from England, from Ireland, from responsibility, and from each other. There are almost no connections. Even the weathervane, that points to something else, is broken—it has a mouse in the cogs. Not only the troubles of autonomy but those of decadence, and all attendant follies, are invited by that house and its condition.

Adorning the pleasure grounds, a dovecote and a peacock house correspond to the castle and its occupants. The dovecote, a reproduction in miniature of the leaning tower of Pisa, shelters amorous birds, who ineffectually pursue each other round the balconies or push each other out. This leaning tower of fat lovers, associated with falling bodies and expressive of decline, takes its place with gilt milk pails and peacocks, traditional reminders of vanity, in a complex of refractions. Pat, the solitary Irishman, feeds the peacocks, and English servants feed the doves. It is no less important that one of the peacocks, killed by the cook's nephew and plucked, cannot be distinguished from chicken. Rejected by the cook and brought back from the dust bin to annoy her, it begins to stink. Edith, stealing peacock eggs, puts them up in waterglass, a preservative. Meanwhile

96

a ring is lost, buried for a while under the dovecote, and mysteriously recovered. Both loss and recovery provoke anxieties; for rings are circles, and circles, as we know, suggest unity and loving while obscurity of loss and return imply impermanence. Not least among these details is Green's use of demonstrative "that," which removes all things, rings, people, and birds alike, to a suitable distance.

What seems at first no more than a picture of Anglo-Irish decay becomes upon contemplation of these and other details another, a more ominous thing. Green's concern seems less with a particular situation than with that of everybody in our world and time—as his title, no less functional than his images and tones, implies. Surely wider than the affair of mistress and lover or the pursuit of servant by servant, "loving," responsible and adult, implies connection, giving, and acceptance, all that is foreign to the house. Only the last sentence promises that community; but this interpretation, leaving assignment far behind, is no more than possible. Unexhausted, the "great consult" of glancing images and rhythms continues to issue rays, perceptible to others perhaps or to me at another time.

It occurs to me at this point that my examples of kinds, though by Irishman, Pole, and Englishman, are all from British literature. Maybe I should have taken Mann's *Death in Venice,* Kafka's *Castle,* Proust's great work, or something by Faulkner. My choice was no more than convenient, and as for those whom I seem to have neglected I shall do what I can with them later on. For the present, let us see how the symbolist novel has evolved.

The great period commenced just before the first war with the appearance of *Death in Venice, Dubliners,* and the first volume of Proust; lasting through the 1930s, it ended—or so it seems—with the works of Faulkner and Green. One of the richest in all literature, this period, which reached its climax with *Ulysses, Remembrance of Things Past,* and *The Magic Mountain,* saw the emergence of Kafka, Lawrence, and Virginia Woolf. *The Trial, The Plumed Serpent,* and *To the Lighthouse* found fitting rivals in *A Passage to India, The Sound and the Fury,* and *Absalom, Absalom!* After these came *Finnegans Wake.* Since those great days, lesser writers, attenuating the tradition, have made it popular; but that some, whether easy of comprehension or difficult, have produced excellent books Malcolm Lowry's *Under the Volcano,* Hemingway's *Old Man and the Sea,* and John Hersey's *Marmot Drive* are sufficient evidence.

The most formidable of these is *Under the Volcano.* Too indirect and devious to be acceptable as a book of the month, it seems nevertheless comparatively simple if placed alongside work of Green. Like *Mrs. Dalloway,* Lowry's book concerns one day; the time is 1938, the place Mexico. The narrative displays the prolonged drunkenness of Geoffrey, the British consul, who has resigned his post and divorced his wife. She returns and, with the aid of his brother, Hugh, attempts a reconciliation, but fiesta and bullbaiting, mescal and tequila improve Geoffrey's condition. Finally, as she searches for him and for death, Yvonne falls under a horse, and Geoffrey is disposed of by fascists. Superficially this sounds like another, more violent and exotic lost week end, but as the jacket warns us, the surface hides a "deeper significance of which the characters and their actions are symbolic." The week end is lost—but with complications.

Of these, the first are subjective. Using techniques of Joyce, Woolf, and Henry James, Lowry records the impressions of his characters in long Proustian sentences that provide a confusion of inner and outer and, through memory, of past and present. Geoffrey's alcoholic hallucinations are interrupted by fragments of external reality: irrelevant conversation, words from a travel folder, posters in the

98

street. Yvonne's flow of experience confuses memory, desire, and the present moment. Such mental complexities are as customary as the use of symbols for deeper meanings.

Geoffrey embodies the intellectual in what was once our society. Spain is falling and fascists are around, but, evading responsibility, he does nothing to preserve the culture to which he is heir. With divorce from Yvonne (who suggests reality or a way to it) and drink his escapes from an increasingly terrible world, Geoffrey symbolizes a ruling class with its learning, charm, and incapacity; and in his drunken snores is heard "the muted voice of England long asleep." Hugh, who has awakened to responsibility, represents the English conscience, but he has awakened too late to the need for action, and the aid he plans for Spain will be ineffectual.

Swedenborg and the Cabala are invoked and, as we might expect, the book is filled with incidental correspondences: the dying Indian for whom no one cares to assume responsibility; the Ferris wheel and the infernal machine at the fiesta; the fractured stone, which implies Geoffrey's marriage and his world. Over the town broods the symbolic volcano and under it yawns the symbolic chasm, the meaning of which is fixed by a recurring quotation from Dante's *Inferno*. As Geoffrey broods in the outhouse, haunted by memories of his day, he thinks he occupies a private hell, but, as Lowry suggests, his hell is ours, and the heavy atmosphere of his nightmare circumscribes our own. The fiesta commemorates the dead. Less propaganda than vision, this book is richly textured and intricately composed. Its course is that of tragedy: a great man (great because he embodies our culture) falls through an inherent flaw, and we are moved by pity and fear.

Under the Volcano is among the most elaborate of recent novels—

exceeded in respect of machinery by Philip Toynbee's *Prothalamium* alone—but it is far from being one of the most mysterious. In this respect it is exceeded by *The Marmot Drive,* a simple tale which, nevertheless, gives the illusion of depths. Like John Denham's seventeenth-century Thames, John Hersey's book is both deep and clear—yet, unlike that river, apparently bottomless. The hero, the Selectman of a remote Connecticut village near Yale, has a long-cherished ideal of driving woodchucks into a pen. By zeal he makes the reluctant community share his great design, which is put into operation on the day Hester, his son's fiancée, comes for a visit; but the drive fails, he is overwhelmed with guilt, and the villagers, relieving their more complicated feelings, whip him in the good old way at the ancient post on the common. In his simplicity, he takes the punishment as due him for the failure of his plan, then goes home to plan another drive, more communal than the last. His other passion is old clocks with wooden works; and as the story ends, a clock without a face contemplates its gears upon the floor.

The drive and its failure reveal the Puritanical sadism of the villagers, but the Selectman, emerging as hero and victim, gains in stature. As for Hester, seeing her own inadequacy, she knows herself at last. But what of those clocks, the speck in Hester's eye, the abandoned church in the woodchuck woods, the curious woodchuck stone, found and lost again, and what of the woodchucks themselves? For the Selectman, woodchucks with their long teeth and underground habits may be an almost unconscious image of the community he tries to direct. That the villagers are almost aware of this unflattering correspondence is not unlikely. For us, the crusade and its particulars, suggesting all communities and all zeal, present a vision of man in society. Unassigned, the supporting images play an enigmatic part in a moving yet otherwise inexplicable pattern.

That such indefiniteness is not to every taste is proved by a reviewer who recoiled from the "abominable allegory" as if at supper offered toad.

It would be unfair to conclude from other recent examples that the symbolist novel, having exhausted its possibilities, is decaying at last. Working in the enormous shadow of the great ones, some of the surviving symbolists, Rumer Godden or Jean Stafford, for instance, may seem reminiscent; epigraphs from Eliot and images from Virginia Woolf may replace invention. The trouble, however, may be that such novelists, less decadent than minor, are unable to create a context for borrowed symbols; for whether fresh or old, symbols do not work alone but in concert with each other and with other elements. Moby Dick would be a minnow without his Ahab.

The Stuffed Owl

*A*MONG SYMBOLIC parts the image is principal. Before we approach it, however, or, passing from the simple to the complex, proceed beyond image to other parts and to the whole, we must reconsider the meaning of image. Earlier I called the participating image an epitome of the whole or all but its epitome. It is fitting, before we receive that, to consult authority and establish usage; for nothing is slipperier than a word. The imagist school, founded by T. E. Hulme, promoted by Ezra Pound, and adorned by T. S. Eliot, may offer help.

In "Notes on Language and Style," a posthumous paper published by Eliot in his *Criterion* (July, 1925), Hulme, a Bergsonist who preferred analogy to logic as a way of expressing and knowing, defines the image as an analogy, offered to the senses, expressing vision. Composed of definite words, his analogy is a solid thing which, taking the form of a metaphor or an unattached concretion, not only makes the poet's thought and feeling apparent to himself and the reader but, preceding thought and feeling, creates them. As defined by Hulme, therefore, an image is not unlike a symbol. Both are solid analogies, but whereas our symbol, presenting itself, suggests something indefinite, his image, suggesting something almost as definite as itself, seems limited if not altogether assigned. These notes, though fragmentary, may approximate what Hulme said in his seminar on imagism.

Ezra Pound attended it. For him, in *Gaudier-Brzeska,* a Vorticist manifesto, the symbol has a fixed traditional meaning; yet, however definite, a symbol such as cross or crown invites "mushy" technique. The image, on the other hand—such as the triple sphere at the end of Dante's *Paradiso*—has "variable significance." Particular, precise, and impersonal, it is "that which presents an intellectual and emotional complex." His symbol seems our sign and his image our symbol.

Feeling his definition inadequate, however, he turns to autobiography and further example. One day in the *Métro* he saw beautiful faces of straphangers as a nonrepresentative color pattern. No painter, he went home to find expression in the image, the poet's pigment. There, after an attempt which proved of "secondary intensity," he composed the following *hokku:*

> The apparition of these faces in the crowd:
> Petals, on a wet, black bough.

This image, he continues, which records the precise moment when a thing outward and objective transforms itself into a thing inward and subjective, is a "radiant node or cluster or vortex from which and through which and into which ideas constantly rush. . . . In decency one can only call it a vortex." A radiant thing and a vortex, as he seems aware, are opposites, one going out and the other in; but since his vortex, which receives and confuses the reader's ideas, remains alone at the end of the definition, we might assume that Pound's image is like those ink blots where neurotics find what they think is there—or like Moby Dick among critics. Pound's *hokku,* plainer than his definition, suggests, however, that his image is an analogy, a metaphor in this case, that embodies feeling if not idea.

T. S. Eliot, a disciple of Pound and Hulme, commended the metaphysical metaphor for combining idea and feeling. His "objective correlative," amounting to a definition of image, is a verbal formula outside poet and reader for presenting something inside them but to neither alike. However uncertain, therefore, the "heap of broken images" in *The Waste Land* is a way of objectifying spiritual conditions.

In his lectures on the poetic image, Cecil Day Lewis, who is closer to Pound though somewhat less precise, says that the symbol, standing for one thing alone, is denotative, whereas the image is "infinitely resonant." Despairing of definition, he concludes that "images are elusive things." Inclining somewhat to the other side—if one can speak of sides in a matter like this—Caroline Spurgeon, famous for removing Shakespeare's images from context, classifying them by subject, and making charts, defines the image as a word picture used by a poet to "illustrate, illuminate and embellish his thought." Both that venture and this definition are dubious.

W. B. Yeats, a greater critic than these, seems almost as perplexing. "I have no speech but symbol," he says in one poem, and in another: "I have but images, analogies." Since in his essay on Swedenborg he identifies correspondences with symbols, and correspondences are analogies, he appears to identify image and symbol. Those daemons, therefore, who came to bring him images for poems were bringing symbols. This raises a further question: is the image-symbol an element of a poem, the poem itself, or both? In "Byzantium," a poem that suggests the nature of a poem and its composition, Yeats starts with "unpurged images." Next, an image, evidently purged and more image now than man or shade, has power to summon something both alive and dead, the work of art maybe. Calling complexities from time to itself and composing them, the image seems at once an element of a work, the work, and the creative imagination. In "Ego Dominus Tuus," Ille, the Roman protagonist, calling to his own opposite, seeks an image, which, like Eliot's objective correlative, is at once impersonal and evocative. In "Phases of the Moon," another didactic poem, Yeats is rebuked by Robartes for having spent his life in the pursuit and capture of "mere images," images "that once were thought." Such images, once thought from the poet's point of view, perhaps, if not the reader's, may be elements of poems, but since Yeats calls them perfect and immovable, it is likely they are poems, too.

Applauding the insights of Hulme, Eliot, and Yeats, and the example of Pound, we are now in a position to reconsider the image. My approach to definition, though based upon example, welcomes authority. The image, like the symbol of which it is a principal kind, appears to be a verbal embodiment of thought and feeling. An analogy ranging in scale from the relative assignment of metaphor to the unassigned, the image presents what it carries. The word image may refer to the symbolic whole or to an element depending for part of its burden upon context—like that stuffed owl on Mr. Bloom's mantelpiece. It is to image in its capacity of functioning part, however, that I shall confine myself in this chapter; for my image, less than the whole, is a constituent symbol.

Take, for example, this image from Eliot's "Love Song of J. Alfred

105

Prufrock": "men in shirt-sleeves, leaning out of windows." One of many parallel concretions, this one acts with them and with elements of other kinds to create by interrelationship the figure of the hero and the vision he embodies. By itself this image suggests loneliness, frustration, despair, and, since a window is for looking out of, longing. Shirt sleeves and window leaning, implying class and deportment beneath those of Prufrock, who, nevertheless, sees himself in this lonely figure, are enriched by relationship with other images. There is contrast between those covered arms and the arms, elegantly braceleted and "downed with light brown hair," that Prufrock has just imagined. He sees the shirt-sleeved man at dusk, a time of day that connects him with the opening conceits of evening, the patient, the streets, and the catlike fog. The following image of the lonely "pair of ragged claws" at the bottom of some sea and that of rolled trousers, suitable for wading but not for deeper excursion into the waters of life, enlarge the man at the window as he enlarges them. These images and others, together with tone, rhythm, questions, statements, and periodic deflations, work upon each other and upon the whole until something emerges, at once the sum of the parts and, beyond that, the result of their interaction. We are moved, as Eliot observes at the end of "Preludes," another sequence of "sordid images," by "fancies that are curled around these images"; for what they compose is an embodiment of our extremity. Qualified by the nature of the elements, this vision includes the sexual, social, and spiritual plight of the individual and, what is more, the state of the times. "The Love Song of J. Alfred Prufrock" has proved popular because through it we conceive more about ourselves and our reality than we can through the most discursive of daily papers or the littlest of little magazines. Prufrock's man at window is an element of this vision and its epitome.

106

Baudelaire's giantess is a larger example. Like Prufrock himself, a body qualified by elements that surround it, she is central in the composition she informs:

La Géante

Du temps que la Nature en sa verve puissante
Concevait chaque jour des enfants monstrueux,
J'eusse aimé vivre auprès d'une jeune géante,
Comme aux pieds d'une reine un chat voluptueux.

J'eusse aimé voir son corps fleurir avec son âme
Et grandir librement dans ses terribles jeux;
Deviner si son cœur couve une sombre flamme
Aux humides brouillards qui nagent dans ses yeux;

Parcourir à loisir ses magnifiques formes;
Ramper sur le versant de ses genoux énormes,
Et parfois en été, quand les soleils malsains,

Lasse, la font s'étendre à travers la campagne,
Dormir nonchalamment à l'ombre de ses seins,
Comme un hameau paisible au pied d'une montagne.

By a pun which involves *gea* or goddess of earth, Baudelaire's *géante,* who plainly becomes the landscape by uniting with *campagne* and *montagne,* enters regions of myth and fruitfulness and takes her place with Mrs. Bloom, the "gea-tellus" of *Ulysses.* The relationship of hero and giantess serves to expand them both. Two similes, those of the voluptuous cat at the feet of a queen and of a hamlet at the foot of a mountain, and two actions, crawling over her enormous knees and sleeping in the shade of her breasts, fix their strange encounter. In it we may see mother, son, and all the troubles of Oedipus, the masochist and his lady, and the relationship of man to whatever else woman can embody, the metropolis, perhaps, or things as they are. Not only the relationship, however, but the attitude of

107

the hero serves to solidify our giantess. His tone, as remote from her as he himself is close, contributes to the ambivalence that determines our view. Classical and distant in rhythm and diction, the poem is decadent in theme. This quarrel of grand manner with outrageous substance serves to present adoration and Swiftian disgust, gratification and horror, abandonment and reservation. Attitudes, tone, and relationship alike help to create the atmosphere of dream that clothes enormity and makes it more portentous.

Opening another aspect, *verve* in the first line, from Latin *verbum,* means poetic power or imagination. Nature the image maker creates the giantess as the poet the poem, which, becoming one with monster, reveals the monstrousness of all creation, whether biological or literary. The poet-hero's attitudes toward these creations, however mixed, unite at last in acceptance. "I accept the universe," said Margaret Fuller—but the feeling and idea of more than such acceptance are embodied in this poem. Though "La Géante" and "Prufrock" are alike in being visions of reality, Eliot rejects the reality he apprehends while Baudelaire, with greater understanding and humanity, accepts what we are stuck with, and his image is the symbol of that complex acceptance. By itself neither acceptance nor rejection constitutes merit; but the depth, quality, and scope of what an image incorporates or forms are among its values. Nothing but these forms could acquaint us with the realities and attitudes they present.

Giantess, Bostonian Prufrock, and even the man in shirt sleeves make it plain that person may serve as image. That is no more than we might expect; for if symbol is embodiment and image is a kind of symbol, a body may serve as image. Even Gerald Scales in *The Old Wives' Tale* strikes Sophia (if not us) as "the very symbol and incarnation of the masculine and the elegant." Indeed, body, person, or character as image is the most familiar kind. In his *Autobiography*

108

and *Essays* Yeats is the philosopher of embodiment and in his poems the poet.

A little after the commencement of the new century, Yeats confessed that once he had been interested in disembodied states of mind, lyrical moments, intellectual essences. Now, however, the contrary impulse had come and he was interested in dramatic embodiment alone. In the short essays called "Discoveries," where he proposes the "thinking of the body," to give a body to "something that moves beyond the senses" in words as subtle, complex, and "full of mysterious life, as the body of a flower or of a woman" becomes his purpose. For example of such embodiment he takes girl playing guitar. Her voice, movements, expression all say something delightful that cannot be presented by speech or by another, less personal image. Like Dante in the *Convito,* says Yeats, he found "unity of being" in the "perfectly proportioned human body." It is true that Dante found an image of divine wisdom in the body, an organic harmony of part answering to part, but Yeats, extending Dante's hint and applying his own experience of drama, began to write poems that embodied all his concerns. What he called "the whole man—blood, imagination, intellect running together" became a favorite image. Fishermen, dancers, and horsemen abound in his poems from this time on.

That wise and simple man, his fisherman in grey Connemara cloth (could this mean bawneen?), casting flies with authority and craft at dawn in some mountain stream, is at once the image or mask of Yeats and the image of an audience remote from bourgeois ignobility for whom he will write cold, passionate poems. By the aid of rhythm, diction, and tone, the gentleman fisher presents Yeats's new ideal far better than essay or autobiography can. The fisher is the poem Yeats commends or else its concentrate. That "upstanding" man reappears in "The Tower," but the dancer, having once attracted Yeats, reappears more frequently. Outdancing thought in "The Double Vision of Michael Robartes," she presents by movement and body all that Yeats meant by unity of being; for how could he or anyone else tell dancer from dance? The dance of the ivory image in the Crazy Jane poem not only reconciles complexities but embodies the nature of art and love. As for the horseman who appears on Yeats's proud epitaph at Drumcliff, he is the image of whatever is unlike our democratic world. The "fierce horsemen" who ride from mountain to mountain, like all lovers of horses and women, are aristocrats and artists as far as reference goes, but beyond that they suggest a complex of feelings by body, action, and demeanor as they pass, casting a cold eye on life and death. Bodies, however, can present more than ideals. The Gore-Booth girls, whose house pleased Yeats as much as their politics displeased him, seem when withered, old, and gaunt "an image of such politics." Thought of any kind, as Michael Robartes observes in one of the poems, "becomes an image and the soul becomes a body." Person as *persona* or mask becomes impersonal image.

Becoming general, particular heroes, as both Kenneth Burke and W. H. Auden observe, have always expressed their age. Bunyan's Christian, concentrating in his person the sensations and aspirations of dissent, is a fine example. Childe Harold, Manfred, Captain Nemo, Ahab, the Count of Monte Cristo, and even Wordsworth's feeble-minded boys embodied not only the interest that early romantics took in what Auden calls the "exceptional individual" but the aesthetic, ethical, and religious preoccupations of the time. In these images poets concentrated their darkest, most unsociable feelings and readers found correspondence for their unuttered and maybe unutterable ideals of exploratory quest or mysterious revenge.

110

After second thought, later romantics required heroes of a less heroic kind to embody what they saw within themselves or around them. George F. Babbitt and the late George Apley represent their classes, and we see something of ourselves and of our time in each as we do in all outstanding characters; but a representative is not necessarily a symbol. A senator may represent Wisconsin without symbolizing that state of milk and beer, but if he embodies and presents what he also represents—a wing of his party or a general tendency—he may serve as its symbol. In this sense Babbitt and Apley are as symbolic as Faulkner's Sutpen and Sartoris, who represent aspects of the old South, and his Snopes, who represents an aspect of the new. But character as image is more suitably represented by figures more general than these, and, in recent times, somewhat less heroic than all but Snopes. Such images embody feelings we are almost afraid to acknowledge about ourselves and our situation. The clowns, burghers, knaves, and fools who have wandered through poetry for the past seventy or eighty years reveal our secret convictions about man. As Wallace Stevens's doctor of Geneva, confronting the sea, pats his "stove-pipe hat," uses his handkerchief, and sighs, we find his act and character repulsively congenial; but Auden's "sinister tall-hatted botanist," stooping at the spring to empty his phial, is closer to our fears and our capacity.

Though these images tell us what we are like, our recent favorites have been the betrayed, cuckolded man and the lonely artist. In his notes for *Exiles,* Joyce, the greatest exploiter of both these images, says that since the publication of *Madame Bovary* "the centre of sympathy appears to have been esthetically shifted from the lover or fancyman to the husband or cuckold." Joyce's Richard in this play is an example of the symbolic cuckold, and Mr. Bloom is a greater one, but these are only two of many. Heroes of Proust, Evelyn

111

Waugh, William Sansom, and many others demonstrate the adequacy of this terrible image. It is easy enough to see the relevance and appeal of cuckolds for men in our position, but what of artists? Portraits of the artist—Ernest Pontifex, Stephen Dedalus, or Tonio Kröger—may project the writer's sense of exile and his pride in making rather than destroying; but these portraits must also please the frustrated rebel and creator in the rest of us. To explain the charm of Ernest Pontifex is simplest of all; for that successful young rebel, enjoying his unearned income, mocking his father and the world while clipping coupons, is a bourgeois dream, as acceptable in our time as Monte Cristo in his.

Commonly, as Baudelaire's giantess and other giantesses prove, we embody our needs, if not ourselves, in the image of woman. Whether she is cruel and overwhelming like Salomé or that Ledean body Yeats adored, benign and overwhelming like Mrs. Ramsay or Jung's *anima,* or just overwhelming like Mrs. Bloom, she flatters our irresponsibility and gratifies our desire for retreat, support, and center. From Shaw's Ann, full of life-force, to Mann's Mme Chauchat (with those Kirghiz eyes), woman as image seems almost everywhere. Under other auspices *Lady Chatterley's Lover,* with its emphasis upon man, might have appeared as *The Lover's Lady Chatterley.* Lawrence was exceptional—and so is Eliot, whose women, in the earlier poems at least, are of two principal kinds: revolting or ineffectual. On one hand we find "female smells" in bedrooms and, rising from effluence to source, pneumatic Grishkin in a drawingroom; on the other we find the hyacinth girl and a company of intercessors. Whereas Dante ascends from adorable woman to the heaven she embodies, the preliminary ascension of Dante's adorer seems powered by stamping woman back into Bleistein's slime, whence she came. Not that Eliot is against embodi-

112

ment; for the Incarnation brings *Four Quartets* to a kind of climax, and Celia on her anthill is exemplary.

Impersonal images range in kind from metaphor, comparatively assigned, to images limited by context alone and those that seem to lack assignment. "As and is are one," says Wallace Stevens in "An Ordinary Evening in New Haven." I too find no useful distinction between metaphor and simile; in point of fact some of the "metaphors" we find most agreeable, Donne's compasses and Eliot's patient etherized upon his table, are similes. Similes tend to be detachable and decorative, but when, as in these instances, they are intrinsic and functional, nothing is improved by separating them from metaphor. As we have noticed, symbol, metaphor, and simile are of a kind, and the proper distinction among them is degree of assignment.

An abundance of similes in *Mrs. Dalloway,* while enriching texture, presents character and connection. When Mrs. Dalloway and Septimus, her double, compare experience to brandished plumes, they are somehow united. Analogies of searching for pearls or diamonds at the roots of grass or of fish who inhabit deep seas support a major theme of spiritual exploration. A metaphor of spider's thread, elaborated for page after page, reveals not only the attachment of Clarissa to her friends, especially Peter Walsh, but an element in Clarissa herself that is almost sinister; for, as we know, female spiders, spinning threads, consume the male. Such metaphorical assistance, found not only here, of course, but in the works of Shakespeare, James, Faulkner, and Proust, conditions much that we receive, however unconscious of it we may be or—as when some beast springs from his jungle and by fearful symmetry or the light of burning clarifies all—however conscious.

Except for such as these, metaphors in poems are more conspicu-

113

ous and more nearly essential. Hopkins's "Wreck of the Deutschland" is a great metaphor, built in part of subsidiary similes and metaphors. The poet's experience during his anxieties and that of five foundering nuns form the basis of a vast analogy determining a structure which, like any metaphor, may be expressed by an equation: the relation of Hopkins to God is that of the principal nun to God. Her shipwreck is a metaphor for his spiritual trouble and its relief. "Lightning and lashed rod" in the second stanza, applying to both the elements of this equation, serve as its sign. Metaphors of the hourglass and the well, suggesting time and approximate eternity, present the poet's position as man and priest. The simile of the "lush-kept plush-capped sloe," crushed against a palate to flush and fill the being, suggests communion, which, since it is receiving God, supports the major theme. The vision of "pied and peeled May" that occupies the twenty-sixth stanza is heaven by natural correspondence. These analogies and that of the figure five, an exercise in Sir Thomas Browne's "mystical mathematics," exceed nineteenth-century ideas of decorum; but if one is holy enough, equations of sloe and God as of Virgin and gas have nothing irreverent about them—as Eliot proves when he pursues that conceit of the wounded surgeon plying his steel in Sir Thomas Browne's hospital.

Although we know Eliot as a symbolist and although his methods and those of Hopkins coincide at many points, we do not think Hopkins a symbolist. Yet the sloe may be considered the symbol of what it is equated with and the wreck the symbol of private experience. Equation does not limit as narrowly as we suppose or as its structure implies. The resemblance of elements is only partial at best, leaving scope for unlimited suggestion, and beyond apparent limits the metaphor is indefinite. As the sloe flushes our being full we find more than reference in that vegetable.

114

Finding delightful possibilities of vagueness in the strictest of equations, the symbolists of France made more use of metaphor and simile than we commonly suppose. Take Mallarmé's sonnet on his cigar:

> Toute l'âme résumée
> Quand lente nous l'expirons
> Dans plusieurs ronds de fumée
> Abolis en autres ronds
>
> Atteste quelque cigare
> Brûlant savamment pour peu
> Que la cendre se sépare
> De son clair baiser de feu
>
> Ainsi le chœur des romances
> A la lèvre vole-t-il
> Exclus-en si tu commences
> Le réel parce que vil
>
> Le sens trop précis rature
> Ta vague littérature.

As the pivotal word *Ainsi* makes plain, octave and sestet are halves of an odd comparison between smoking and writing a poem. Unclear at first, the simile yields its secret or some of it upon examination. As one smoke ring abolishes another, so the images of a poem are lost in what they create; and the ash, preserved by the knowing smoker, is less their residue than their origin. Equivalent to actuality, the ultimate source of both rings and images, the ash must not intrude among them lest "its sense, too precise for vague literature, will erase it." This poem, which recalls Verlaine's remarks about vagueness, is a symbolist manifesto, not altogether serious—as we may gather from tone and diction; but what they called vague, we call indefinite. However definite in form, Mallarmé's curious little equa-

115

tion creates something almost as evanescent and impalpable as the rings of smoke it celebrates.

"Les Phares," a construction of another sort, consists of parallel metaphors; but Baudelaire is less notable for analogies limited by equation than for those apparently limited by explanation. "Andromaque, je pense à vous!" the opening analogy of "Le Cygne," establishes grandeur and places the bird among ancient sufferers as, frotting the dust of city pavements, it longs for rain or almost forgotten rivers. Surely this should be enough to confirm the swan as exile, but not contented with image and context, Baudelaire proceeds to examine what he has presented. Failure to exhaust the meanings of the swan and its plight is implied by his final admission that the oppressive "image" corresponds not only to things he has mentioned but "à bien d'autres encore!"

Poets writing in English have also tried and failed to explain their images away. The octave of Hopkins's sonnet on spring presents that season by a vision of juice and joy as luscious and suggestive as anything in English literature, but the sestet, like the second half of something from the bestiary, makes a meaning of the octave explicit. It is true that "cloy," "cloud," and "sour" thicken discourse by a fugitive suggestion of syrup or some other juice; but for all that the sestet is discursive enough to prove the insufficiency of discourse for what it tries. The poet's effort to impose limits upon symbol is rebuked by the limits of logic.

Some recent poets have amused themselves with the machinery of explanation. Thus, in "Le Monocle de Mon Oncle," a sequence, Wallace Stevens begins a poem with what he calls a "parable" or a "trivial trope" that baffles understanding. Offering enlightenment, he ends the poem with another trope as obscure as the first. Maybe this metaphorical semblance of explanation intimates his sense of its

116

futility. In any case, we are left with two all but unlimited images to account for instead of one, but a poem, as Stevens says in "Man Carrying Thing," should "resist the intelligence almost successfully."

That the image does not resist it entirely is due most often to context; for images limited by explanation or even by pseudo explanation are less common these days than images limited by context alone. It may be that in *St. Mawr* Lawrence, overcome by a preacher's impatience, explains the meaning of his central horse, which proves too substantial to be diminished, however, and of a brightness too bright to be impaired. Lawrence, I repeat, is exceptional. Most images today, whether in poem or novel, are allowed to stand alone, teasing our understanding by nondiscursive relationship with what surrounds them. Let us think again of that stuffed owl on Mr. Bloom's mantelpiece.

Attendant images, those that give additional body to narrative, are conspicuous in *Mrs. Dalloway,* to which for a moment we may return. Peter's knife, for example, is always in his hand. "Shredding and slicing, dividing and subdividing" like the clocks that send their mechanical circles through the air, this instrument, insignificant alone, takes from contexts all kinds of implications and comes to suggest at last not only sex and intellect but aggression and defense. Like the flowers Mrs. Dalloway buys and accepts or her narrow virginal bed, this increasingly heavy knife takes its place in the great theme of separateness. Any of these images could be omitted without destroying the theme, which with their help accosts our feelings more warmly and directly.

Still other images, finding less support from context, are almost like Wallace Stevens's "old song that will not declare itself." Peter, the knife-bearing man of *Mrs. Dalloway,* hears an old woman singing outside an entrance to the tube, her voice "of no age or sex, the

117

voice of an ancient spring," her mouth a mere hole in the earth, bubbling through skeletons and root fibers, yet proclaiming for those who enter the Underground a primeval May. Peter gives her a shilling, but aside from receiving such bounty her function remains unclear. Possibly she is a symbol of life, persistent through skeleton and root, like the old woman in the room who fixes Mrs. Dalloway's attention that evening. There is also the image of the kite in Somerset Maugham's story of that name—though I know it only from the moving picture. What the kite means to its flier or what it may mean to us, though discussed by legal gentlemen at the end, remains obscure and fascinating. Most enigmatic of all, however, is the camera at the end of Mann's *Death in Venice:* "A camera on a tripod stood at the edge of the water, apparently abandoned; its black cloth snapped in the freshening wind." An artist is no camera; yet somehow the image corresponds to dying Aschenbach and concentrates the feeling of abandonment—not only his but that of society. Appropriate but almost entirely unassigned, such images move us while they rebuff our reason.

In respect of this—and speaking of tripods—such images are not unlike a piece of sculpture by Reg Butler, entitled "The Oracle," lately exhibited at the Museum of Modern Art. This object, intended for display at a technical college near an airfield in England, appeared in New York without its intended context. A rusty metal thing on three legs with a sort of tail and neck, it is far from representative, however reminiscent its form may be of insects, crustacea, mechanical contraptions, or anything at once primitive and advanced, vital and mechanical. According to a note fixed to its base, the sculptor wanted the thing to be "suggestive" and "evocative," but of what he does not say. By title, its only limitation, it may bring to mind the oracle on that tripod at Delphi, who, according to Heraclitus, "neither utters nor hides his meaning, but shows it by a sign."

In Proust's *Remembrance of Things Past,* a work extending in time and almost too vast for apprehension as an object, there are similar objects, the three spires, for example, in the first volume. Proust prepares the way for this vision by a significant reference to Baudelaire, in whose tradition he works, and by a general discussion of objects which seem "to be concealing, beneath what my eyes could see, something which they invited me to approach and seize from them, but which, despite all my efforts, I never managed to discover." "Teeming, ready to open, to yield up to me the secret treasure of which they were themselves no more than the outer coverings," such objects, providing "unreasoning pleasure," have littered his mind with "a confused mass of different images, under which must have perished long ago the reality of which I used to have some foreboding, but which I never had the energy to discover and bring to light."

Given a lift in Dr. Percepied's carriage, young Marcel encounters an image that he does not abandon without thorough exploration. He observes the twin spires of Martinville, lit by the declining sun, and behind them a third spire, that of Vieuxvicq, and as his movement in time and space continually alters the aspect and relationship of the three spires, their mobility and luminosity entrance him, affording the special pleasure he has always found in images that seem, like Carlyle's symbols, "at once to contain and conceal." Contemplation and analysis yield at last a little of what the "vision" offers him. Taking out pencil and paper, he composes a prose poem, rhythmic, descriptive, and filled with similes of girls and flowers. This trifle, which clears up nothing for us, relieves his mind of its "obsession" with the steeples and their mystery, and his words, an "equivalent" for the experience, permit its recapture. Since what pleases him now

119

is less those steeples than his words, "what lay buried within the steeples . . . must be something analogous to a charming phrase."

Omitting the attempt at analysis, Joyce would have given the images alone to make of what we could. Even if he had included its literary equivalent, a poem by Stephen perhaps, he would not have talked about it. But Proust's analysis, less penetrating than it seems, also leaves us where we were, and discourse proves as non-discursive as image. Those steeples, filled with mysterious suggestions, seem an analogy for something, maybe something having to do with the setting sun and changing relationships in time and space. What Marcel finds is an analogy for an analogy. His prose poem on steeples is less an analogy for steeples than for his feeling about them, and we are left, as we are after reading Stevens's "Monocle," with two undeclared analogies.

For his little poem Marcel has decomposed experience, transposed it into words, and recomposed it in a way that recaptures something of the original experience. Not altogether pleased with his verbal equivalent, which must have seemed to him at last as inadequate as it seems at once to us, he revises it years later (in *The Captive*). That he returns to it shows how the experience continues to haunt him. It also comes to mind when in another carriage, this time near Balbec, he observes three trees. Apparently "double in time," they prove even more enigmatic than the steeples, which he does not begin to understand until the last volume. Although such "signs" and "hieroglyphs," he says, have no meaning unless one extracts it, discursive analysis is not the way; for the greater part of the meaning must come to us from some spiritual analogue, a moment of revelation or the work of art, a better one presumably than his first attempt.

Since the "privileged moments" he has been enjoying are at once the occasions and the concrete embodiments of what they evoke, it occurs to him that his experience of the steeples is not unlike them. There is a difference, however, between the *petite madeleine* and the steeples: the privileged moment unites sensation with memory; the experience of the steeples unites sensation with a promise to which something within him responds, and, evading his intellect, holds out to his unconscious a hint of capacity and future achievement. It becomes plain to him, as it does to us after we have put the last volume down, that the image of steeples is an epitome of his book as well as a clue to one of its meanings. The changing relationship of viewer and objects in time and space, lighted by the setting sun, anticipates the disclosures of the last great party. Steeples become analogous now to people or parties, the shifting point of view is like his own, the sunset seems social and the prose poem the transformation of time and change by the work of art. A symbol that waits to disclose that much of its burden for fifteen or sixteen volumes, and then depends upon context and inference, is all but unassigned—altogether unassigned for those who tire before the end. For those who endure, the discovery of steeples, uniting a sensation of the last volume with a memory of the first, is a moment as privileged as any of Marcel's.

Symbols that precede their attendants are even more mysterious in plays. To a member of the audience, whether in orchestra or balcony, or even to a critic on his aisle or a reader in his closet nothing could seem less definite than gin and water in Eliot's *Cocktail Party*. In the first act of that comedy the Unidentified Guest asks for gin and water, odd but possible in a society where Martinis seem unnatural. A few minutes later he asks for his peculiar drink again, and our attention is entirely engaged not only by a third request but by a song about drinking gin and water. In something by Noel Coward, to which Eliot's play bears a superficial resemblance, both

121

song and repeated demand would serve comedy alone; but as we know, *The Cocktail Party* was composed by a symbolist. Even without this knowledge we might wonder if the Guest's beverage is more than mildly diverting or if the cocktail party itself is more than convenient. Why, moreover, does Edward, the host, persistently forget his guest's preference? And what of the flat champagne that others choose? The first act fails to appease our curiosity about the mixture of gin and water, which, though seeming important, lacks certain import; and the last act, disclosing another cocktail party, increases our uncertainty. Here the Guest, now identified as Sir Henry Harcourt-Reilly, an analyst or confessor, prefers plain water without gin; for this, he says, is a different occasion. "To what does this lead?" asks Edward as if our spokesman; and as the Guest himself remarks: "nobody likes to be left with a mystery."

Recollection in anxiety after we have reached our homes or beds may find the theme a limiting context for the perplexing image. Sir Henry has commended two ways of adjustment, martyrdom near anthills and making the best of a bad job. It seems possible that his preference in drink embodies and predicts these ways, which like Celia's experience can only be "hinted at in myths and images." Gin is a spirit, and water, as we know from "Dry Salvages," may serve as an image of life in time. At the first party gin and water may indicate a choice and at the second plain water may celebrate Edward's "appointed burden." These words, which seem almost Calvinist, remind us that gin implies Geneva, an element in the thirty-nine articles. The juniper, which flavors gin, is an evergreen, and tree implies the cross. Like the Church of England, a cocktail is a mixture, and a party, however secular, is a kind of communion. These possibilities, too ingenious, I am afraid, though suggested by the play as a whole and by what we know of Eliot's habit, remain indecisive.

122

Far from signs, the images are no more than adumbrations, of which the ritual that closes the second act is one of the more perplexing examples. As Sir Henry and the other angels pass the decanter and parody the litany, is their drink straight gin? Eliot likes to leave a little fruitful mystery around. In a poetic play, he said, "you get several levels of significance," plot for the simple, character for the thoughtful, words and phrases for the literate, and for those with sensibility "a meaning which gradually reveals itself," according to "different degrees of consciousness." Symbols like gin and water, water, and possible gin are among the instruments of this gradual but never final revelation.

No less inviting, Ibsen's wild duck is even less definitely assigned. There she sits in the attic, displaced and injured, one wing broken by shot, one leg twisted by the dog that retrieved her from the depths of the sea where she had sought refuge. Around her in the attic are rabbits, hens, foreign books, dried Christmas trees, and a clock that works no longer. Now and again Ekdal, scouting among the Christmas trees, shoots a rabbit, but the old sportsman cherishes the sitting duck, which, indefinitely suggestive, is a center of values. To old Ekdal, once a hunter of bear, his duck in the attic recalls not only the freedom he has lost but his present injuries and frustration. Gregers, whose father shot the duck and injured Ekdal, is impressed by the duck's timelessness (now that the clock has failed), her descent to the depths of the sea, and her return to light in the jaws of a dog. In the dog he sees himself and in the duck, clinging to weeds on the bottom, he sees an illusion to be destroyed. Hialmar, the victim of this illusion, sees the duck as himself until, enlightened by Gregers, the retriever, he turns against darkness and aqueous depths. Relling also finds the duck an image of illusion, but the necessary life-illusion that Conrad was to call the "destructive element" in

123

which, although it destroys us, we must immerse. Identifying the duck with herself, Hedwig sacrifices both by suicide. Gina observes that there is too much fuss about a duck that is duck to her and nothing more. To each his duck—as if Ibsen's design were to display the nature of symbol. Plainly the bird is unitive, revelatory, and variously significant, but what we are to make of her is more than we can say; for we are wiser than those Norwegians. All we know for sure is that the duck embodies the meaning of the play and, by the aid of action, speech, and immediate context, presents it.

Yeats praised Ibsen's "wild duck in the attic" and Maeterlinck's "crown at the bottom of the foundation" as "vague symbols that set the mind wandering from idea to idea, emotion to emotion." But once in a while he felt lost in a "darkly splendid world" of "unintelligible images," and it seemed safer on the whole to use "a symbolism handled by the generations." If Ibsen's duck were a swan or an eagle, it would carry a more intelligible meaning; for swan, eagle, rose, moon, tree, and the like are traditional images. Beyond fixed reference, such images permit personal enlargement and mix the virtues of mystery with the assurance of old directions. What is more, the past has conferred beauty and richness upon them. "It is only by ancient symbols," says Yeats in his essay on Shelley, "by symbols that have numberless meanings beside the one or two the writer lays an emphasis upon, or the half-score he knows of, that any highly subjective art can escape from the barrenness and shallowness of a too conscious arrangement, into . . . abundance and depth. The poet of essences and pure ideas must seek in the half-lights that glimmer from symbol to symbol." Traditional images, expressing "personal emotion, through ideal form" become "a mask from whose eyes the disembodied looks." "A hundred generations might write out what seemed the meaning, and they would write different meanings, for no symbol tells all its meaning to any generation." In these and other passages in his *Essays* Yeats, the exploiter of swans, affirms his general preference for images at once assigned and unassigned, personal and impersonal, enriched by the past and open to present expansion. He was not alone; for by image and discourse alike Eliot too was always mixing memory with desire and tradition with individual talent.

A traditional image is either a natural thing, like a tree, or an artifact, let us say a crown. The crown, a hat of distinction, has been symbolic from the start. Not so the tree; for in its original context a tree is a tree, which becomes symbol when removed to an artificial context or when such context has been projected around it. Even when so removed or improved, its meaning is inconstant, differing from time to time and from place to place. In a culture at a time tree may come to mean virtue, let us say, or aspiration; and custom, affirming a general agreement, enriches it. Men of another time and place may find tree an image for home or mother, and for years all will applaud the association as the most normal thing in the world. Traditional images owe such meanings neither to necessity nor to chance, however, but to something in between. Finding a tree the image of mother or aspiration demands something of the tree—maybe quality, appearance, or shape—else the association, lacking felicity, could not endure—still less begin. The traditional images I am concerned with here are those received by European culture since Dante's time or in some cases far earlier, images that seem as natural now as their origins. No doubt they ordered things otherwise in the Ming dynasty or the T'ang, where trees for all I know meant politics or song.

The abundance of images from past times in our time is easy to explain. Dismayed by flux and finding the illusion of stability in

125

images from a solider past, poets have rummaged Dante for roses and Baudelaire for swans. At a time of violent change such images, affording a comfortable sense of continuity and permanence, approximate that union of eternity with time which pleased Eliot and Yeats. At a time, moreover, when the poet feels separated from the reader, the traditional image with its quota of reference is a way of closing the gap between them by partial communication. Although the French symbolists used an occasional image of this sort, they delighted in privacy. Mallarmé's swan is far from typical of his school, but Remy de Gourmont's hypocritical rose, plucked for *Ash Wednesday* by T. S. Eliot, announces our present temper. Even Dr. Sitwell exchanged the façades, the furry grass, the wooden stalactites, and the other ornaments of her French youth for wasteland, sun, and rose.

Like the real toads of Marianne Moore's imaginary gardens, the traditional flowers of contemporary literature seem odd in gardens both commonplace and exceptional. Owing some part of its color and fragrance to Dante and Lewis Carroll, the rose of Eliot's *Four Quartets* becomes through context an image of personal frustration, not unlike those hyacinths proffered in *The Waste Land* to the incapable hero. Like the hyacinth, the narcissus owes fixed meaning to myth and variety to individual requirements. Whereas the "black narcissus" of Rumer Godden's novel of that name seems no more than the perfume ignominiously used by an oriental dandy, it acquires connotations that justify the emphasis placed upon it. Sister Phillippa wants jonquils and daffodils for the convent garden. Like that perfume, these flowers of the narcissus family call to mind the original Narcissus, who, suggesting both Sister Clodagh's vanity and her rebirth, summarizes in one allusive image the principal theme of the novel. The blackness of this flower implies not only a

126

nun's habit and the unworldliness that threatens rebirth but also the period of trial and deprivation that must precede it. This took a while to figure out; but most traditional flowers, whatever their eccentric varieties, are simpler—and so are fruits.

Fruit is traditionally (and actually) sexual, but Lawrence at once improved and exhausted its possibilities. "Every fruit has its secret," he says, telling it in *Birds, Beasts and Flowers*. His pomegranate with its fissure and his heavy, globular, fleshly peach with its groove and hairy skin leave nothing unsaid. As for the fig, an image that Eliot was to use for sensuous temptation in *Ash Wednesday* as in "Prufrock" he had used the peach: "You feel at once it is symbolic," says Lawrence, "It is female . . . it stands for the female part." "Fruit of the female mystery," recalling Eve's leaves together with secular wounds, slits, and lips, the fig with its abundant limitations satisfies those who tire of "the limitations of the Infinite." Lawrence may add nothing but brilliance to tradition; but reference brilliantly embodied becomes more than reference, and tradition, becoming a present thing, recaptures mystery.

Fruit depends from tree, no less traditional. Endowed by the scriptures with reference to knowledge, life, and cross, the trees of secular literature, exploiting this inheritance, proceed beyond it. The "wych elm" that guards Forster's Howards End, a house as symbolic as its tree, may be less elaborately rooted and less great than Yeats's "great-rooted blossomer," but it serves similar purposes. From Hardy's greenwood tree to the rude red tree of Dylan Thomas the trees of literature, like their biological cousins, owe as much to heredity as to environment.

Relieving loneliness, conquering change, and increasing substance by memories, traditional images commonly precede their private renewal. But in the works of Joyce, who liked to do things backwards, particulars sometimes precede the traditional image, which, instead of origin, becomes conclusion. Hidden by the details that embody it, the image is what we must discover and the climax of the tale. "Clay," one of the stories of *Dubliners,* provides an instance of this reversal. It is Halloween, the scene a laundry, and the *décor* apparently naturalistic. Preparing for "her evening out," Maria, whose long nose all but meets her long chin, seems among "big copper boilers" a "veritable peace-maker." The time, her name, her appearance, the equipment around her, and the reference to the Mass for All Saints' Day suggest that the poor old thing is at once witch and Virgin. "Maria is my proper mother," says Joe as if to confirm the second of these suggestions. Her laundry, though Protestant, is dedicated to making dear dirty Dublin clean; her purse is from Protestant Belfast and her attitude, suitable to the relationship of subject to ruler, toward the colonel on the tram is meek. Maria's bewitched frustration is proved no less by her loss of cake and her omission of the amatory second verse of Balfe's song than by her choice at the Halloween party first of the bowl of clay, signifying death, and second of the prayer book. Joyce's design, however, is not to present a frustrated virgin amid naturalistic scenery but through her in her context to create an image to embody and reinforce the meaning of his book. This image, the traditional embodiment of Ireland, is the Poor Old Woman, who served Yeats in *Cathleen Ni Houlihan* and was to serve Joyce again as the milkwoman of *Ulysses.* Having recreated this traditional image, Joyce employs it to offer a vision of Ireland herself and her choice of the decay, death, and submission he has escaped.

"Birds, beasts, men, women, landscape, society, are but symbols, and metaphors," says Yeats in his *Autobiography,* "nothing is studied in itself, the mind is a dark well, no surface, depth only." Such

128

images, living in the "great memory," possess the imagination of man, and once they have possessed it, become "an embodiment of disembodied powers" and repeat themselves in "dreams and visions." The "subconscious life," he says in his essay on Shelley, seizes upon "some passing scene" and moulds it into "an ancient symbol without help from anything but that great memory." By that great memory Yeats means what we call the unconscious and by the images it contains he means what we call archetypes. The traditional image is often though not necessarily archetypal. Freud's houses, trees, birds, and flowers inhabit our dreams while Jung's woman and his other "archetypes" fill those of the less respectable. According to Jung—and on this point Freud would not disagree—an archetype is the imagistic residue of racial experience, which, presenting our deepest concerns, comes from the unconscious where it resides to tease our waking minds. Carrying "memories backward thousands of years," borrowing beauty and "far-off suggestion" from previous usage, as Yeats observes, these images keep "half their secret to themselves."

That such images from the unconscious retain the power to move us, however unconscious of them we may be, is the point of Maud Bodkin's *Archetypal Patterns in Poetry: Psychological Studies of Imagination,* which accounts for the emotional significance of certain poems from the Greeks to Eliot and Lawrence. The archetypal pattern within us "leaps in response," she says, to that in the poem if the poet has availed himself of images that have "taken shape in the fantasy of the community." Concentrating experience, both individual and collective, by his images, the poet unconsciously evokes our unconscious reaction. Miss Bodkin is liberal enough to receive Ernest Jones on *Hamlet* as one of her proofs, but on the whole she follows Jung, who in his *Integration of the Personality* calls archetypes genuine symbols, ambiguous, full of intimations, and inexhaustible.

Under archetype, though some of my examples may be unorthodox according to one school or the other, I include landscape and sea, enclosures such as garden, island, and cave, and in addition city and tower. Uniting the personal and the general and commonly ambivalent, these images, not necessarily symbolic in themselves, become symbolic by context, first in our sleeping minds and then in poems.

Of landscape as image, Yeats, who had much to say about symbols of most kinds, had much to say. Impatient with naturalistic scenery for the stage and with representative painting for the easel, he preferred to regard landscape, liberated from utility or photography, as the image of an "infinite emotion." In the world about him, among the gaunt mansions of Dublin or below Ben Bulben, he sought "a landscape that is symbolical of some spiritual condition." Hopkins, who devoted large sections of his notebooks to details of landscape, invented "inscape," which, suggested by landscape, is the essential and individual quality of a thing. Every landscape, he believed, has its inscape or something peculiar that it embodies and shows forth. But the principal authority on landscape in our time is W. H. Auden, who devoted *The Enchafed Flood* not only to the sea as romantic image, but to desert, island, garden and city as well. His "Paysage Moralisé," a sestina, reveals this preoccupation in five of its terminal words: valleys, mountains, water, islands, and cities. The sixth word is "sorrow," of which apparently the other five are images. Let water (in the manner of Hopkins's sloe) "gush, flush" valley and mountain, Auden prays in the envoy, and let us leave islands for cities. The hero of "Adolescence," one of his better poems, is reminded by landscape of his mother's figure; for Auden is a Freud-

130

ian, and, like the master, tends to regard symbol as sign or symptom. As a disciple of Kierkegaard and Tillich as well, he finds landscape no longer the receptacle of indefinite suggestions but something to be moralized. Not that the arctic, alpine or industrial barrens of his early poems, full of potholes, slag heaps, and rusting equipment, lack suggestive power; but Auden has become so "cold sober" and so fully conscious, like Prospero in "The Sea and the Mirror" or like one going home from the analyst's couch, that he has renounced magic and art for what he calls reality. "The Sea and the Mirror," that curious mixture of prosaic verse and poetic prose, is an obvious analogy for Auden's present commitment to what his Caliban calls "feebly figurative signs"; for Auden's vestigial landscapes, divested of imagination and all other impediments to morality, have become allegorical, fanciful, and significant. While old Yeats, having made his choice, was "raging in the dark," Auden began to lecture in the light.

The sea, which depends for meaning upon temporal or cultural as well as literary context, is commonly ambivalent, implying both life and death. To Freud the amniotic sea is our beginning and, for sons, the end. To Virginia Woolf, as much Bergsonist as Freudian, the sea is flux, time, life, death, something that our fishlike soul swims in. To Conrad the alien sea, an image of our discouraging universe, is what sailors must conquer or endure. As Auden explained at his blackboard at Swarthmore, the sea, however ambivalent, and the desert are iconographical opposites. His Alonso in "The Sea and the Mirror" follows a kind of "tightrope" between the sea of sensuality and pure deed on the one hand and the desert of pure intellect on the other. This reduction to extremes fixes a reference if not the connotation of these areas.

We need not linger by the sea. As symbol it is too familiar to detain us; but the desert, though conspicuous in recent literature, is unfamiliar enough to require contemplation. In Hardy's dramatic triolet, "Winter in Durnover Field," which concerns a number of birds, pecking a frozen field in vain, grotesque frivolity of form and tone quarrel with desperate matter to reveal an attitude toward man's condition, centered in an image of northern desert, that makes the verses seem a *Waste Land* in miniature. The implications of Eliot's more elaborate desert, which reappears with cactus in "The Hollow Men," are personal, social, and spiritual. It was his achievement to provide an analogy not only for his private horrors but for the desolation, infertility, and despair that men between the wars found within themselves and around them. Whatever the poet may have intended, readers as experienced as I. A. Richards saw little hope of rain in a prospect that expressed the lostness of a generation and its moral dessication. The desert to which Eliot is always retiring like a saint seeking a pillar is the most extensive of our century, but that of Yeats, though less familiar, is more promising—if this word may be used for barrens. Nevertheless he may have been moved by Eliot's example; for in the Preface to *The Cat and the Moon* (1924) Yeats says: "The other day . . . I read that strange 'Waste Land' by Mr. T. C. Eliot." Even before this experience, however, the desert had figured in such poems as "Ego Dominus Tuus" and "The Double Vision of Michael Robartes," where Bedouin, Sphinx, stone, and sand acquire importance in his store of images. Far from implying infertility, Yeats's Arabian and Egyptian wastes seem by context to mean abstraction, all that is opposite the complexities of the "gong-tormented sea." In "The Gift of Harun Al-Rashid" Arabian sands under a burning sun give philosophers, djinns, and mathematicians wisdom. The great wheel is but an emblem in those sands; and in "some bookish desert, the Thebaid, or the lands about the Mareotic

132

sea," occupied by ascetics on their pillars, Yeats found triumphs of intellect as great as those attributed to the Sphinx herself. Meanwhile in his oasis amid the sands wise Solomon entertained his Sheba or she him. In Yeats's iconography, one that he shared with many romantics, the moon signifies imagination, the sun intellect and fact. For many years Yeats avoided sun, but a growing desire to unite moon and sun in "one inextricable beam" commended sunny desert as much as moony tide. Joyce's more compendious desert, centered in Mr. Bloom's back yard, is closer to Eliot's and a product of the same year. But though *Ulysses* and *The Waste Land* present the idea and feeling of infertility, they differ in respect of this: Eliot's hero is unable to do anything about his desert, but Mr. Bloom goes out to fertilize his.

Like desert, mountain and tower are generously endowed with reference and connotation. From the time of *Pilgrim's Progress*—to go no earlier—these awful eminences, displaying their archetypal and traditional meanings, have invited individual treatment. Freud's dream, Auden's F6, and the mountain which provides a site for Mann's Hermetically sealed hospital reveal the capacity of the image. Though the tower of Milton's Platonist has little in common with Gérard de Nerval's "tour abolie" or the dark tower to which Childe Roland came, it is equally traditional. However archetypal, the towers of Yeats, Joyce, and Virginia Woolf, and, above all, that of Ibsen show modern improvements.

The Master Builder, rich, complex, and inexhaustible, is one of Joyce's great examples. An old man with two girls, Solness is a prototype of H. C. Earwicker, the hero of *Finnegans Wake,* who also builds and falls from tower. Fear, dizziness, public indifference, and the menace of youth have transformed Solness from a daring builder of churches to a builder of towerless homes; but Hilda, a member of the generation he fears, interrupts his frustrated brooding. Amorous of noble erections and suitably dressed as a mountaineer, she demands those castles in the air that he once promised. She has seen him place a wreath on the pinnacle of his highest tower, but another wreath, ambiguously signifying success and death, would be "tremendously thrilling." Convincing enough but hardly realistic, tower-demanding Hilda seems a projection of Solness's ego, his desires, and his fears. She and the tower reveal not only his exhibitionism but the guilt he shares with other modern heroes and his creative urge. His dizziness on ascending towers is that of achievement and conscience. To become a "free builder," paying the price in suffering, he has had to offer up family and friends, but to become a builder at all he has had to sacrifice the higher reaches of his art to popularity. That his final tower is domestic improves the complication. The exiled, guilty, and all but frustrated artist in our time and the nature of his art have never found more impressive embodiment in character or image. The tower's traditional references to sex, solitude, and aspiring pride allow these brilliant extensions.

More than phallic and proud, the tower resembles castle or house. Such images of enclosure, together with island, garden, cave, and city, are also ambivalent. Implying retreat, isolation or even trap, they are disagreeable but agreeable in implying refuge, creation, and center.

"Consider the subtleness of the sea," says Melville in *Moby Dick*, "how its most dreaded creatures glide under water, unapparent for the most part, and treacherously hidden beneath the loveliest tints of azure. . . . Consider all this; and then turn to this green, gentle, and most docile earth; consider them both, the sea and the land; and do you not find a strange analogy to something in yourself? For as this appalling ocean surrounds the verdant land, so in the soul of man there lies one insular Tahiti, full of peace and joy, but encompassed by all the horrors of the half known life." Consider also the island of Conrad's *Victory,* there to embody Heyst's destructive illusion of apartness and to prove, as he learns in the end, that no man is an island. Baudelaire imagined two islands. One, an image of order, beauty, and peace in "L'Invitation au Voyage" is all that is opposite our world. The other in "Un Voyage à Cythère," an "allegory" of love as an island, is "triste et noire." Promising flowers of Venus, this island proves a desert of venereal horrors in the midst of which the poet finds "un gibet symbolique où pendait mon image."

Among gardens, Adam's is famous, but there are snakes, and in the happy fall, celebrated by Saint Augustine, Milton, and Joyce, garden seems inferior to responsibility and work without those walls. Dante's *Purgatory, The Romance of the Rose,* and *The Faerie Queene* show gardens good or bad. Marvell's garden, joined to Eden by melons to stumble on, is the lobby of Paradise or its earthly equivalent. But most gardens of contemporary literature, those of Eliot or Joyce in particular, are either barren, difficult of access, or contrived by memory alone. Maybe one gains entrance at last, as Alice does, to find the rose a painted thing and the painters flat with terror among their pots.

Caves and burrows are more congenial. Robinson Crusoe in his cave, surrounded by hoarded goods and elaborate walls—and these on an island that is at once refuge and trap—is a bourgeois vision and the symbol of a class. Defoe was unaware no doubt of this possibility in the image he made, but Auden's barflies of *The Age of Anxiety* in their Third Avenue bar know their cavelike retreat an escape from the moral choices of the avenue. More moving images of enclosure, however, were made in Russia and in Prague.

"The Man in the Shell," a story by Chekhov, who, in *The Cherry*

Orchard offered one of the least assigned of contemporary images, reveals a man who always wears rubbers and a heavy coat. He carries an umbrella in a case, and his bed in a boxlike room has curtains to pull around it. When he retires to that room and dies after one excursion into the frightening world, he looks happy in his coffin. The narrator of this discouraging story finds something of this man in those kept by routine, convention, and fear from what surrounds them; but the meaning of the image is less definite and more general than this assignment.

In *Notes from Underground,* a kind of manifesto that anticipates Freud, Jung, and Kafka, Dostoyevsky presents what we might call an introvert. His room and that of Lisa are haunts of a man whose metaphor, elaborated throughout the work, is underground burrowing like that of some animal. His burrow includes the unconscious, the deepest layers of personality, its contradictions, and the unmentionable. Joyce was born on groundhog day, but it was Kafka in *The Burrow* who raised Dostoyevsky's metaphor to symbol. The nameless creature, maybe a mole, who makes and inhabits with fear, trembling, and delight an intricate maze of tunnel and chamber is an image of man in our time. Anxious, possibly paranoiac, this creature, constructing something more than dark refuge, is craftsman and artist too. Hesitations limit his pleasure in what he has made and hoarded; and what seemed a Castle Keep ends as place of terror. When the whistling beast, whose sharp protrusive snout bores the surrounding earth, comes to threaten the security of an autonomous system, the solitary mole knows the guilt of accumulation and retreat. By his image Kafka may have intended the capitalist, the artist, the thinker, the common neurotic or himself, but what he gives us is an image that fits those in private worlds.

The city is a commoner image for our condition or our desire.

136

Baudelaire's "Tableaux Parisiens," crowded with desolating particulars, gave Eliot the idea of hell as a city much like London, which he exploits not only in "Preludes" but in *The Waste Land*. More liberal than Eliot, Baudelaire had another kind of city, that of "Rêve Parisien," a dream of metal, stone, and water without life. Like one of those deserted cities of *The Arabian Nights*, "ce terrible paysage" of stairs, arcades, and palaces is an "image vague et lointaine" that ravishes him. Baudelaire's city, out of nature and promising the placidity of artifice, seems an image of the work of art. Auden's allegorical city has still another aspect. Occupying the end of the path between sensuous sea and abstract desert, the city is the goal of his quest or the heart of the adjusted man's reality. Joyce's city, larger than these, includes them; and, the scene of almost all his works, it becomes symbol as well. Labyrinth and hell at times, his city is also the heart of reality—as we know from Earwicker's long monologue on cities in the fifteenth chapter of *Finnegans Wake*, where allusions and puns, calling to mind the cities of the world, enrich the Dublin Earwicker founded and built as a home for his lady. In the Viconian pattern this chapter concerns the third or human age of man's development. Earwicker's city or man's ripest achievement, good and bad alike, is the image of our world.

Whether traditional, archetypal, or less general than these, images are most important when central in a structure that, limiting and enhancing them, brings out what might have remained potential. In *Heart of Darkness* and "La Géante" central images are improved by supporting structures; but here we may consider others of the kind from another point of view.

T. S. Eliot's song of Harvard is at once simple and exemplary:

> For the hour that is left us, Fair Harvard with thee
> Ere we face the importunate years,

> In thy shadow we wait, while thy presence dispels
>> Our vain hesitations and fears.
> And we turn as thy sons ever turn, in the strength
>> Of the hopes that thy blessings bestow,
> From the hopes and ambitions that spring at thy feet
>> To the thoughts of the past we go.

In these little-known but extraordinary verses, Harvard is the central image, given solidity, feeling, and tone by a supporting structure of abstractions, such as hopes and ambitions, archaic but reverent possessives and adverbs (thy and ere), and a rhythm adequate though a little distant perhaps. The "vain hesitations and fears" of the poet almost cease under the enormous "shadow" of what is not unlike Baudelaire's giantess. Later in life, Eliot was to find substitutes for Harvard, a thing greater and older than himself, in other images, no less central: tradition, Britain, and the Church. Even under the larger shadows of these, however, hesitations and fears continued to give substance to his poems; for, as he complains in "The Hollow Men," between idea and reality, conception and creation, desire and spasm, "Falls the Shadow." But here, "under the shadow of this red rock" (a possible reference to Harvard in *The Waste Land*), the tension between circumstantial accompaniment and the great image that embodies his needs, providing drama, anticipates his later triumphs. Here, in this early poem, he may have said all he had to say, but later poems on "thoughts of the past" proved images and other rhythms a more suitable setting for the central image. However similar in substance and design, the later, more elaborate poems are also closer to the common taste.

Most people would prefer *The Bridge* by Hart Crane, a larger but less audacious poem that does less well what it seems designed to do. Eliot's image of Harvard, surrounded by those improvements, in-

138

cludes and presents all the poet meant and something more. Crane's Brooklyn Bridge, the central image of his structure, seems at first a happy device for uniting its parts; for by nature a bridge unites things. According to his letters, which are so good they seem a dissipation of creative power, Crane was pleased by the "symbolical possibilities" of the bridge and by the harmony it could bring to a "symphonic" arrangement. Effecting "a mystical synthesis" of America's past, present, and future, transfiguring history into "abstract form," his mighty symbol would "condense eternity" and "lend a myth to God." His intention, however, was better than his choice of image; for a bridge that connects the Navy Yard with the borough of Manhattan may not connect Far Rockaway with the Golden Gate. His bridge, moreover, is so alien to Columbus, Pocahontas, and covered wagons (though all crossed something) that it fails to embody them, and the poem, full of such excellent things, falls apart—its center will not hold. The moral of that is that images differ in capacity. A central image, however exciting in itself, must be chosen for its power to function in a structure where it takes back what it gives for its own enlargement and the enlargement of what surrounds it. Though the "curveship" of Crane's bridge fails in that, the failure is splendid.

The Castle of Kafka's *Castle* shows what a well-chosen image can do. When K. arrives, the Castle on its hill above the village is so densely veiled in mist and dusk that he seems staring into emptiness. Next morning, however, it appears to be a rambling pile of small low buildings, more like a wretched little town than his idea of a castle; yet it has a tower, broken at the top and pierced with tiny windows that have "a somewhat maniacal glitter." The preposterous structure seems oblivious to all below it, and when he looks up later on, the contours of the Castle seem to dissolve and "the gaze of the

139

observer could not remain concentrated there but slid away." That the central image, lacking better description, remains uncertain is not without importance; for it owes part of its power to indefiniteness and the rest to relationship with other things.

Something is added to the image by reports of those who have been to the Castle's outer offices and something by hearsay. The Castle is occupied by officials in intricate hierarchy. The lower ones, who are all we hear of, seem involved with documents so complicated and so numerous that files become inadequate, and papers, spilling out, are lost. To what end this busy, scrupulous, and apparently inefficient bureaucracy devotes itself is far from plain. "What a strange business!" says Olga, whose brother may or may not be a messenger for the Castle, "It's almost incomprehensible." Communication between Castle and village is difficult. The snow is too deep to permit ascent. The telephone emits noises or contradictions; officials on descents to the village sleep or play with model railroads; and letters, though not to be ignored, cannot be taken literally. It is impossible to determine whether K. has been appointed Land Surveyor; a document may have been misplaced or K. may be intruding. We must conclude, as he observes, "that everything is very uncertain and insoluble."

Convinced that acceptance by the village is the way to acceptance by the Castle, which seems and is a community, K. pushes and debates what others accept, trying by reason to master the irrational. The landlady tells him in vain that he has no understanding of Castle or village. His efforts and frustrations, however, enhance the central image; and so do the characters of all connected with the Castle. The two bearded yet childish creatures, sent from above to act as K.'s assistants, may seem ineffectual or absurd; but who can tell the purposes of those in the inner offices or, for that matter, the outer? The

140

abominable proposition made to a girl from the village by Sortini, an official, proves the Castle not only beyond reason but beyond common morality.

We share with K. and the family of Barnabas a feeling that immorality, confusion, and nonsense may have a meaning we can never fathom. Some critics of Kafka try to make *The Castle* an allegory of this or that, but most, better on the whole than critics of Melville, abandon such endeavors. K.'s efforts to join the community and the redness of all that tape up there on the hill suggest a social or political interpretation; but this surface proves no more than a carrier of further meanings. K.'s refusal to wait for grace and Sortini's immoral proposition suggest that Kafka had Kierkegaard in mind— as we know he had—and that the Castle is no more than Kierkegaard's "Absurd" or "Wholly Other." Those who incline to Freud— as Kafka did—may find in ruined tower or all those beards a father image. "The Judgment" and what we know of Kafka's relationship with his father support this view, but the image of the Castle, although including these possibilities, is far more general than any of them. The great image, not altogether to be grasped, embodies total reality: social, psychological, and divine. Man's loneliness, his aspiration, and his desire to know what he cannot know are present in K.'s troubles. But if *The Castle* reveals man confronting the universe, how does it differ from *Moby Dick?* The difference lies in the character of the image and its surroundings. Reality discovered by Ahab and a whale is different in feeling and quality from reality discovered by K. and a castle; for the nature of reality depends upon that of its embodiment. Einstein is said to have found *The Castle* too complicated for him; but he is accustomed to another form for apprehending what we are faced with. Even for those within our form there is choice of images.

E. M. Forster chose caves as the central image of *A Passage to India,* a great novel that takes its place without embarrassment next to Kafka's inconclusive and significantly unconcluded story. Announcing the image almost in the manner of Joyce, whom Forster detests, the first chapter begins "Except for the Marabar Caves . . ." and ends with "the Marabar Hills, containing the extraordinary caves." Division into three parts, *Mosque, Caves,* and *Temple,* places the caves as central to a structure of three principal elements; but subordinate images, hints, and actions cluster around the center with their loads of complication. Everything enters this service: being bumped at night on the road by an unidentified beast, Professor Godbole's inarticulate song, and the untouchable punkah wallah, who, at the trial, ignorantly pulls his cord and agitates the dust, mindless, aloof, eternal, reducing Western machinery to nothing. Mysterious, these parallels to the caves prepare us for their deeper mysteries or confirm them. Images of light and dark, sun and moon, join the horrid chorus as the Marabar Hills and their hollows creep nearer at sundown.

Of incredible antiquity—whether geological or archaeological we are never sure—those caves, singular yet plural, seem older than time itself or spirit. Polished and circular, these enclosures have something "unspeakable" about them and bear so little relation to other things that the visitor "finds it difficult to discuss the caves, or to keep them apart in his mind." Beyond good and evil, they seem at once meaningless and charged with meaning. Their finiteness, denying while implying infinity, suggests that the abyss itself may be mean and petty though none the less abysmal. The worst thing about them, however, is an echo that seems to say courage, fidelity, and filth are identical, that nothing has value. If one recites a proposition by

Euclid, an ode to an urn, or some obscenity, the comment of the caves, confusing all, is "Boum."

Temple, cave, and mosque—each presents a universe. Though temple and mosque are caves of a sort and related by shape to the caves of Marabar, God is there. The universe projected by the mosque is formal and limited—almost like the world of Englishmen, but that of the temple is a "divine mess." Midway between cave and mosque, the temple with its "holy bewilderment" symbolizes something that is neither the definite meaning of the mosque nor the prehuman indifference of the caves. "God si Love" on a placard expresses not only confusion but compromise; and the Temple comes last to reconcile abysmal cave with tidy mosque. Yet over the horizon lies Venice, an image of shapeliness and all its human joys, an image perhaps of Forster's own distaste for monstrous or disorderly things.

Action and character also support the caves. Rising to a melo-dramatic climax within them, the action declines from there, revealing character, which in turn reveals the caves. When his attention is called to them, Ronny, an English official, says: "I know all about them, naturally." His ignorance is greater than that of Dr. Aziz, the Moslem, who, though thinking the caves a suitable place for a picnic, asks: "By the way, what is in these caves? Why are we all going to see them?" Though Dr. Godbole, the Hindu, seems to know something about them, he cannot or will not reduce what he knows to discourse. Mrs. Moore, canonized by Indians for knowing, knows so much about the caves that, finding the universe a horror instead of an expression of love as it has seemed in the mosque, she goes away to die without telling what she knows of "something very old and very small," something before time and space, "incapable of generosity." As for Adela, who has her sexual hallucination in the

143

caves, she is enabled by them to renounce a "suburban Jehovah" at last and to see herself incapable of love. Reborn in the cave, she becomes conscious of what has been her unconscious nature.

What then, with all this support, do those caves mean? It is plain that they include the primitive, the unconscious, and the sexual. An image of India, deeper than mosque, temple or individual Indian, except perhaps the punkah wallah, they show why Englishmen once found that country disconcerting; for how can the mind take hold of a thing so indeterminate? But below these references, the caves shadow forth our discouraging universe, all that Hopkins feared as "time's vast womb-of-all, home-of-all, hearse-of-all night." A great image, like castle or whale, the caves present man's feeling about all things. That Forster knew, understood, and admired *Moby Dick* is evident from a fine passage on the "inexplicable" whale in *Aspects of the Novel;* but no sooner is a conception of such things "put into prose," as he remarks in *A Passage to India,* than it becomes "untrue."

The Trotting Mouse

*A*CTION reveals as much as image can. Simile: as the Irishman, having made his tea, trots a mouse on it to show its density, so the poet uses other actions for showing other things. In the last chapter we took the "objective correlative" as a definition of image; but as Eliot says in the essay on *Hamlet,* where he announced his correlative, "a chain of events" may also serve as the "formula" of a particular feeling.

When Aristotle says in the *Poetics* that plot is the imitation of an action, he means by plot the arrangement of incidents, but he does not say what action is, or what he said has not survived. To Aristotle's distinction between action and plot Francis Fergusson devotes an appendix which, however profound, is equally inconclusive; for the word action is an "analogue," not to be defined but to invite the guesses of readers. Since *The Idea of a Theater* is a study of action, the word recurs, and from Fergusson's usage or his remarks in passing we may guess that action, though sometimes what is done, is more often the idea of doing manifested in events: "by 'action' I do not mean the events of the story but the focus or aim of psychic life from which the events, in that situation, result." Distinguishing "story" from "plot" in *Aspects of the Novel,* E. M. Forster finds story plot's basis: story, displaying events in sequence, means "and then," whereas plot, including causes and effects, means "why." Only a man of letters and dealing moreover with a looser art, Forster prudently avoids the word action that Fergusson, who owes allegiance not only to Aristotle but to Kenneth Burke, philosophically confronts.

Like everything Burke writes, *The Philosophy of Literary Form: Studies in Symbolic Action* is filled with useful observations and fine things. By symbol he seems to mean an equation or a representation; but he is an authority on action. Words like "tactics," "dialectics," "drama," and "strategy" abound since poems, as if playing a part on some stage, seem kinetic to him. As an action of the body can reveal a man's character, so the poem, a similar action, represents a state of mind or "the dancing of an attitude." Literature as action, a pleasing insight, may alter the critic's approach, but for my purposes here Burke's idea of symbol is sometimes a little too limited, and, since any "overt structure" is an act, his idea of action a little too general. At this point, moreover, I want to separate image and action, which his philosophy confounds.

By action I intend nothing so deep as everything but only something doing. Dictionaries call action "the process or condition of doing," a gesture, a movement of the body, an enterprise, a deed, an event or series of events, either actual as in our daily affairs or virtual as in literature. Becky Sharp, leaving Miss Pinkerton's academy for young ladies, opens the window of her carriage and throws Dr. Johnson's Dictionary into the garden. Ahab seeks a whale; Jason steals the Golden Fleece; Kafka dreams. These are actions as I take the word; for my concern is not with distinctions among story, plot,

146

and action but with action, both great and small, as symbol. As for movement and action, I wave my hand to a distinction between them without making it.

At first glance, contemporary literature of the more formidable sort may seem lacking in action. The reader of Mickey Spillane would find nothing doing in the novels of James, Proust, Joyce, or Woolf, and if curiosity took him that far, in the poems of Valéry or Stevens, for, abandoning the habit of Aristotle's poet, poets of our day seem to imitate action no more. But that reader, accustomed to spectacular actions, might miss those that are there: someone enters a room or raises a cup of tea. Such actions, however, acquiring importance from context, may strike another reader as more impressive than the crises, at once overt and intestinal, of a novel by Mickey Spillane. We must remember, moreover, that Conrad, Faulkner, and Hemingway brought action back with a violence perceptible to the most hardened reader, and E. M. Forster always includes one great, melodramatic, and revelatory action. Gide's "acte gratuit" is more of a problem. When Lafcadio pushes an unknown man from the train, is his act not only gratuitous but meaningless or is it a revelation? Is meaninglessness its meaning? Except for the last, which remains obscure, all these actions may serve as well as image to present our inner life or other things. Under action I propose to take not only single acts like these but those great chains of events found in voyage, dream, and myth. Even some of Jung's archetypes, that of rebirth, for example, are active; and when in Freud's unconscious, we climb ladders or fall from them like Finnegan himself.

Those apparently melodramatic episodes in the novels of E. M. Forster should prove good examples of the single act. When the kidnaped baby dies in the wreck of a carriage, the surprise for reader and characters alike is tremendous. Murder in Florence and even

147

Ricky's casual death on the railway lines, shaking things up and reordering them, as Lionel Trilling has pointed out, not only focus the themes and refract them but by their suddenness reveal a violence which, though implicit and growing, had not come to light. Showing forth this violence and those characters, the incidents release the tensions—if I may change my metaphor from optics to mechanics.

Of all these shocking little actions, the death of Leonard Bast is worthiest of notice. That outsider, having become an insider in one sense at least, is overcome by guilt as he enters Howards End, where under blows from the flat of a sword, he clutches a bookcase, pulls it down on his head, and dies beneath books. In this accident, which discloses the Wilcoxes, of course, and Bast himself, even the slightest details seem important. Why is Bast killed in a Wilcox house by Schlegel books and the flat of a Schlegel sword wielded by a Wilcox? Plainly a sword in the hands of a Wilcox represents authority; for Wilcoxes are the rulers of England and use the property of others for ends whose respectability may require the flat of a sword rather than its edge. The books belong to the Schlegels, who represent the culture to which Bast aspires, but whether death by books implies the peril of an alien culture and Bast's temerity or his final union with culture in a moment of triumph is unclear. The house, owned by Wilcoxes, adored by Schlegels, and entered by Bast, represents the tradition of old England; and the problem of who shall inherit it underlies the plot. That it comes to the posthumous son of Bast is no less ironic than his death—though victory of a sort for a sort of culture.

We may ask if this action, so rich in detail and plainly significant, is more than machinery to advance the plot. In her essay on Forster in *The Death of the Moth* Virginia Woolf finds the episode of the bookcase a true symbol, combining reality and mystery after the manner of Ibsen, but she qualifies her praise. The trouble with Forster, she finds, is an intellectual anxiety which, intruding at each climax, makes him point the moral too emphatically. It is true that most of these climactic episodes seem a little contrived; but although they have more significance than mystery, every symbol has some significance, and the death of Bast is not altogether unsuggestive. I should call it a symbol of the more limited kind, almost totally different from the great, unlimited symbol of *A Passage to India*. Having made that after all those experiments with carriages and bookcases, Forster, knowing he had done it at last, wisely sat on his laurels.

Ulysses differs from the early work of Forster in being filled with trivial events, which resemble his, however, in tempering significance with mystery. Of these Mrs. Bloom's getting out of bed and onto pot, the only action of the last chapter, is conspicuous. In a context at once flowing and static but more static than flowing, Mrs. Bloom's indecorous movement is improved by solitude; and in a book so inactive on the whole that throwing a biscuit tin becomes gigantic, her movement, coming at the end, gains importance from position. Held by the indecorum, solitude, and finality of her action, we take notice and ask why Joyce put her potting there, what it means, and what it does. He put it at the end, I think, to gather, contain, and radiate themes and associations already established.

If water, as Joyce has made plain, suggests life and making it suggests creation, Mrs. Bloom on her pot seems the creative imagination, Stephen's Muse as well as Bloom's reality. But Mother Grogan's "tea and water pot" of the first chapter—if we remember it—suggests something more. This ambiguous utensil connects the water of life with tea, which becomes through recurrence and context an image of family communion. By the help of Mother Grogan's confusion,

Mrs. Bloom is also making tea to unite Bloom and Stephen, her family, with herself. Becoming splendid now, her act brings other things to bear—even the arrival that morning of the schooner "Rosevean" from Bridgwater with bricks. Bringing Bloom's nautical surrogate home, this three-master also includes the other two members of Joyce's trinity. "Rosevean," which combines Rose, Eve, and Anne, suggests Mrs. Bloom, who bridges water while making it. Bridgwater, associated with Stephen in the second and third chapters, promises fulfillment to that "disappointed bridge" when he sees the ship proceeding up the life-giving river. The bricks carried by this ship may be building materials of a future artist and, similar in kind to Molly's rock, the substance of her pot. Her rock is Gibraltar, the entrance to the Mediterranean or the center of the earth and gateway to the fertile East. Calpe, Gibraltar's name in Greek, means urn or, more suitably in this context, water pot.

All this, piddling as it is, makes Joyce's method plain. A multitude of definite but unapparent correspondences adds to the meaning of each image or act. The astonishing thing about his method, however, is that no matter how definite the associations upon which image or act depends, no matter how conscious or carefully contrived, the result lacks the effect of contrivance that injures Forster's early novels. Mrs. Bloom's action, given meaning by all these associations and many more, seems as unpremeditated as a summer shower and no less suggestive of life itself.

Since life is encountered less commonly on portable and compendious oceans than all at sea, we favor the voyage for man's adventures in reality or his escape from it. Noah was a voyager, and irresponsible Jonah enlarged the possibilities of travel. Explorers too, leaving home for other reasons, found the seas congenial. Ship and sea allow varieties of meaning that tradition has confirmed. The motion and permanence

150

of the sea, its depth and vast extent make it an image of refuge, danger, mystery, infinity, of all that is alien and welcoming. The sea is our origin and our end, and, whether in poem, dream, or myth, voyaging on it has always seemed our necessity; for life is a voyage and we embark in ships of society or self. Nature and tradition alike commended the voyage to romantics, who, escaping or exploring, were never so happy as when at sea—whether they took to it to find themselves or, lost in deeper mysteries, the nature of things. Ishmael gives all their reasons as he leaves Manhattan for Nantucket, for chowders of clam or cod, and for oceans crowded with whales.

Shelley's Alastor is such a voyager and so is Poe's Arthur Gordon Pym of Nantucket, but the Ancient Mariner is more famous than either. Coleridge regretted the open "obtrusion of the moral sentiment" in a work of imagination, but Robert Penn Warren has saved "The Rime of the Ancient Mariner" from its creator. Far from being a moral allegory as the final tag has led many besides Coleridge to suppose, his voyage, says Warren, is symbolic. Symbols bring things together, and in the great images of albatross, sun, and moon Coleridge united his ideas of nature, imagination, and morality. Killing the bird is a sin against a unity recovered through love. Warren's commentary, one of the best on the romantic symbol, leaves little more to say about this voyage; and I gladly turn to voyages where I feel more at home. Feeling at home on voyages seems less unsuitable when we recall that romantics feel most at home away from it.

A commentary on voyaging, "Le Voyage" by Baudelaire reveals the disparity between illusion and reality, imagination and fact, the hopes of children "amorous of maps" and the memories of ancients coming home. Most of us embark our infinities on the finite sea, driven by impatience with shores or by the dangerous perfume of some woman, but true voyagers leave for the sake of leaving. What-

151

ever the cause of departure, we are alike in our expectations; for our soul, like Joyce's schooner, "est un trois-mâts cherchant son Icarie." Interviewed on our return, we list islands and idols, though we know them now as opium dreams. No matter how far we go, we encounter sin, and the world becomes "Une oasis d'horreur dans un désert d'ennui." Even such bitter knowledge, however, cannot keep voyagers home:

> Nous voulons, tant ce feu nous brûle le cerveau,
> Plonger au fond du gouffre, Enfer ou Ciel, qu'importe?
> Au fond de l'Inconnu pour trouver du *nouveau!*

To discover something new in the gulfs of the unknown became the delight of romantic voyagers, and this poem, for all its reservations, is their manifesto.

Plunging into Baudelairian gulfs was the daily occupation of Rimbaud, whose "Bateau ivre" ranks among voyages with *Moby Dick*. Far less limited than "The Rime of the Ancient Mariner," Rimbaud's wonderful voyage proves the symbol of voyaging as adequate for feelings of expansion and retreat as for moral and philosophical ideas. Leaving English cottons to their merchants and Indians to their sadistic distractions, Rimbaud floats down his river and out to sea, where, lolling in his beautiful vomit, he survives hurricane, calm, and reef as he ascends the waterspout or fathoms the whirlpool. Waves like "shudders of shutters" roll him to incredible Floridas, where he beholds flowers like panther eyes, and to marshes where monsters rot among black perfumes. But intolerant of static poles and zones, the sea, lifting waves like carnivorous flowers, washes him on again through violet fogs, azure snots, and blond-eyed birds. That glorious freedom is interrupted, however, by a sudden regret for parapets of Europe, and he finds himself ashore at last, a child again,

152

his only sea a puddle on the sidewalk in the embalmed twilight. Prison hulks are no longer to be ignored by boats as frail as butter-flies.

It is a voyage to be sure, but what can it mean? Though unassigned, the trip permits several interpretations. It is plainly an equivalent for transcendental experience. Confusion of surface may serve to indicate the derangement of senses that, according to Rimbaud's letters, must precede illumination: "j'ai vu quelquefois ce que l'homme a cru voir." Knowing Emerson and the rest, we might expect that sort of thing, but there are other aspects, equally affirmed by images. While presenting delight in expansion, the poem may also imply the comfort and guilt of regression; for references to mother and infant abound. Childish concern with Cooper's Indians and Verne's maelstroms is attended by the presence of mother in the "hysterical cow houses" and the "lactescent" depths through which drowned men sink. The return to shore in this case would be from womb to what Freud calls the reality principle. Not only an ambivalent celebration of retreat, the voyage may imply making love or imaginative flight, a day dream or the writing of a poem; it may mean flight from society and frustrating return. Whatever it implies—and all these possibilities are assured by images—it is a form for inflation and deflation, the fate, alas, of all romantics. By all its conflicts of desire and failure, wish and fear, imagination and fact, the poem presents the condition of young men.

Although André Gide's *Le Voyage d'Urien* (du Rien?), an early work in poetic prose, seems indebted to both Baudelaire and Rimbaud, it is far more definite than most romantic divagations. Without apparent aim beyond voyaging itself, Urien and his companions set out from an exotic port, touch at tropical islands, filled with dangerous women to whom several succumb, fret awhile in the

153

doldrums, and in the glacial regions of the Pole reach journey's end. On a bank of weeds in the Sargasso Sea, Urien discovers Ellis, under a cerise umbrella, reading a book on metaphysics; but this young lady proves to be a fraud, and it is not until his arrival in the North that the authentic Ellis, a kind of Beatrice, appears on a cake of ice. Under her direction the voyagers, aware at last of God and of their own capacities, attain a more or less tolerable valley and, forgetting voluptuous islands and boring seas, accept things as they are. Plainly an allegory of growing up, this voyage is saved from the obviousness to which it seems committed not only by bizarre humor, which troubles the atmosphere of dream and moral earnestness by equivocal title, cerise umbrella, and jesting Envoi, but by the suggestiveness of the scenery. Each island, desert, or sea, the embodiment of a condition or stage of development, seems an interior landscape or what Gide called, in a contemporary note, an equivalent for a state of mind: "Emotion and manifestation form an equation; one is the equivalent of the other."

By the time Hart Crane wrote "Voyages," his best poems, he had enjoyed *Moby Dick* for the third time; and Rimbaud, whom Crane had read more times than that, seemed the "last great poet." In spite of their ecstatic confusion, however, Crane's voyages are different in kind from those of *Moby Dick* or "Bateau ivre." It is true that, fascinated by water, Crane found it symbolic. Amorous of sailors, he walked over Brooklyn Bridge to keep a weather eye on the harbor and found himself a room, overlooking it, whence to observe what he called "leewardings." The poems in which he celebrated these interests, however, are ruminations rather than narratives, and the voyage, central in "Bateau ivre," is reduced to allusion. "Adagios of islands," "crocus lustres" of stars, and "poinsettia meadows" of the tides, too pretty to suggest Rimbaud, are metaphors. Each poem of the overheated suite may embody his love, but voyage and sea seem materials for decorators.

Dylan Thomas's "Ballad of the Long-legged Bait" is another thing entirely. "The old ram rod," as he came to call himself, knew Melville, of course, and he had read Rimbaud in translation. A hint was enough for him, however, and his poem is not only a faithful parody of "Bateau ivre" but an original extension with richness and glory of its own. As the "fishermanned boat" puts out to sea, the skipper's "whale-blue eye" turns from dwindling shore to the business of the voyage. Out comes his rod. His bait, a long-legged girl "with his hooks through her lips," swerves and dips in the wake among sea horses, rainbow fish, and amorous whales. The hand on the rod is firm, but the boat, apparently without rudder or compass, is almost as drunken as Rimbaud's. As it plunges from tropic to pole, the bait explores the chambers of the deep, embraced by the octopus and scuttle-fished by the crab-backed dead. When he winds his reel at last, he finds to his dismay that he has a heavy haul of countryside and town. His anchor goes down through the floor of a church, and, "lost on the land," the fisherman stands at the door of his house "with his long-legged heart in his hand." This remarkable fishing trip, obscure at first reading, becomes clear enough at second or third. As Rimbaud used the voyage to present the feelings of romantic youth, so Thomas, like Gide, used it to present the passage of man from youth to maturity, or, specifically the details and stages of his own adjustment. As Thomas put it one day in a bar on West 23d Street (though his intention fails to exhaust the meanings he created): a young man goes out to fish for sexual experience, but he catches a family, the church, and the village green. Indeed, he himself is caught by his bait. The ambiguous tone of the last stanza, as the stranded catch stands at his door, expresses wry

155

acceptance. Maybe the sea with all its wonders and delights is gone and the old ram rod is "dying of women" now, but that fate, less desperate than it seems, is not altogether inconvenient.

W. H. Auden, an authority on literary voyaging, examines it at length in *The Enchafed Flood*. In early times, he says, voyaging, though neither voluntary nor pleasant, seemed the death that must precede rebirth, but among romantics the voyage answered a variety of needs. To some, like Baudelaire, who left for unknown destinations for the sake of leaving, not city but sea seemed man's condition. While some, such as Captain Nemo, found at sea a pleasing freedom from responsibility, others, like Melville, found a particular voyage an elaborate "synecdoche" for life in general, since going to sea permitted exploration of self and the rest of reality. By now we should be familiar with these possibilities of voyage as suggestive action, but Auden proceeds beyond them to journey and quest. The journey on land, adopted by Christians as a way of presenting the ups and downs of spiritual life, is found in *Pilgrim's Progress* and many other allegories, though less common than voyaging in recent times. Whether to regard Mr. Bloom's wanderings through Dublin as journey or voyage is a question—one that Auden fails to put and, of course, to answer, but he is very good on quests, which may be defined as journeys or voyages with a purpose or goal. Ahab's voyage is a quest, and so, I suppose, are most voyages, however unaware of purpose sailors may be. I hardly know whether to place Dylan Thomas, starting out for fish and ending as catch, among questers or voyagers; for like most excursions, his is a little mixed. In "K's Quest," an essay on the "genre," Auden surveys journeys with salvation, self-knowledge, or something else as goal. From fairy tales, where the third son sets out to do what his elders failed at, and

156

quests for the grail, Auden proceeds to the detective story, a quest for "innocence," and the novels of Kafka.

Not content with discourse, Auden illustrates his points in discursive verses. In "The Quest, a Sonnet Sequence," he devotes twenty short poems, most of which are fourteen lines in length, to the necessity and perils of questing. Compelled by anxiety, the pilgrim sets out after some preparation and follows the way until, coming to a crossroads, he has to make a moral choice. Some pilgrims have taken the left or negative way, but our hero, passing desert, water, tower, and city, traps for some, finally arrives at the garden of his desire: "All journeys die here." This one was conceived on looking, with enormous Alice, through a door into a garden. Necessity and choice, predestination and grace, and all the other matters that have haunted Auden since he found Kierkegaard's Absurdity congenial, become almost as concrete in this allegory as that compulsive image. Many of his other verses have quest for theme. "Doom is dark and deeper," an early example, concerns a man compelled by Marxist or Freudian necessity to leave his home for desolate landscapes and strangers. His goal, set before us by Anglo-Saxon attitudes, is return in order to reform what he has left. In "The Sea and the Mirror" Prospero dreams of "some tremendous journey" through "imaginary landscapes," and waking, finds "this journey really exists" for him and all of us. In his monologue, later in the symposium, Caliban elaborates with more than metaphysical persistence a metaphor of life's journey, but, as he says, his "derelict factories," friendly steam rollers, alternative routes, and scenery from modern nightmares are "merely elements in an allegorical landscape." Those barflies in *The Age of Anxiety* undertake an imaginary journey on their stools. As anxious as any of his heroes, Auden is at too much pains to make his points,

157

and, despite approximations of surrealism, most of his later work lacks magic, which, to be sure, Prospero, his spokesman, abjures. Obscurity must not be confused with magic; for Auden's intelligent verses are obscure enough.

For the real thing in recent quests we must turn to novels. *To the Lighthouse* by Virginia Woolf offers the best and least discursive kind of questing. Of it, as Mrs. Ramsay says of something else, one might say: "Beneath it is all dark, it is all spreading, it is unfathomably deep." The first sentence of the book proposes an expedition to the Lighthouse on its rock in the bay near the Isle of Skye. Mrs. Ramsay and her son James want to go, but Mr. Ramsay, supported by Tansley, insists that it will rain: "There'll be no landing at the Lighthouse to-morrow." James's disappointment is matched by Mrs. Ramsay's annoyance with these rational negations. There is no expedition on the morrow; time passes, Mrs. Ramsay dies, and it is only after ten years or more that the quest is proposed again, by Mr. Ramsay this time, to James and Cam, his children, now reluctant. It is his quest now ("He had all the appearance of a leader making ready for an expedition") and seemingly his alone: for, as Lily thinks, "There was no helping Mr. Ramsay on the journey he was going." Into the boat he drives his children and away they sail. He lands, the journey is over, but why was it undertaken? Who are those Ramsays and what of the Lighthouse?

Of the four important people on this quest (Mrs. Ramsay, Mr. Ramsay, James, and Lily Briscoe, a visiting painter), Mrs. Ramsay is central, not unlike Mrs. Bloom in function, though different in degree. The book is "about life, about death, about Mrs. Ramsay." There she sits in her window, like a queen, accepting tributes silently, enjoying her triumph. She is "irresistible," thinks Lily: "Always she got her own way in the end." This enormous figure, sitting there, abundant, beautiful, like a flower, brings pure being to mind. Ignorant, not clever at all, she has the wisdom of Forster's Mrs. Wilcox and Mrs. Moore, who know and are. It is fortunate for all concerned that, instead of living to eighty-six or ninety as such women do, Mrs. Ramsay also dies young—in her later fifties.

When with her, Mr. Bankes, a scientist, feels the ordering of chaos he enjoys on solving a problem; but, as Lily observes, Mrs. Ramsay "led her victims to the altar," an ambiguous service that includes sacrifice as well as matchmaking. Good at bringing people together and composing them, she makes of dinner party a coherent thing that shines against black flux outside the windows. Victorious over that and serving stew, she helps a guest to a "specially tender piece of eternity." Indeed, her gift is for arranging times and people into approximations of eternity, for "making of the moment something permanent," as if to say, "Life, stand still." When she has gone, things fall apart again. For all her great accomplishment, however, Mrs. Ramsay alive is still unsatisfied; for, though mistress of flux, she demands peace and stability beyond her power to create. It is for this reason apparently that she looks from her window at "that stroke of the Lighthouse, the long steady stroke, the last of the three, which was her stroke," and, saying, " 'We are in the hands of the Lord,' " becomes one with the light, praising herself in praising it; for "she was stern, she was searching, she was beautiful like that light."

Poor Mr. Ramsay, at once venerable and pathetic, is so unsure of himself that he demands praise and sympathy of his vague and necessary wife. When she is occupied with other things or at those times she sees through him, he lopes up and down the terrace, facing the limitations of intellect, the failure of his books, and other horrors. Nevertheless this vain, lovable man gives his wife part of what she needs in partial return for her bounty. They illustrate "the inade-quacy of human relationships," their "extreme obscurity," and our essential solitude, yet "That is marriage," thinks Lily, observing them together: "And suddenly the meaning which, for no reason at all, as perhaps they are stepping out of the Tube or ringing a doorbell, de-scends on people, making them symbolical, making them repre-sentative, came upon them, and made them in the dusk . . . the symbols of marriage." As Mrs. Ramsay, apart from him, composes flux by humanity, so he composes it by intellect; but no less dissatis-fied than she, he needs something more, that a distant goal may offer. Lily, who observes the failures and triumphs of these two, tries to compose flux in her own fashion, on canvas, in paints, by arranging masses. Apparently more nearly final than theirs, her com-position requires no Lighthouse to complete it, but as she approaches her vision she keeps an eye on that tower and questing Mr. Ramsay, whose landing is her moment of approximation.

The Lighthouse is a suitable goal; for in it each quester can see himself and what he wants. An "enormous distance away," it be-comes an image of man's remoteness and solitude. Sometimes it is lost in haze; at others it seems "a silvery, misty-looking tower with a yellow eye that opened suddenly and softly in the evening"; and at still others it rises "stark and straight, glaring white and black," a bold tower on a bare rock with waves breaking around it. When as a child James sat with his mother at the window, the Lighthouse seemed misty and attractive; but now, approaching it on Mr. Ram-say's expedition, its other aspect is apparent. The solidity, strength, and starkness of the Lighthouse confirm some obscure feeling about his own character and about external reality, and, looking at the tower, he thinks that all things are "like that." This realization, a realization of self, marks his sudden maturity. Having hated his father and loved his mother in the familiar pattern, he suddenly forgives his father and abandons Mrs. Ramsay's maternal window for this father image in the bay. Stable amid the waves, a light in darkness, bringing order to night and confusion, the tower suggests the ideal of Mr. Ramsay, a philosopher seeking the absolute, and that of Mrs. Ramsay, composing dinner parties; for the Lighthouse seems all that is hostile to flux, whether of wave or time: "In the midst of chaos there was shape." That explains the interest of Lily, trying at her easel to control the disorder of impression and to place her chosen elements. Instead of one tower, then, we have many, and, thinking of one or another, James concludes that nothing is "simply one thing."

Since the tower is remote, paternal, and severe, it may also serve as an image of any absolute. As we have noticed, the Lighthouse makes Mrs. Ramsay think of God. Tansley, who opposes the expedition, is an "atheist," and Mr. Ramsay, however desirous of truth, is also skeptical. About to land at the Lighthouse, he stands, like a tower himself, "very straight and tall, for all the world, James thought, as if he were saying, 'There is no God,' and Cam thought, as if he were leaping into space." At that moment on shore, Lily says, "He has landed. . . . It is finished," while Mr. Carmichael's hand falls as if to drop a wreath of asphodels, a gesture that makes Mr. Ramsay's landing seem his death—not necessarily actual of course. In the boat he has been reading and thinking. Maybe at last he has followed the letters of his alphabet from frustrating R to final Z, and attaining his absolute, leaves time, like a god, for a kind of eternity. Time is intolerant of absolutes, and Mrs. Ramsay, a genius in time, finds the peace and harmony of her desire in actual death.

Having also forgiven her father in that boat, Cam sees him no longer as tyrant but as hero, "leading them on a great expedition,"

161

plainly that of life. If the expedition is also the pursuit of one's desire, whatever it may be, we must ask why Mrs. Ramsay, who is central, fails to go along. Perhaps we are to take Mr. Ramsay as her surrogate and Lily's too, as Septimus serves Mrs. Dalloway. Mr. Ramsay's success may include all; and that it does so aesthetically if not logically is plain from our satisfaction. Or it may be that Mrs. Ramsay, almost self-sufficient, has no need of suggestive abstractions, however much they fascinate her. In that case her failure to accompany the voyagers is the important thing; for inaction may be as revealing as action. Such uncertainties should not plague us, who know that quest and lighthouse, though surrounded by limiting elements, retain an indeterminate number of possibilities. A narrow interpretation of the quest as a religious allegory, let us say, would be partial, serving only to diminish the richness of movement and shape, the richness of something, as one of the minor characters says, "as if it were Constantinople seen through a mist . . . 'Is that Santa Sofia?' 'Is that the Golden Horn?' " By a happy coincidence Yeats sailed to Byzantium, leaving fish, flesh, or fowl for some artifice, that very year.

Mr. Ramsay's voyage out is supported by incidental actions, metaphors, and other images. In the boat about to land at the Lighthouse, having read and thought awhile, Mr. Ramsay raises his hand mysteriously and lets it fall "as if he were conducting some secret symphony." This revealing gesture remains more mysterious, however, than James's dreams of action in that boat: "He had always kept this old symbol of taking a knife and striking his father to the heart." Having "sought an image to . . . detach and round off his feeling in a concrete shape," he imagines a great wheel crushing a foot in a garden. These Oedipal fancies make James's Lighthouse a hunted father and a father found. Less narrowly assigned, repeated analogies

162

of waves, fish, birds, and flowers (the "red-hot pokers," for example) enlarge the general theme by parallel or other reinforcement. Of these images two are conspicuous. The urn of geraniums on the terrace, at which the philosopher pauses to knock out his pipe, seems to offer life and death; and the austere kitchen table, an image for Lily of Mr. Ramsay's abstractions, anticipates the Lighthouse. Such objects, as her comment shows, are potential: "to feel simply that's a chair, that's a table, and yet at the same time, It's a miracle, it's an ecstasy." Lily is always asking what life means. There is no answer, but such nondiscursive images and actions are ways of apprehending; for, as she says, "how could one express in words these emotions of the body?"

By comparison Hemingway's *Old Man and the Sea* is simple, but this moving story, which a wit dismissed as "a poor-man's *Moby Dick*," is not so simple as that. Like Ahab, Hemingway's old man puts out to sea in quest of a great animal. There, however, the similarity ends; for differences in image, action, and supporting devices carry other meanings. The old man goes out so far and gets so big a fish that he cannot bring it home, but the great attempt brings out his fortitude, endurance, and craft. His bleeding hands secure the noble fish; his aching arms refuse to quit a hopeless battle with the sharks that leave his catch a skeleton. Shouldering his mast, defeated but not disheartened, the fisherman goes home, thinking his trouble going out too far; but it was also catching something too big. What can that fishing mean? A critic, seeing the sharks as hostile critics, saw the story as an allegory of Hemingway's attempt to write a greater book than he was able. It is possible to see that meaning in a quest which, however, is far less limited than such an interpretation makes it seem. Hemingway's particular action is so suggestive and so general (as recurrent analogies of Joe DiMaggio, African

163

lions, and Jesus help persuade us) that it fits any of man's great endeavors and more dignified defeats, marriage, for instance, or thinking things out.

Faulkner also celebrates man's courage and endurance in *As I Lay Dying,* but, a larger artist than Hemingway and grander in manner, he mixes the heroic with the gruesome and the hilarious. A journey to bury Ma among her kin in Jefferson provides him with theme, structure, and symbol. Although to get her there in spite of smell and high water is the common purpose, each of the journeying family has a purpose of his own, and each his peculiar difficulties. "It's a trial," says Pa, "But I don't begrudge her it"; even farmers along the road admit, "He's getting her into the ground the best he can." However local the journey of Pa's company and however limited its object, its meanings are general; for their journey is that of life, their goal a grave. Rising from her coffin, Ma speaks of "significant shape," words that together with "myriad," Faulkner's favorite, describe the journey and its meanings. That Ma in her coffin seems either a fish or a horse adds suitable mystery to a familiar shape.

Hunt for bear in deep woods is the expressive pattern of "The Bear," another of Faulkner's quests and one of the more curious. The first part of this three-part story may seem, like *The Old Man and the Sea,* another but landlocked variety of the hunt for Moby Dick; the second and third parts, inconsistent in method with the first, may seem discursive and eagerly moral; but first impressions of Faulkner are inadequate. Let us look again at the opening narrative on which the sections of commentary are based. Around 1880, the great forest near Jefferson is still primeval, though crossed by a small railroad and menaced at one edge by a sawmill; and in this forest lives a bear like a "locomotive" or a "thunderclap," who seems like Blake's Tiger the forest's concentrate. To hunt the enormous

164

beast is vain, but the sportsmen at the hunting lodge never stop trying. Ike, the boy, is inducted into forest lore by a half-breed that he may be worthy of the great pursuit. Monomaniacal perhaps, this boy is no Ahab, nor is he intended to be; for when worthy at last, he becomes an observer and leaves the killing of the bear to dog and half-breed. Taken by themselves the images of forest and bear and the action of hunters and hunted provoke thoughts and feelings about man's conquest of nature and, beyond these literal matters, man's pursuit of any large enterprise. That the hunting boy, whose preparation for life is one of the central themes, becomes an observer, leaving the hunt to a dog (as if Ahab had delegated his to a shark), is a significant departure from the expected, and so are the funeral rites over dog, bear, and half-breed that follow a now ambiguous victory. Maybe there are several ways of looking at that hunt.

The boy is at pains to point one of them out. Contemplating the ruin left by the once negligible railroad and sawmill and the encroachment of cotton fields, with their odor of slavery, he regrets his "ravaged patrimony, the dark and ravaged fatherland." Forest and bear, his teachers, become the symbols of what he has learned and lost, symbols too of the heart of America. The land, he concludes, is not ours to buy and sell but a trust now violated. This discourse, which follows the story of the bear and returns to it now and again for strength, seems at first to diminish it by social, economic, and moral applications. Faulkner himself is moved by guilt and concern to intrude, as he does in *Intruder in the Dust,* with discourse that may seem to impair or, at least, to limit, what he has created by action and image. Though he shares the boy's ideas about the land, it is the boy in this case who expresses them. His response to experience is a legitimate part of the drama, and his interpretation need not fix our own, but, working with it, may enlarge it a little;

for, working with symbol, discourse may create an effect beyond that of either, and, becoming part of the action, may add something to the whole with which we are confronted. The improvement of bear by hero's discourse is a larger and more suggestive thing than bear alone.

Quest, unaffected by discourse, is one of the elements of *Light in August,* which begins and ends with the image of the road and Lena going along it. Though hunting on the first road, she is too nearly central to persist in that, and on the last is only traveling. But Christmas, whose hunt for self is presented by images of street and corridor, is a quester to the end. The book is filled with suggestive action (murder, arson, lynching), but what most impresses me is an action in the past. Hightower's obsession with his grandfather's raid upon Grant's stores in Jefferson may have been no more in fact than raiding a henhouse but, improved by long remembrance, becomes the symbol of glory and loss for him and serves us as an embodiment of the South and its fixation. In his pulpit, where the memory moves him most, "it was as if he couldn't get religion and that galloping cavalry and his dead grandfather shot from the galloping horse untangled from each other." Old men and women of the congregation did not like his "using religion as though it were a dream. Not nightmare, but something which went faster than the words in the Book."

Dream, whether fast or slow, is an action of images. That structures of this kind are symbols composed of symbols has been agreed from earliest times. The Old Testament is filled not only with dreams but with interpretations by amateur and expert. In the age of reason, to be sure, they thought dreams silly and unworthy of notice; but after science led men away from reason, along came Freud to support old agreement by system. Men of letters, always solicitous of dreams, had used them as motive or frame. Christian's

166

progress from here to the holy city, for example, is undertaken "under the similitude of a dream." With the romantic movement such similitudes became at once more authentic in appearance and less definite. The dream of Anna Karenina, seeming an actual dream, contains and presents her desperate situation. The dreams of Svidrigailov in *Crime and Punishment,* even more terrible, reveal his deepest conflicts and those of Raskolnikov as well. That symbolist writers since Freud have found dreams congenial is not surprising. It is my purpose here to consider their use of dream, first as an element in a larger structure, and second as the structure itself, a field so large that choice is forced upon me.

If we did not know the effect of Freud on literature, we could deduce it from *To the Lighthouse* and the works of Kafka. That what Freud pointed out was there before his time is plain from "Bateau ivre" and *The Wanderings of Oisin.* Since literature seems to illustrate Freud's principles, we might profitably recall that he found it equivalent to dream or, at least, to daydream, which has the same machinery. His dreams, as everybody knows, are designed to carry and hide unconscious motives, preferably bad. To reveal and conceal, not only the function of Carlyle's transcendental symbol, is also that of Freud's libidinous dream, which exploits the irrational, primitive, and childish parts of our personality. The latent or real content of a dream is what we have repressed, and its manifest content or what we remember is the latent in disguise. To prevent our knowing what we are, the censor uses symbols, which by a kind of compromise satisfy the demands of social ego and disreputable id. Since the symbols of dream are parallel to neurotic symptoms, a neurotic washing hands or walking the white line down the middle of a street is not altogether unlike the dreamer or the man of letters.

Dream-work or the making of symbols involves displacement, con-

167

densation, and secondary elaboration. The last and simplest of these is giving an air of coherence to latent disorder. Displacement or disguising important matters by making them seem peripheral is closer to our concerns—as the death of Mrs. Ramsay in a parenthesis makes plain. But what should move us most is condensation, which seems the process of all symbolism, even the more nearly conscious varieties. Taking elements commended to his notice by some similarity of function or feeling, the dream-worker combines them in one image or act. This rich composite of meanings, though designed to conceal them, invites attention by its brilliance. If symbol implies putting together, Freud's account of this unconscious work may shed light on the origins, process, and nature of literary symbolism, without, however, explaining it away; for origins do not determine things entirely, nor is likeness identity. However analogous to dream symbol, the literary symbol is not dream but art or an element in a work of art. Belonging as much to the external world as to the internal, the literary symbol, mediating between them, follows not only the demands of the unconscious but social and aesthetic necessity.

The symbols of Freud's dreamer and those of Kafka or Baudelaire invite analysis, but the analysis appropriate to one is not necessarily appropriate to the other. In *The Interpretation of Dreams* Freud spreads his cases before us. Addressing himself to examples of dream, which are somehow analogous to literary texts, he resembles Wilbur Marshall Urban and the "ontological" critics in assuming that all can be explained, but like an old scholar among books he also goes outside the text before him to consult the dreamer's life and habits. Following one method or the other, he pursues puns, verbal echoes, associations, events of the day before, memories of a remoter past; finds parallels in myth and fairy tale; and ends at last in those child-

168

ish enormities where all dreams start. He takes the "universal" symbols of ladder and tower into account, but most of his analysis concerns "accidental" images or actions peculiar to the circumstances of the dreamer. After this ingenious exercise, he announces: "The meaning of the dream immediately becomes clear to me," but that his analysis fails to exhaust it is apparent from a reexamination of one of Freud's own dreams by Erich Fromm in *The Forgotten Language,* an excellent account of dream and myth. The later analyst, who liberally departs from Freud's dogma now and again, finds that the machinery of repression celebrated by Freud kept the master from interpreting the dessicated flowers, an image of his dream, that might have revealed an unnatural reduction of love to science.

The dreamer and his problems are beyond the critic of literature; for he lacks a couch, and, unable to rely on the writer's conscious statements, has to confine himself to text alone or what he may discover by accident or circumstance. The literary symbol, like a dream before Freud has got around to it, remains mysterious—and I like it so, preferring dreams before an analysis that turns image and action to sign and discourse. Freud's value to men of letters is calling attention to dreams and showing their symbolic possibility, but critics of symbolist literature had better let his kind of analysis alone. My purpose is not to discover Freud in literature or to examine it by his light, but, as I have said before, only to consider what he confirmed: the use of dream as symbol.

Fascinated with dream and vision, pre-Freudian Yeats used what he got from them for poems. Images and actions from Henry More's *Anima Mundi* opened up more than intellect could; for the memory of nature, having stored all that man had thought or felt, returned it in our sleep. Yeats was as pleased by the intensity of images from this great receptacle as by what his occult studies told him of

169

their import. In later life, however, though still persuaded that the materials of dream "are forms existing in *Anima Mundi*" and mirrored in our minds, which created them, he allowed that the great memory and "what we have begun to call the subconscious" are one. Maybe from the self, the revelation of dreams is from an "age-old memoried self," call it what you will. "All art is dream," he said in a later essay, and in a play he said: "A dream is body."

Since embodiment was his aesthetic principle, some of his poems faithfully embody dream, "The Cap and Bells," for example, in *Wind Among the Reeds*. This "beautiful and coherent" dream, he says, has always meant a great deal to him, but "as is the way with symbolical poems, it has not always meant quite the same thing." For Freudians, if not for Yeats, the meaning of his dream-poem is almost painfully apparent. The pity, however, is that for them his garden, window, queen, and the jester's gift of cap and bells, losing mystery and variety, diminished and denuded now, mean one thing alone. To be ignorant of Freud seems better for those who prefer poems to ideas, and, content, like Yeats, with the manifest structure, can let the latent tease.

Fascinated in his turn by the dreamy poems of *Wind Among the Reeds,* Joyce used dream as symbol in *A Portrait of the Artist.* Of the many dreams and waking visions in this novel, three stand out, that of dead Parnell near the beginning, that of a wasteland of goats and cans in the middle, and that of a cave of fabulous kings and little people at the end. Functional in the pattern of country, religion, and family, these three dreams are what Stephen calls "epiphany"; and though Joyce differed from Yeats in knowing what his visions were about, his knowledge does not limit their suggestiveness or our pleasure. In *Ulysses* Stephen, Bloom, and Haines have prophetic dreams, of the sort which, in spite of Freud, Fromm allows. The dream

170

shared by Bloom and Stephen predicts their relationship with Mrs. Bloom—as we shall see. Haines's dream of the black panther, somewhat more obscure, is a vision of Bloom, who, dressed in black, is to walk from the library with "step of a pard." Since, as A. M. Klein has pointed out, Haines means hate and the panther is a traditional image of Christ, it becomes plain, if we carry these observations a little farther, that Haines's dream is the earliest adumbration of Christ-Bloom, whose daydreams of the Orient, hateful to devils, present the fertility he is to restore. Hallucinations in the Circe episode, not to be taken literally, are symbols of Bloom's deepest being, which, had he lived near an anthill, might have commended him to Dr. Harcourt-Reilly at some party.

A dream in *Mrs. Dalloway,* which takes method from Joyce, departs from his pattern, to the ghostly applause of Sir Thomas Browne and other "oneirocritical masters." Having seen the great lady, Peter Walsh falls asleep on a bench in Regent's Park. He dreams of Mrs. Dalloway, we learn, but his dream, presented indirectly, takes the form of an extended simile. Whatever it may have been in detail, his experience is as if a solitary traveler in a forest should approach a great female figure at the end of an avenue. Like Baudelaire's giantess, Jung's *anima,* or Robert Graves's matriarchal "White Goddess," this figure is a little overwhelming. "The death of the soul," cries Peter as he awakes. If dream is analogy for something latent, what Virginia Woolf has done is to give us a general analogy for a particular one. Suggesting at once the feeling of his dream and its interpretation, her simile helps us to apprehend both Peter and his Dalloway.

Of dreams as elements in novels, the richest and most rewarding, with the possible exception of Joyce's Circe, is Hans Castorp's vision in the snow, at once the center, summary, and climax of *The Magic*

171

Mountain. Hans leaves the Berghof on skis for a lonely adventure among snowy mountains. Lost and facing death, he has the dream that, presenting and solving his problems, completes his development. To understand his experience we must review time, circumstance, and previous action.

The sanitarium among its mountains is far from the flat lands and their realities. It may be a question for professional thinkers, as Mann says, "whether the hermetically sealed conserve upon its shelf is outside of time," but the sanitarium, a jar of this kind, is certainly outside it, though it preserves the familiar materials of time and space. Sealing himself from reality, our "simple hero" faces it as never before; for, concentrated now, it is isolated for examination. What is more, mountains, however remote, afford a view.

"Hermetic," the most important word of the novel, means not only sealing up but alchemical transmutation as well. Since, as Mann tells us, his novel is a *"Bildungsroman"* or the story of a young man's development from bourgeois simplicity to maturity, Hermetic plainly refers to the change he undergoes. "You, of course, do not know," says Hans to Clavdia, "that there is such a thing as alchemistic-hermetic . . . transubstantiation, from lower to higher, ascending degrees, if you understand what I mean." Not only transmutation but ascent along the ladder of being with which we are acquainted seems involved in this condescending announcement. Later, Mann refers to Hans's "hermetic career," and observes at the very end, as his hero lies in the mud, that his story is "neither short nor long, but hermetic." The Berghof is a "magic mountain" because Hermes-Thoth, the god of magic, presides over Hans's "hermetic enchantment."

Like some base element in its alembic, Hans is transmuted by several agents, chief of which are three people: Naphta, Settembrini,

172

and Clavdia Chauchat. The Jesuit and the humanist, endlessly debating, show the possibilities of reason and its ends; but while those philosophers talk, Clavdia shows herself. Her eyes, her X-ray picture, and her embodiment of disease and love lead Hans to regions where her pencil becomes a significant image and her habit of slamming doors a significant action. Shaped by these three and by what they suggest of body, reason, and music, Hans is ready for adventure in the snow.

A quest with no known goal but maybe with the secret hope of one, exploring the snowy back premises of the Berghof becomes a symbol of inner exploration, a part of what Hans calls "taking stock." Out he goes into the blind, white, whirling nothingness, which, at once transcendent and deathly, is like the sea and the sands of the shore. As equivocal as the sea and as monstrous, snow implies both life and death, but death predominates; for snow, composed of geometric crystals, is so antiorganic that "the living principle shuddered at this perfect precision." Facing alien indifference, "a fitting theatre for the issue of his involved thoughts," Hans has his vision. He sees a Mediterranean shore of "spacious sunny bliss" where beautiful people pass the hours in pastoral pursuits. His heart goes out to them; but at their back is a temple where hags, dismembering children, feed. Awaking with rapture and horror from this dream of love and blood sacrifice, Hans finds the storm over, the sun out, and an open slope before him.

If a symbol is a form that puts things together, this vision in the snow is a good example. Presenting all the scattered things that Hans has learned from his teachers, his dream reconciles them at last and provides knowledge beyond the capacity of his waking mind —as if to justify Erich Fromm in his idea of dream as insight. Before Hans starts down that significant slope to the Berghof, he

173

draws conclusions "in utter clearness" from his enlargement: "I have dreamed it out to the end," he thinks. "I have come to my goal." Death, life, disease, and love, which used to quarrel in his mind, are aspects now of a great harmony.

His commentary, though seeming to weaken the symbol he or the general soul created, belongs to a larger structure. Whatever that dream may be to us, it is first of all an expressive thing for Hans and his reaction to it is part of the drama. His commentary rather than the symbolic action it concerns marks the climax of his development. If climax, however, why does it come so far from the end of the story? There are several reasons for that. As Mann ironically points out, Hans forgets most of his insight on his return to the sanitarium. Peeperkorn, who renews the vision by another embodiment, is still to come. The theme, moreover, is not only the development of Hans but the decline of Europe, which he must share. War and the duel between Settembrini and Naphta, though implicit in the vision, must unfold.

That much for work including dream; but sometimes dream, including work, is equal to it. For work as dream I could take *Finnegans Wake,* but, having mentioned it elsewhere, prefer something less familiar and less obvious. There is *Alice in Wonderland,* of course, and there are stories of Llareggub, a backward land that Dylan Thomas roamed in sleep. I shall take *The Trial* by Franz Kafka.

Action and atmosphere, image and situation establish this book as dream. K.'s mysterious arrest is no more than we expect by night, and his execution by tall-hatted officers, while the figure at the window pities or invites, seems all nightmares' end. Between these extremes we visit buildings only sleepers know—up narrow stairs, down tenement corridors, through kitchen or bedroom we pass to court-

174

rooms with balconies so low that occupants must bend their heads. This maze of oppression and enclosure acquires additional strangeness from the bourgeois reality around it and the rational tone of the dreamer. Never was dream more manifest or suggestive of something latent, but the nature of that is the question.

Taking it literally, Marxists have found Kafka's dream a sign of bourgeois decadence and incipient fascism. Surely, however, those courts, however complicated and incompetent, are no more like our directorate of income taxes, shall we say, than like what we know of Soviet Russia. Moreover, since the manifest content of a dream is never its meaning, we must look below the surface to find what it implies. Maybe the legal complication disguises and dimly reveals the problem of Law and Grace or a Kierkegaardian drama as most commentators, including Max Brod, think. Psychologists, on the other hand, think the dream an adumbration of man's deepest motives, and there is much to support their view. Consider those bearded men with badges whom K. encounters in the lowest court, and the man who carries the janitor's wife up the stairs, certainly father images from Freud. Erich Fromm, whose analysis of *The Trial* is most fascinating of all, finds "arrested," the verb in the opening sentence, equivocal, meaning not only seizure by police but psychic frustration. Carrying on from there, Fromm finds K.'s refusal to admit his guilt or to discover his crime and his reliance on others for help the signs of a maladjusted personality. Whether social, religious, or psychological, these interpretations are more or less justified by manifest absurdities; but each is partial.

Kafka implies as much by the parable repeated to K. in the dark cathedral. From a pulpit with canopy too low for comfort, the Priest tells K. of the man who, denied admittance at the gate, waits there all his life and finds at its end that the gate was for him alone. This

175

discouraging story is unalterable, says the Priest, but interpretations differ. As the story seems an epitome of the book, these interpretations, various yet incomplete, seem the attempts of critics. K. is no wiser as he gropes his way in the dark from that cathedral—nor are we after reading essays on Kafka. *The Trial,* of course, is a shape for the feeling we have when facing what surrounds us, whatever it may be. Some of us feel guilty nowadays or, denying our guilt, feel anxious at least, and the rooms and corridors we grope through for relief are so perplexing we despair of it.

Enough of that. Myth to Freud seemed same as dream, except more public. As a disciple put it: dream is myth of an individual and myth a dream of the race, but Bronislaw Malinowski disagreed. In *Myth in Primitive Psychology,* he holds a Viennese parlor no place to study myth; for myth is alien to the bourgeois mind. To confine one's study, moreover, to classical myths, as Freud commonly did, is not only to take the divagations of scribes for the real thing but also to take text without context. The place to study myth is on some island where myth makers are busy, chanting their compositions at dances or around the fire while a fitting audience, entranced, sucks marrow bones, preferably human. So studied, myth proves to be a cultural device of great practical importance. A narrative of primeval reality, it confirms and strengthens tradition by precedent, supplies a retrospective pattern of moral values, and, while supporting magic and ritual, confers order and unity upon the tribe. This satisfaction of needs and justification of custom has nothing to do with symbolism. A myth of the South Seas may have caves and snakes, but lacking Freud's middle-class Western unconscious and its symbols, the maker of myths means caves and snakes by caves and snakes, and that is their only meaning. Discouraged symbolists may recall that other authorities, no less great, find myth symbolic.

Without denying its cultural importance, Ernst Cassirer in *Language and Myth* finds myth a symbolic form which like language, religion, science, or art creates a world and a way of seeing it. As remote as possible from the mode of discursive logic with its distinctions, myth concentrates experience by analogy; for, like language, myth has its roots in metaphorical thinking. Among primitive people, myth is a way of making the moment permanent, of celebrating its mystery and power, and of releasing conflicts by objectifying them. Among modern people, where myth survives as an imaginative device, useful for poets, it becomes a form of self-revelation. In his *Essay on Man* Cassirer sees myth, now freed from primitive beliefs, as symbolic action.

Both myth and dream, says Erich Fromm in *The Forgotten Language,* "are important communications from ourselves to ourselves." The "symbolic language" by which myth and dream are presented is one "in which inner experiences, feelings and thoughts are expressed as if they were . . . events in the outer world." It is a pity that Fromm's example of an outer event is Jonah in the whale; but we guess what he means. That the experience so symbolized is indeterminate is plain from his interpretation of Oedipus. Whereas to Freud this myth meant "nothing more" than the fulfillment of infant wishes, it seems to Fromm a conflict of loyalties to matriarch and patriarch. Accustomed, however, to disagreements over meaning, we welcome an agreement on myth as symbol, which, after all, is what we are after. Let us ignore the South Seas and, accepting myth around here as symbolic narrative, proceed to peculiarity and function.

I see no great differences among voyage, dream, and myth, the principal actions of this chapter. Voyages need not be myths, to be sure, but those of Odysseus, Jason, Jonah, and Noah are commonly held to be. If, combining the definitions of Malinowski and Cassirer, we find that myths involve religion and society, so, we must agree, do the voyages of Ahab, the Ancient Mariner, and that sailor in the drunken boat. There may be differences, however, in acceptance. Whereas the ancient voyages, approved and repeated by the community, became traditional as well as expressive, recent voyages are more or less private. Myth and dream present man's central problems, but the dream, however general its images, concerns problems of the individual, whereas myth finds those of the community important. Both, on the other hand, involve the individual's relationship with men and things around him. If differences between modern dream and ancient myth or between this voyage and that may be traced to cultures, Odysseus differs from Ahab as Homer's time and place from ours.

For the function of myth in the primitive community we may stray to philosopher or anthropologist. Our concern, however, is with myth in recent times. With ritual it may serve to support belief, but even for those without it, myth retains something of its old potency. Serving the individual as it once served the group, myth may unite him with tradition or society, and, in literature, while uniting the conscious mind with the primitive or the unconscious, myth may express the inner by the outer, the present by the past. Of myths in literature today there are two kinds: old ones revived and modern approximations. Ignoring the latter here, since I have approached it elsewhere, I shall content myself with ancient myths as modern symbols. Patina and temporal dimension give them some advantage over other symbolic actions.

Thésée, one of the last works of André Gide, is old myth with modern improvements. By his own account, Gide's Theseus is no less unscrupulous than responsible. Uncanonical conversations with

178

Daedalus, Pasiphae, and Oedipus prove his shrewdness; and the business of black sails, the affair with Phaedra, and the marooning of Ariadne his indifference to common morality. Yet he did much for mankind: after killing monsters of all varieties, he founded a city and established law. "For the good of future humanity," he says at the end, "I have done my job. I have lived." We do not need the assurance of Daedalus that hero becomes symbol, but what Gide's Theseus and his adventures symbolize is a question to which, although no authority on Gide, I hazard an answer. It seems to me that in embellishing this myth and making of it something gay and malign, he saw it as his own career. Retelling ancient story, he presented in less discursive form than his autobiography allowed an estimate of self, a testament, and the justification of his work.

Le Traité du Narcisse (*théorie du symbole*), one of Gide's earliest works and one composed under the spell of Mallarmé, is dedicated to Valéry. Nevertheless, this commentary on symbolism, disguised as an improvement on ancient myth, is closer to Plato and Carlyle than to Mallarmé at his most transcendental. Having become Gide or any poet, Narcissus, satisfied no longer with his image in the flux, tries to attain the static, crystalline paradise beyond appearances; but flowing, manifested things and reflections of himself keep him from a reality he can approach through art alone. Appearances are symbols, revealing Platonic ideas, which are more important than the things that manifest them; and the object of the symbolist is the crystalline idea that his symbol represents. The approximate paradise of art shows "all forms in a reciprocal and symmetrical interdependence," like that of Eden before Adam's curse; and like Eden, this aesthetic paradise is free from time. Although the image of a timeless heaven anticipates Yeats's Byzantium and the image of crystal, a precipitated, many-sided, transparent form, anticipates

179

Wallace Stevens's crystal, Gide's aesthetic, centered in a transfigured Narcissus, seems too otherworldly to satisfy later poets, who found embodiment of greater value than idea; and the true Narcissus, as Gide's later works prove, stares at an image in the pool.

Public myth for private use is not at all uncommon in our time. Finding the story of Jesus congenial, D. H. Lawrence improved it, much as Gide improved his myths, to fit his own situation and desire. The hero of *The Man Who Died,* a disillusioned savior, rises from the tomb, and, disgusted with humanity and his mission, resolves to preach no more, but a cock and the sun, both of which arise in the morning to challenge death, make him see possibilities in resurrection. So inspired, he begins to adore the life of the body and some unspecified life beyond it. Maybe, he thinks, a woman can help. A priestess of Isis is convenient, and she, finding him not unlike Sir James Frazer's dismembered Osiris, invites him into her flowerlike temple, where rituals and "female mysteries" engage him until, "I am risen," he ambiguously declares. Though forced to flee the displeasure of slaves and common people, he will come again, he promises, like Spring itself. This instructive but unorthodox mixture of two myths served to celebrate Lawrence's own discouragement and hope. Maybe Freud was right about myth as wish-fulfillment, but that Viennese, however poetic he may have been, had no way of commending the art that makes *The Man Who Died* one of the most moving of Lawrence's stories.

Myth allowed these vain men not only to exploit their parts but to exhibit them; for familiar myth, like traditional image, can be understood—or almost. Unfamiliar myths, however, or myths of any sort employed by those who laid themselves less bare or else by those who moderated the pleasures of exposure by subtlety, lack this virtue. For these writers and their readers myth, unbuttoning no buttons, remains as indeterminate as most symbols. Yeats's addiction to myths both local and obscure is a case in point.

"There is for every man," says Yeats in his essay on Shelley, "some one scene, some one adventure . . . that is the image of his secret life." That Cuchulain and his deeds served Yeats in that capacity is plain. Acquiring more than Irish significance by the aid of a mask, Cuchulain, he thought, could become "an image seen in reverie by some Orphic worshipper," and we may be sure that Yeats thought himself that. Treating his Cuchulain almost as liberally as Lawrence his Jesus, Yeats dedicated work after work to the image and actions that obsessed him. In *The Only Jealousy of Emer,* a poetic play in the Japanese manner he had learned of Ezra Pound, Cuchulain is disclosed, supine. Washed ashore after fighting the waves, and waterlogged now, he is nevertheless the object of three contending women. Emer's sacrifice saves him from Fand, the lady from the sea, but leaves him to Eithne, his latest mistress. Far from being a savior, the defeated hero is saved by another's heroism.

That Yeats saw himself in this symbolic inaction is likely enough and that, just married and "coming home to a mortal woman" after "loving an immortal goddess," as Cuchulain had done, he saw something of his wife in noble Emer is even likelier; but the personal bearing of the play is unimportant. We know that Yeats's theater was designed to restore heroic ideals to Ireland. Patriotism may have helped to shape Emer's fine renunciation and Cuchulain's plight; but these are local matters, and to please us, unless Irishmen or scholars, the import of the play must be more general. A prose version called *Fighting the Waves* and an essay explaining it confirm what action, image, and context suggest and direct our notice to what we might have missed in the labyrinths of Yeats's verse. The essay makes it apparent that the waves, the central image, suggest all that is inimical to mankind and that Emer's action, more effectual than Cuchulain's fight, is man's victory over flux, regression, and machine. Liquid or aquatic now, modern man, says Yeats, has abandoned limit, line, and principle for a deluge of experience, the dangers of which have been affirmed by "a German psycho-analyst" who "has traced the 'mother complex' back to our mother the sea." Going back to the play with this help, we can see it now as a humanist's defiance of romantic flux. As for the machine, which is equally dangerous, it seems suggested by Fand's metallic costume and the nature of her dance on coming from the sea. The prose version relies less on "elaborate words" than on music, dance, and gesture, such movements as lighting imaginary fires—on symbolic action in short —to create this complex of feeling and idea.

What an audience without help of preface made of Emer's action is more than I can say. Sharing my doubts about the adequacy of his form, Yeats stepped before the curtain to make a speech whenever he had the chance. In *It Isn't This Time of Year at All!* Oliver Gogarty reports one that preceded a performance of *At the Hawk's Well,* a similar play, in Gogarty's drawing room: " 'Perhaps I had better adumbrate the suggestions—not their significance, for that would be to limit them. . . . I know you would not have me be explicit.' " After limiting actions and images a little, Yeats continued: " 'I have found a form that does its work by suggestion, by complexity of rhythm, color, gesture, symbol, not by direct statement!' " That he said something of the sort is affirmed by "Certain Noble Plays of Japan," an essay on his kind of play: "I have invented a form of drama, distinguished, indirect, and symbolic." Leaving realism to common people, he offers expressions of the body and "distance" to aristocrats who, in those drawing rooms, enjoyed a doubtful experience.

182

Our specimens so far have been of ancient myths retold and changed in the retelling for modern purposes, but myth as parallel to a modern story is more common. Dylan Thomas's "Altarwise by owl-light," a sequence of ten dazzling sonnets, is a good example of this. After recovering a little from our amazement, we notice that the octaves follow the sestets and ask the reason of this backwardness —a clue perhaps to a further inversion, that of method. Although in most narrative sequences, story or statement orders the images, here no customary surface greets the eye, but only a quarrel of contraries which must create theme and parallel. Eliot's "Rhapsody on a Windy Night" may be a series of creative images—harmonious, however—while Thomas's action of images, before we apprehend its work, seems discordant alone.

Most of the contending images in these sonnets are from the Bible, especially Genesis and the Gospels, and from marine biology; but, having spent an hour or two with *The Interpretation of Dreams,* Thomas put all his images through Freudian machinery to make artificial dreams. It was his delight to reduce the dreams of acquaintances to obvious signs, but the sonnets before us are products of the opposite process. Like all the poems of what Thomas himself called his womb-tomb period, his sonnets are true to elementary Freud, but, however Freudian, an image from the Bible in a poem by Thomas retains its Biblical significance—so that, as he says: "I, in my intricate image, stride on two levels." All the images of these early poems are ambivalent: the word "bones" means death and sex; the ladder of cross-bones in the second sonnet is at once Jacob's ladder, making piratical love in a Freudian dream, and the formation of the embryo; the "triangle landscape" is sexual and, since delta and pyramid are triangular, Egyptian. Womb and tomb, making love and dying are the furniture of these poems, but perhaps we should

183

resist his invitation to translate; for the meaning of his images is less important than their action and appearance. "I took my marrow-ladle / Out of the wrinkled undertaker's van": it is best to enjoy this surrealist picture. If we translate, we get womb and tomb, birth and death; for translation of anything from early Thomas results in more of the same thing. Left as they are, however, his images are brilliant and functional. Signs no more but symbols with an element of significance, they may now create the theme.

The theme of these sonnets, like that of most of his early poems, appears to be Thomas's own development from conception to adolescence or maturity. He loved the moment of his begetting, his sojourn in the womb, and all his troubles with love and poetry. Indeed, as Thomas hints in the first sonnet, "Altarwise by owl-light" is the life of "a dog among fairies." Since that dog is Thomas's idea of himself among contemporary poets, his sequence becomes another portrait of the artist as a young dog. Of the parallels that support the theme two are important: a voyage and the life of Christ.

References to Odysseus, Jonah, and Moby Dick, together with medusae, sea nettles, and jellyfish compose a voyage of life. If men are bones on some beach, women are marine invertebrates. The "stinging siren's eye" and "the bagpipe-breasted ladies in the dead-weed" serve as Homer's Sirens, mothers, Muses, invitations to love, and pictures by Dali. That *The Odyssey* and Christ may get along agreeably together in "a Christian voyage," as Thomas puts it in the tenth sonnet, is not without example. We have only to think—as Thomas probably did—of Mr. Bloom. This brings us to our immediate concern: the use of myth as parallel to a process of embryo, child, and poet.

Jesus is so evident in the sequence that some readers have mistaken parallel for theme. Starting in the garden as a "hangnail cracked

184

from Adam," he is hatched on one leg as "a gentleman of wounds." These references to the fall of man and the cross attend Thomas's beginnings in that "cavern over the black stairs." After two-gunned Gabriel announces adolescence, the Lord's Prayer and the crucifixion present the bother of writing poems. The entombment, equated with "oracular archives" of Egypt, is the printing of hieroglyphic poems, which, done at last, allow Thomas to balance the globe and, like his tremendous predecessor, lie down with Capricorn and Cancer. The "old cock from nowheres" (both resurrected Christ and erected Thomas) has achieved his destiny. Not Christ in the sense Lawrence intended, but Christ as every man and poet, Thomas comes from and is nailed to a "rude, red tree," at once the cross, the tree of knowledge, and a poem.

That *Ulysses* inspired this kind of parallel is made more likely by an apparent reference to Joyce in "To-day, this insect," a poem on fables, at the end of which, "Greek in the Irish sea," an ageless voice tells of a "cross of tales behind the fabulous curtain." We are no less familiar than Thomas was with figures on that curtain: the parallels of Odysseus, Christ, Hamlet, and Don Giovanni, but that of Moses is unfamiliar enough to secure our notice. During the conversation at the newspaper office, Moses appears first as Michelangelo's statue, "that stony effigy in frozen music, horned and terrible, of the human form divine, that eternal symbol of wisdom," then as rebel against Egyptian priesthood, leader of the chosen people from the house of bondage, and bearer from Sinai of tables "graven in the language of the outlaw." The latter references apply to Stephen Dedalus, exile, outlaw, and rebel against priesthood; and Michelangelo's statue seems to promise, as it describes, the book Stephen will write. But his parable of the plums, *"A Pisgah Sight of Palestine,"* complicates the Mosaic parallel by reference to Bloom, who, like the Moses of the

113th Psalm, is to lead Stephen from the house of bondage to sight of the promised land without getting there himself. That Bloom's dimensions are increased throughout the book by the analogy of Moses is plain to the attentive reader. Mulligan calls him "Ikey Moses," someone at Bloom's trial shouts, "Moses, Moses, king of the jews," and Bloom's genealogy that ends with Christ begins with Moses, whose vision, like that of Bloom's seafaring surrogate in the coffee stall, may also have been impaired by sand in the Red Sea. The parallel of Moses is one of many devices for establishing the unity of Bloom and Stephen, and, by making each more general, enlarging them. References by each to "fleshpots of Egypt," Mosaic vessels associated with Bloom's bathtub, Plumtree's Potted Meat (by way of the parable of the plums), and Mrs. Bloom's pot, affirm their connection with its occupant. This allusive yet elaborate parallel with all its ramifications is not so solemn as that of Jesus and D. H. Lawrence. The disparity between Bloom and his fabulous analogue is not only illuminating but comic.

To Thomas Mann such half serious, half comic parallels seemed "parody" of myth, as Henry Hatfield points out. Long before Joyce discovered its values, Mann used the technique in "Tristan" and "The Blood of the Walsungs." When in the first of these ironic stories a pretender to literature falls ineffectually in love with the wife of a business man, the parallel of Tristan, Isolde, and King Mark is established by Frau Klöterjahn's rendition of Wagner's *Tristan* on the sanitarium piano. The parody of Wagner's *Die Walküre* in the second of these stories is more elaborate and far less frivolous. Siegmund and Sieglinde, twins, lead a life of "rare uselessness" in their father's mansion. These spoilt exquisites, adoring each other, keep the inelegant world, to which they owe their luxury, at a distance. Siegmund has a passion for washing that would in-

186

terest Freud, who drew much of his clientele from this class of society. Sieglinde recoils with distaste at the thought of marriage to her crude intended. Safe in a "warm little silken-lined retreat" of a carriage with drawn blinds, the twins go to a performance of *Die Walküre,* the story of their namesakes, Siegmund, Sieglinde, and of a bear rug for incest. On their return home, a bear rug on the floor of Siegmund's boudoir, near his chaise longue, gives them an idea. Their incest, more refined than that of Wagner's primitives, may make the existence of Sieglinde's fiancé "less trivial," says Siegmund, rising from that rug; but incest, however perfumed, is the symbol of narcissism, not theirs alone but that of their world. Since action and parody combine in Mann's story to create a vision of the self-centered, decadent society that was to produce two wars, the Wagnerian accompaniment is not without political point.

Some parallels in recent times, Faulkner's *A Fable,* Eric Linklater's *Laxdale Hall,* and Gore Vidal's *Judgment of Paris,* for example, are more obvious and less revealing than Mann's, but most are slighter and more allusive. Consider the ghostly intrusions of Parsifal in *The Waste Land* and *The Waves.* In Eliot's poem Parsifal is there, somewhere behind the scenes, by virtue of a quotation from Verlaine, a footnote on Jessie L. Weston, and a ruined chapel. Though these suggestions are supposed to bring to mind the quest for the grail and the recapture of fertility that form the implicit structure of the poem, they did not bring these matters to my mind until I had read a monograph on the subject. Reappearing as Percival in Virginia Woolf's novel, that hero is equally remote. A leader of men, who falls on his empty head from a horse in India and dies, her Percival, never around in person, occupies the uneasy minds of the six speakers, of whom, as their center and their dream, he makes "a six-sided flower." If they represent becoming, he is being. Though what this

187

has to do with the grail I shall never know for sure until I find a monograph; maybe he has found the grail of reality while they are still looking.

The allusion to Narcissus at the end of Faulkner's *The Sound and the Fury* is less baffling. After Benjy attends a nondiscursive Easter sermon with Dilsey, his grave, hopeless bellow expresses "all voiceless misery under the sun." To restore peace, Luster gives the idiot a single narcissus, and, since its stem is broken, puts a splint on it. Benjy holds his flower, his eyes "serene and ineffable" until his carriage turns unfortunately left at the Confederate monument. Once this sinister choice has been corrected, Benjy's eyes become serene again as he holds his broken flower. Easter and Narcissus together imply the hope of renewal that Dilsey seems to embody. Splints for the symbolic flower, however, hold questionable promise.

From myth to ritual is but a little step—either way. Which of the two follows the other depends upon one's school, but nowadays most agree that myth is there to justify ritual or symbolic action at its lowest and most acceptable extreme. Those "vague acts of the priesthood" that pleased Stephen Dedalus "by reason of their semblance of reality and of their distance from it" pleased Eliot more; and in his plays ritual seems more important than the myth it celebrates. The mumbling of women in *Murder in the Cathedral,* no more discursive than Benjy's sermon, puts me in mind of churches as it is meant to do, and though the echoes die, my longing for a missal persists. Parodies of liturgy interrupt *The Cocktail Party* and bring *The Family Reunion* to a bad end. It is idle to transpose them into thought; for Eliot's rituals are what he feels. Even Yeats when young longed for "a new ritual, the glimmering of new talismans and symbols," for priests of literature who with "a little waving of the hands, a little murmuring of the lips" could charm their congregations.

188

Later, he found the ceremony of his desire in the Noh plays of Japan. His own plays, based on them, seemed "verse, ritual, music, and dance in association with action." But drama sinks with alacrity to its origins, and examples of ritual from novel or poem might prove more remarkable.

The Plumed Serpent by D. H. Lawrence is what we want. "Weary of fixed meanings," Kate, the heroine, seeks "the presence of that which is forever unsaid." This longing for a nondiscursive form is satisfied in part by the myth of Quetzalcoatl, the reborn god who emerges from his pale, milky lake to change the world and bring mystery back. The images of bird, snake, sun, and morning star that attend his reappearance, promise a union of above and below, but the rituals devised by Don Ramon, those endless ceremonies of drum, dance, hymn, and mindless sermon, prove more enchanting. It is clear that the myth of Quetzalcoatl is there to support these rituals, which carry the central meanings. The very structure of the darkly splendid novel is ritualistic, as undulant and hypnotic as the bird tread of the dancers; and all Lawrence ever felt or thought is presented by the ceremony of his prose.

Though E. M. Forster, keeping aloof, does not participate in the rites he describes, those that ensplendor the last part of *A Passage to India* are almost as brilliant and expressive as Lawrence's. In the Hindu temple old Godbole, who dodges the definite, superintends the birth of a god who "is, was not, is not, was," and, as one might suppose, his ceremonies lack precision. "A frustration of reason and form," they prove formlessness a form for the ineffable. "How can it be expressed," Forster asks, "in anything but itself?" For the participants these rites are a revelation, a way of apprehending what cannot be apprehended, of ravishing the unknowable, and of "making in each man, according to his capacity, an emotion that he

189

would not have had otherwise." To us the shapeless shape that Forster constructs presents feelings and ideas that, as we have noticed, release the tension between formal mosque and abysmal cave.

By tone, rhythm, and structure "Ceremony After a Fire Raid" by Dylan Thomas parodies the movements of a ritual. The incantatory opening reveals the death of a child; the second part is a discursive meditation; and the third and most glorious is a hallelujah, the meanings of which are confirmed by references to priest and service. An atheist and a Presbyterian too, Thomas brings, as with a common prayer book in his hands, assurance of eternal life—all the joy of man's desiring and all that woman hankers for.

Strange Relations

*T*o FIND how symbols put things together we must look more steadily than we have and from another point of view at matters touched upon before; we must also notice other arrangements and other devices. This chapter is about allusion and quotation, effects of juxtaposition, elaborated themes, and structures both large and small—all these not only as significant shapes but as ways of joining part to part or, sometimes, the work itself to other things. The end of a progress through these matters is structure as symbol.

Allusion and quotation may seem far from this end. No more symbolic in themselves than a tree or climbing a ladder, they too, becoming suggestive through context, may serve not only as bearers of gifts and inviters of guesses but, looking two ways, as importers of things from outside the work to enrich it. When in *The Waste Land* Eliot makes Marvell or Dante say what he means, he unites times, places, and other cultures with our own, or, as he says in "Tradition and the Individual Talent," the pastness of the past with its presence. Functioning among the quotations he arranges, those from Dante or

Marvell unite the arrangement with something else by reference to it. If the reference is plain to us, we enjoy a double experience; if not, we must be contented with what we have before us on the page. A greater deprivation awaits the literate; for, contented with identifying the reference, they may stop short of finding what it brings to its new setting and how it works there.

In view of Eliot's proclaimed distaste for Milton, the allusion to him, the quotation from him, and the imitation of him in *Four Quartets* improve their effects by surprise, a characteristic, says Eliot, of the best literature. Except for the last word, which seems ambiguous, "One who died blind and quiet," a reference to Milton in "Little Gidding," is not unkind. Maybe as Eliot sat waiting for the gifts of faith, hope, and charity to descend, charity descended; or maybe the reference marks a change of policy. That this is the case is plain from another document, but before we get to that, let us consider "East Coker," where "dark dark dark" is quoted from *Samson Agonistes* and "vacant interstellar spaces" recalls Milton's "vacant interlunar cave." What that quotation and this distortion are doing in Eliot's poem is the question. References to darkness and blindness, they bring the condition of Samson and Milton, together with its moral and political causes, to bear upon the condition of Eliot's captains, bankers, and eminent men of letters, who with the rest of us are going into the dark, not the benign darkness of St. John of the Cross but an emptier kind. These suggestive references, which combine the inadequacies of three times and places, are supplemented by three Homeric similes, another surprise; for Eliot had found such detachable devices revolting. His three similes offer three more kinds of darkness: that of a theater when the lights go out, that of the London Underground, and that of another etherized patient. These similes, however, are less Homeric than Miltonic, as

192

the context proves; and imitation of Milton becomes another reference, this time not only to his physical, religious, and political darkness but to his poetic method, which unaccountably emerges into light. Working as a footnote to this emergence, Eliot's latest essay on Milton applauds his similes and the rest of a poetic suitable now for modern poets to use and critics to adore. Therefore the three Miltonic similes of "East Coker" seem at once an example, a manifesto, and a symbol of this change of heart, which, to be sure, we might not have apprehended from the text itself without the essay. But Eliot, whether as man or poet, has always relied upon external support. Essays and footnotes outside the text become the context of his quotations, which, looking out more often than in, give equal testimony of his habit.

The epigraph of *The Waste Land,* however, looks in as much as out. This curious mixture of Latin and Greek, quoted from Petronius, may be translated as follows: "I myself saw the Cumaean Sibyl hanging in a bottle, and when those boys asked, 'Sibyl, what do you want?' that one replied, 'I want to be dead.'" The reference is not to Petronius but to his Sibyl, who, like Tennyson's Tithonus, having asked and received immortality without youth, consequently aged and shrank until bottled for convenience. It was that Sibyl in her happier prime who directed Aeneas on his journey to the underworld, and here she hangs at the entrance to Eliot's underworld to point the way for us. A suitable directress in her present condition, she also serves as the image of ours, an image of living death; for we are bottled Sibyls hanging on the wall, incapable of prophecy or motion. By reference the quotation brings these ideas and feelings to the poem, but by mixture of Latin and Greek the quotation also creates an air of pedantry, which thickens as the poem proceeds, to warn us we are lighter than we think. Beyond that the Sibyl antici-

193

pates the women of the poem: Mme Sosostris, the hyacinth girl, the hysterical woman at her dressing table, and all the rest, as degenerate and powerless as their shrunken original. Brilliantly functional, she concentrates the feelings and persons of the poem while introducing them. Without her work the poem would succeed, but it becomes more meaningful as, persisting in memory, she directs us through the structures she orders and includes. Finding her and putting her where she hangs are among Eliot's happiest achievements.

Without my context I could do little with Eliot's. To one of my students, better at Sibyls than I am, I owe the identification of Petronius and to another a possible reference of Father Hopkins's Sibyl. "Spelt from Sibyl's Leaves," one of the most terrible of sonnets, presents agony by ponderous, grinding, overloaded movement, by images of dapple-ending night and naked nerves, and by reference to the Sibyl, who, though bottled, can scatter a few applicable leaves. This reference to his "oracle" is plain enough, but there seems to be another, suggested by the action of winding a horn, which, together with the general feeling, brings Thomas of Celano's famous hymn to mind:

> Dies irae, dies illa
> solvet saeclum in favilla,
> teste David cum Sibylla.

Converted to Christianity by Vergil no doubt, Thomas's Sibyl presides over the day of judgment, announced by the winding of a horn:

> Tuba, mirum spargens sonum
> per sepulcra regionum,
> coget omnes ante thronum.

194

If this is the reference Hopkins intended, as the text certainly implies, it increases the horror of his condition by Christian as well as natural and classical despair. His theme, however, is not the day of wrath, as the pious might wish and as the student who had this admirable insight maintained; rather the day of wrath has been imported by horn and Sibyl to reinforce the suggestion that Hopkins feels like the damned. Composed of these references and the rest of his machinery, the poem, a symbol of his feeling and idea, shows it is Hopkins he mourns for.

Let the celebration of my ingenious students conclude for the time being with an example from *Ulysses*. The end of the Eumaeus episode had puzzled me for years. As Stephen and Bloom proceed from the cabman's shelter to 7 Eccles Street *"to be married by Father Maher,"* the driver of the "sweeper car . . . simply sat in his seat near the end of lower Gardiner street *and looked after their low-backed car."* Since Bloom and Stephen are not in a car, their departure in one seems odd until the literary allusion has been identified. The passages in italics, as my student pointed out, are from "The Low-backed Car," a ballad by Samuel Lover, which tells of a couple off to get married by the priest. Using quotation to enrich one context by importing another, as Eliot was doing, Joyce suggests by this device that Stephen and Bloom, having met and agreed, are now off to be united in the following chapter, where over the kitchen table at number seven they will symbolize their atonement with cocoa or god-food. Consubstantial at last, Bloom will become Blephen and Stephen Stoom. While anticipating and suggesting this union, the image of the lowbacked car brings two chapters together. There is no clearer example of symbol in this capacity.

Nevertheless *Ulysses* shows more elaborate examples of constructive and suggestive reference. It may be that the discovery of Mr.

Bloom is the climax of the enormous comedy, but it is plain that Mrs. Bloom occupies the center of things. Stephen's understanding of that is his final triumph, a triumph to which Mr. Bloom leads him. An allusion to Dante leads us to knowledge of what Stephen finds. This allusion, together with many plainer references, establishes *The Divine Comedy* as one of the principal, yet least apparent, parallels upon which *Ulysses* is founded and to which it owes something of its richness, massiveness, and depth.

The plainest reference to Dante in *Ulysses* is Stephen's ironic account in the Eumaeus episode of the impetuosity of Italians: "we have the impetuosity of Dante and the isosceles triangle, Miss Portinari, he fell in love with and Leonardo and san Tommaso Mastino." Why Beatrice is an isosceles triangle, though difficult, is not beyond all conjecture. Maybe she is isosceles rather than equilateral (like Mrs. Bloom and the mark of Bass's ale) because she has almost no bottom. St. Thomas Aquinas, Dante's philosopher, is described as a mastiff (Mastino) here, and elsewhere as "the bulldog of Aquin," because during the middle ages by a Latin pun on their name the Dominicans were known as dogs of God. Joyce, who had a horror of dogs, was turning at this time from Aquinas to Bruno, and he had turned already, as Stephen proclaims in *Stephen Hero,* from Dante to Ibsen. But Joyce found Dante more useful than Bruno or Ibsen as a parallel for Stephen's quest. This parallel, suggested less by allusions than by quotations, implies that Telemachus-Hamlet-Stephen in search of a father or rather in search of himself is not unlike Dante.

It is likely that in Dante's four meanings, literal and allegorical, Joyce found a hint for making Stephen more general. Since, as he remarks in the library: "His own image to a man with . . . genius is the standard of all experience, material and moral," Joyce's prob-

196

lem was how to free his hero from personal attachment and, while retaining the details of autobiography, to raise him to symbol. Literally, Dante is Dante; allegorically he is everyman searching for "peace and ardor." So Stephen, while literally young Joyce, is symbolically every young man in search of maturity and adjustment. Using a hint from Dante, Joyce made the personal quest of an exiled aesthete the quest of mankind for humanity. If we take his quest aesthetically, Stephen finds the subject matter of his future art and his creative power; if morally, his adolescent pride yields to mature compassion; if socially, he begins to understand his oneness with common man; and if religiously, he finds in mankind a substitute for God. His success, which like his quest is far from being a mechanical parody of Dante, is symbolized by his meeting with Mr. Bloom and a little later by his apprehension of Mrs. Bloom.

In the Aeolus episode Stephen, meditating the rhymes of the poem he has written on the beach, quotes four fragments from the *Inferno:*

> . . . . la tua pace
> . . . . che parlar ti piace
> . . . . mentrechè il vento, come fa, si tace.
> . . . per l'aer perso . . . .

Literally these fragments are examples of rhyme and of Stephen's learning, but in the matter of Homer, since they concern Paolo and Francesca, these fragments agree with the other references to wind in that gusty chapter. Morally, since Paolo and Francesca occupy the second circle, these lines refer to lust, one of Stephen's dearest sins. But these lines from the *Inferno* are followed immediately by two fragments from the *Paradiso:* "quella pacifica oriafiamma" and "di rimirar fé piu ardenti," both of which concern the mystical rose of Dante's vision. By way of these quotations we rise from human lust to divine love, from time to eternity, from Francesca to Mary, a progress suggesting that of Stephen from the lust and pride of the *Portrait* to the charity implied by Joyce's presentation of Mrs. Bloom.

Mr. Bloom is at once God, humanity, and the subject of Joyce's art—or rather he suggests them, but having discovered Mr. Bloom, Stephen leaves him. As Mr. Bloom accompanies his guest to the back yard, Stephen silently intones, in the words of the 113th Psalm, the departure from Egypt for the promised land: *"In exitu Israēl de Egypto: domus Jacob de populo barbaro."* Serving not only the parallel of Moses but also that of Dante, Stephen's choice of psalm is at once the most obscure and the most significant allusion to him and his symbolic method in Joyce's work; for by his choice Stephen seems to imply the Epistle to Can Grande, in which, dedicating the *Paradiso* to his patron, Dante used this psalm to illustrate his fourfold method:

To elucidate, then, what we have to say, be it known that the sense of this work is not simple, but on the contrary it may be called polysemous, that is to say, "of more senses than one"; for it is one sense which we get through the letter, and another which we get through the thing the letter signifies; and the first is called literal, but the second allegorical or mystic. And this mode of treatment, for its better manifestation, may be considered in this verse: "When Israel came out of Egypt, and the house of Jacob from a people of strange speech. . . ." For if we inspect the letter alone the departure of the children of Israel from Egypt in the time of Moses is presented to us; if the allegory, our redemption wrought by Christ; if the moral sense, the conversion of the soul from the grief and misery of sin to the state of grace is presented to us; if the anagogical, the departure of the holy soul from the slavery of this corruption to the liberty of eternal glory is presented to us.

Preparing the learned reader for a new *Paradiso* and suggesting the fourfold method, this allusion prepares him for more than one meaning. Dante's explication of the psalm also summarizes Stephen's triumph and one of the central meanings of *Ulysses*. Led by his Moses from bondage to the realization of his humanity, Stephen is free at last to achieve eternal glory by art.

Emerging from the door of Bloom's house into that infertile garden, which they proceed to water, Stephen and Bloom look up at the "visible luminous sign" of Mrs. Bloom's window while Mr. Bloom elucidates "the mystery of an invisible person, his wife Marion (Molly) . . . , denoted by a visible splendid sign, a lamp . . . with indirect and direct verbal allusions or affirmations: with subdued affection and admiration . . . with suggestion." Her lamp, casting on the ceiling a pattern of "concentric circles" as if to imply Dante's final vision of the Trinity, appears to imply Stephen's enlightenment and his vision of ultimate reality. As Dante was led to his vision by St. Bernard, so Stephen is led to his by Mr. Bloom. It seems likely that in one of his capacities Mr. Bloom serves as St. Bernard, and it is likelier that Mrs. Bloom is Dante's mystical rose, symbol of heaven and of the Blessed Virgin. Or rather, to give the relationships their due, St. Bernard and the rose expand the meanings of Mr. and Mrs. Bloom.

The Virgin as rose and queen of the rosary is a principal theme of the chapter on Gerty MacDowell, who, as she sits on the beach, blushes a glorious "rosebloom." Meanwhile Father John Hughes, S.J., conducting in the church nearby the men's temperance retreat, celebrates the rosary and gives benediction: "pray for us, honourable vessel, pray for us, vessel of singular devotion, pray for us, mystical rose. . . . and many who had erred and wandered, their eyes wet with contrition but for all that bright with hope for the reverend father Hughes had told them what the great saint Bernard said in his famous prayer of Mary." St. Bernard, whose devotion to the

Virgin is singular, comes next to St. Leopold in the procession of saints in the preceding chapter. Leopold, whose devotion to Mary-Marion seems as great (though by no means singular), is described in the Ithaca chapter as "centripetal"; for, like Dante's Bernard, Bloom, looking up at Marion's lamp, is drawn to the central petal.

As for roses: Joyce's *Portrait* and *Ulysses* are a garden of those blooms, which traditionally suggest woman, eternity, and creative ecstasy. In the *Portrait* as Stephen wakes one morning and composes a poem, his moment of creation is presented in terms that associate it with his girl, with mystical ecstasy in general and, in particular, with Dante's vision of the enormous rose. The overblown flowers of the wallpaper form a "roseway from where he lay upwards to heaven all strewn with scarlet flowers." In *Ulysses,* though flowers are everywhere, they flourish in greatest profusion in the chapters of lotus eating and siren song. The answer to Lenehan's riddle (What opera is like a railway line?) is Rose of Castille. Lenehan associates his riddle with Miss Douce, the barmaid, who wears a jumping rose on her satiny bosom; but Bloom, perverting Lenehan's question to "What railway opera is like a tramline in Gibraltar?" associates it with Marion. She is from Spain; she is connected with Bloom's castile soap; and she is certainly a rose; but why she is a railway is unclear unless it is because she is a common carrier. She is a rose—and that is partly why, I think, Joyce chose the name of Bloom, which, as Marion lies abed, she finds suitable.

The affair of "Penrose" confirms the rosiness of Mrs. Bloom. During the Lestrygonian episode, Mr. Bloom, frustrated by a defect of memory not altogether without Freudian significance, tries to think of the name of that "priestylooking chap" with weak eyes, "Pen something." Later, meeting the blind piano tuner and helping him across Dawson Street and into Molesworth, Mr. Bloom suddenly has it: "Penrose! That was that chap's name." Since the priestlike piano tuner with his stick and his quarrel with the world is one of Stephen's surrogates, it becomes plain that Penrose is another. Stephen the penman accounts for the first syllable of Penrose, but what of the second? This is suggested by Virag in the Circe episode: "Read the Priest, the Woman and the Confessional. Penrose." Already connecting Bloom and Stephen, Penrose now looks forward to Molly and her monologue. The Ithaca episode reveals Penrose as one of Molly's lovers; in the last chapter she thinks of him in terms that associate him with Stephen; and a little later she thinks of Stephen himself, who, she hopes, will become a lover and write about her: "They all write about some woman in their poetry." If Mrs. Bloom is the rose, the second syllable of Penrose refers to her. Connecting Bloom, Stephen, and Molly, Joyce's trinity, Penrose, acquiring and shedding new meaning, now suggests that Stephen, her most Platonic lover, will use his pen to celebrate the rose. This pen, like Mann's pencil, has more than one meaning, and so has that rose, but such implications, whether sexual or religious, serve only to make the domestic structure firmer, funnier, and more intricate.

As she lies abed Marion thinks first of Bloom and then, as if to provoke associations, of Mrs. Riordan, the Dante of *A Portrait of the Artist*. She recalls the white rose she wore when Mulvey's letter came, how as a girl in Gibraltar she was a rose, and at the end of her rumination she thinks: "I love flowers Id love to have the whole place swimming in roses." As her thoughts rise to the tremendous affirmation, she is lost in an ecstasy of red roses and flowers of the mountain. Creative power, the river and mountain of life, the fecundity of nature, and the wonder of God are united in these ultimate symbols.

That Marion Bloom was born on the 8th of September helps to

establish her significance; for that is the feast of the Blessed Virgin's nativity. Though neither the Blessed Virgin nor the mystical rose, she is like them in symbolizing unity, reconciliation, and peace. As human Mr. Bloom is compared to God, yet is not God, so human Mrs. Bloom is compared, with Dante's help, to the rose of God. Not to be taken literally, these analogies are correspondences that carry the meaning of the book. The same holds for Stephen's vision of her lamp. Although he recalls Dante's vision by analogy, Stephen's enlightenment is humane; but his vision of this world corresponds to Dante's vision of the next. After his mystical vision of heaven, Dante returns to write his comedy, and, after his mystical vision of humanity, Stephen, now mature Joyce, leaves Bloom's back yard to write his.

Ulysses, which tells of the flowering of Stephen's genius, is the fruit of that genius. Since Mrs. Bloom is the heart of the book, she is not only flower of vision but fruit of creation, the melon or "creamfruit" that Mr. Bloom offers the still frustrated poet in a dream. Her fruitiness, accepted at last by Stephen, is established by Bloom's final act of the day: he kisses her "plump mellow yellow smellow melons . . . with melonsmellonous osculation," a correspondence for which not Dante but Mr. Bloom is responsible. That, aside from melons, the growth we have been botanizing upon comes from the seeds of quotation and allusion is additional assurance of their fertility.

Taking what she could from Joyce, Virginia Woolf called *Ulysses* "an illiterate, underbred book," and in her *Diary* she also recorded her dismay when Tom (she called Mr. Eliot Tom) found *Ulysses* as good as *War and Peace*. Finding in her books the technique of quotation common to Eliot and Joyce, therefore, is no surprise. When Mr. Ramsay, striding up and down his terrace, shouts " 'Someone had blundered,' " we share the sense of failure and courage he shares with that noble six hundred. There is a quotation in *Mrs. Dalloway,* however, that is not only revelatory but constructive:

Quiet descended on her, calm, content, as her needle, drawing the silk smoothly to its gentle pause, collected the green folds together and attached them, very lightly, to the belt. So on a summer's day waves collect, overbalance, and fall; collect and fall; and the whole world seems to be saying "that is all" more and more ponderously, until even the heart in the body which lies in the sun on the beach says too, That is all. Fear no more, says the heart. Fear no more, says the heart, committing its burden to some sea, which sighs collectively for all sorrows, and renews, begins, collects, lets fall. And the body alone listens to the passing bee; the wave breaking; the dog barking, far away barking and barking.

Before we get to " 'Fear no more,' " the embedded quotation, we might pause to compare this passage, one of her most beautiful, with a passage in *Night and Day,* the last novel she wrote before turning from discourse to symbol:

As she ran her needle in and out of the wool, she thought of the various stages in her life which made her present position seem the culmination of successive miracles. She thought of her clerical father in his country parsonage, and of her mother's death, and of her own determination to obtain education, and of her college life. . . .

Though both passages concern sewing hands and idle mind, that from *Night and Day* catalogues the contents of the mind whereas that from *Mrs. Dalloway* offers the quality while suggesting the substance of a mental state without its particulars. Rhythm, sound, and that wonderful simile conspire to give the feeling of peace—as of an afternoon nap. " 'Fear no more,' " the quotation from *Cymbeline,* works in this congenial setting.

Mrs. Dalloway, who reads no books, reads the opening lines of Shakespeare's dirge for golden lads and girls on her way to buy flowers that morning as she pauses before the window of a bookseller, where the book lies open. Appealing to something deep within her and haunting her throughout the day, " 'Fear no more' " brings from source a deathly air that, surrounding her, as she sits and sews, proves her meditation one of death. In the Preface, Virginia Woolf says she had once meant Mrs. Dalloway to die at the end of the book; but in it as it stands, Septimus, her surrogate or double, dies instead. Hearing of his death at her party, she feels drawn to one who has "completed her" and vicariously enjoys his suicide; for, in love with life, she is in love with death. That it was Virginia Woolf's purpose to provide Mrs. Dalloway with Freud's death wish is made probable not only by the Preface but by the fact that as Freud's English publisher she had published *Beyond the Pleasure Principle,* his statement of the death wish, shortly before commencing her novel; but that Mrs. Dalloway's death wish was not altogether a bookish fancy is proved by Mrs. Woolf's own inclination.

" 'Fear no more' " serves not only to reveal and confirm Mrs. Dalloway's deepest desire but to connect her with the death-wishing double whose triumph she envies. Lacking the advantage of a bookseller's window, Septimus thinks nevertheless of the very quotation as he lies before his suicide on the sofa in the sitting room: "his hand lay there on the back of the sofa, as he had seen his hand lie when he was bathing, floating, on the top of the waves, while far away on shore he heard dogs barking and barking far away. Fear no more, says the heart in the body; fear no more." Septimus, whose identity with Mrs. Dalloway is established by this passage, is one of many doubles in recent literature. There are the hero and his double in Dostoyevsky's *The Double,* the captain and his guest in Conrad's "The Secret Sharer," Swann and Marcel, the host of doubles or surrogates in *Ulysses,* and many more. In every case, one of the pair may be considered a projection and, in a sense, a symbol of the other. Crazy Septimus presents the hidden nature of sociable Mrs. Dalloway.

By virtue of the name itself, juxtaposition seems an even better way than quotation of putting things together. That it is also a variety of symbol is implied by the approval of Coleridge, who, in *The Statesman's Manual,* rejecting mere balance or compromise of two powers, favors a "living and generative" union, "a creative overflowing" in which "the two component counter-powers actually interpenetrate each other, and generate a higher third, including both the former, *ita tamen sit alia et major."* The two contending elements become "the image or symbol" of what they generate. Hegel, another romantic, had a similar idea, and Mallarmé, inspired by Hegel, speaks in "Crise de vers" of instituting an exact relationship between images in order to detach from them a third aspect, "fusible et clair présenté à la divination." After such assurance can we doubt that one plus one may equal three or that placing two things side by side may create and present something else?

The great authority on doing that is Sergei M. Eisenstein, whose word for putting two things creatively together is "montage." Two pieces of film placed together, he says in *The Film Sense,* "inevitably combine into a new concept, a new quality, arising out of that juxtaposition." The result, less a sum of the parts than a creation of a third something qualitatively distinguishable from its components, must be foreseen by the artist and subordinated to aesthetic and political purpose; all contributing elements must be selected to "evoke in the perception and feelings of the spectator the most complete image of the theme itself." His insistence that the suggestion must be limited and the spectator's necessary participation directed sounds communal enough, but Eisenstein, as his apologies show, had been suspected of

205

formalism and a preference for art. Certainly the examples of montage by which he illustrates his points are unexceptionable. Consider this sequence from his picture *Strike:* (1) the slaughter of a bull; (2) the slaughter of a crowd of striking workers; (3) an ax; (4) a gun. The participating Russian knows what to make of these.

First applied to the movies by D. W. Griffith, montage has aesthetic applications beyond his scope and, indeed, beyond that of any single art. Griffith's disciple Eisenstein finds montage in *Paradise Lost,* in the portmanteau words of Lewis Carroll's "Jabberwocky," and in *Finnegans Wake.* "We must study Joyce," he said.

We might follow Eisenstein's advice for a moment before turning to less obtrusive matters. The pun, one of the central means of poetry, is the medium of *Finnegans Wake,* and puns, as Eisenstein observes, are telescoped montage or montage by superimposition. "Are we speachin d'anglas landadge or are you sprakin sea Djoytsch?" asks Joyce. However dazzling such collocations of elements (French, German, land and sea in this case), they serve immediate context and general theme. Beyond that, they issue richly indefinite suggestions that would never do behind the curtain. Joyce's combinations, what is worse, are witty and almost always funny. "Jesuistical," which puts Jesuitical and casuistical into one portmanteau, is montage at its simplest and most rewarding. "Wednesbury" is more complicated. A place name in its context, it acquires the idea of time by confusion with Wednesday; Woden, wed, and bury, referring to religion, marriage, and burial, the three stages of Vico's temporal pattern, include a major theme of the book. Analysis, which yields these elements, gives no idea of a whole greater, as Eisenstein says, than the sum of these parts—a thing for immediate apprehension, which, however, is improved by simultaneous awareness of the parts. The quickness Joyce demands of his readers is rewarded more readily by montage of phrase. "Ramrod the meaty hunter" needs no commentary, nor, if you let your mind play on it awhile, does the following union of Descartes and Pope: "Sink deep or touch not the Cartesian spring!" That Joyce had the movies in mind, as Eisenstein had Joyce, is certain not only from his establishment of Dublin's first movie house but from references in *Finnegans Wake*, his "allnights newseyreel." At their meeting in 1930, Eisenstein and Joyce must have had plenty to talk about.

Montage in its more customary sense of juxtaposed images or incidents is everywhere in Joyce's work. Sequences in *A Portrait of the Artist* may be diagrammed as Eisenstein diagrammed his scenarios. Take this sequence at Clongowes Wood College: (1) the sound of cricket bats, compared to water dropping in a bowl; (2) a conversation about "smugging" in the urinal; (3) the dainty nails of "Lady" Boyle, a smugger; (4) the cool white hands of Eileen and the Virgin's *Tower of Ivory;* (5) the college urinal and graffiti on its walls; (6) a conversation about punishment; (7) the sound of cricket bats again. There are no transitions; Joyce makes no comment; Stephen concludes nothing; but from this collocation of elements arises a kind of nameless nastiness that fixes our impression of the school. Montage as symbol was never more instructively displayed, except perhaps in the less subtle but no less excellent scene at the agricultural fair in *Madame Bovary*.

Yeats, who based much of his philosophy upon warring contraries, speaks in his *Autobiography* of their acquiring sex and engendering: "All creation is from conflict." That he applied the principle to poems is evident from "Oil and Blood," a montage of two elements. In the first stanza the bodies of holy men, lying in elaborate tombs, give forth a sweet-smelling oil; in the other stanza vampires full of blood lie under trampled clay, in bloody shrouds, their lips wet. These

207

images, at once similar and dissimilar, are given the semblance of logical connection by "But," the opening word of the second stanza. Not logic, however, but creative contiguity explains the feeling of the poem. As for idea: the two visions produce a composite vision, larger than either, that carries an indefinable commentary upon man's life and times.

Dylan Thomas professed Hegelian method. Taking an image, he said, he placed it alongside another and let them generate a third. I have never been able to trace the process among the dizzy juxtapositions of his early poems, but his general practice seems related to montage. The "barley dark" and the "milking moonlight" of "In the White Giant's Thigh," for example, owe their effects to the transfer of epithets from the context where they are at home to one a little alien to their habit. Epithet and noun, nothing much in themselves or alone, become creative lying together. The opposition of two times in "Poem in October," which might seem similar in kind, is softened so much by discourse that it lacks the impact of naked montage. Times, however, are among its better materials as the work of Eliot proves.

"Sweeney Among the Nightingales," a poem of two times, owes tidiness and mystery to the abrupt collocation of its elements. Eisenstein would have reduced the poem to this scenario: (1) Sweeney in a whorehouse; (2) a nightingale singing near a convent; (3) another nightingale singing in another place at another time; (4) the murder of Agamemnon. That the arrangement is pleasing is shown by the fame of the poem, but neat quatrains, promising sense, present uncertainty instead. The man in mocha brown is puzzling, but what bothers and delights us most is the suggested though improbable association of Sweeney and Agamemnon. That they are unalike is at once apparent: the one a modern vulgarian, the other

208

an ancient hero. As their strange connection stimulates thought, it may occur to us that the two are alike in being troubled by women. Sweeney, who has avoided some feminine conspiracy against him, is shrewder, however, than Agamemnon, who has succumbed. Is that why nightingales, presumably letting Sweeney alone, stain the noble shroud with droppings? We toy with these while the montage does its work. What it creates is not that union of feeling and thought Eliot once promised but feeling alone, a feeling so unthinkable that its only expression is what created it. Whereas the arrangements of past and present in "Burbank with a Baedeker" and *The Waste Land* are definite enough to invite discourse, nobody has made much sense out of Agamemnon and Sweeney, who resist the intelligence more than "almost successfully."

Suggestive conjunctions of a less mysterious sort make up lost time for Proust. Otherwise his privileged moments, at once the cause and essence of his book, are not unlike Eliot's temporal montage. The cup of tea in the first volume, the uneven paving stone, the sound of spoon on plate, and the feel of a napkin in the last, together with several experiences between—the scent of hawthorn, for example—carry and reveal all Proust had to say. Although these moments, involving taste, sight, hearing, smell, and touch, are present, their magic comes from sudden correspondence with forgotten sensations in the past. The privileged moment is a montage of two sensations and two times or, to put it as the great "amphibian" of past and present commonly did, of sensation and memory. Their momentary contact calls from the unconscious a forgotten past and allows the artist recovering it to make it permanent. The first two volumes of *Remembrance of Things Past* explore times opened by a cup of tea. The rest was disclosed and opened for exploration by those moments at the final party.

The fusing of two sensations from time is out of it. At such moments, as Oliver Gogarty would say, "it isn't this time of year at all." Yet Proust appears time's celebrant, not its refugee. In a way he is both, and what happens when, after long absence, he attends the great party at the end, is paradoxical. His discovery that all he knew as young are old now, that he too is time's victim, is accompanied by a release from time in privileged moments and consequent art. Those liberating moments, the climax of his search, are akin to moments in the rose garden, by the pool, or in the chapel that free Eliot, expert in times present and times past, from time and, uniting it with the timeless, approximate eternity. Proust too relies on gifts. No effort of intellect or will, such as those expended in vain upon the three trees, will give what must be given; for involuntary memory must open reality's door.

In those conjunctions of sensation and memory bringing gifts we can call sensation the "signal" (as Proust does) or stimulus of memory, or, preferring their concurrence, we can call them equal interacting elements of a montage. There they are, side by side, and out of their rapport comes something that gives ecstasy and indifference to death, something radiant and disengaged from utility. Though sensation and memory, the creators of this happiness, are in time, they bring not only what Eliot desires but what Yeats knew when stepping ashore at Byzantium or Mr. Ramsay at his Lighthouse. Proust called this creative relationship of elements metaphor, but symbol seems a better term for an analogical interaction that embodies what it presents: the ecstasy of timelessness and that of art, another timeless, ecstatic revelation of ultimate or inner reality. Art, analogous to its cause, is a more elaborate embodiment of what privileged moments offer. "Truth will begin," Proust says in the last volume,

210

only when the writer takes two different objects, establishes their relationship . . . and encloses them in the necessary rings of a beautiful style, or even when, like life itself, comparing similar qualities in two sensations, he makes their essential nature stand out clearly by joining them in a metaphor, in order to remove them from the contingencies of time, and links them together with the indescribable bond of an alliance of words. . . . The relationship may be uninteresting, the objects mediocre and the style bad, but without that relationship there is nothing.

He follows this account of what we might call creative montage by attacks on naturalism, which is limited to description of surfaces, and on political, sociological, and moral purpose. Poetic, mysterious, and profound, art is a "spiritual equivalent" of reality. Deceived by long passages of commentary, critics used to call Proust a rational analyst of society, a mistake as great as that of those who found him devoted to time. His quest was for the timeless, and it is no less plain that far from being an intellectual analyst, he was an enemy of reason, basing his work, like many romantics, on sensation, memory, and mystical or even primitive intuition. Intellect, present in his purposely tedious analyses of what is given, is there as collaborator. Serving to examine what one already has, it is a poor substitute, he says, for impression. Since writing with the intelligence, he continues, deprives a work of depth, we must follow imagination and sensibility through deep realities within us to capture "timeless joy"; for time is "incarnate," and people and places, fixed in actuality by name alone, abide in memory.

Baudelaire was another who united memory and sensation for exploring a rich interior. After the ecstasy at the last party, Proust thinks of Baudelaire again and resolves to reread his poems in order to claim a share in a "noble literary heritage." Recent French critics, Arnaud Dandieu and Emeric Fiser among them, see Proust, as he

211

saw himself, an heir to the symbolist tradition; but also preferring the word metaphor to symbol, Dandieu calls Proust's work an enormous metaphor, parallel to the little metaphors of the privileged moment. Whatever my preference in words, I cannot quarrel with that.

"Thinking of a relation between the images of metaphors," as Wallace Stevens puts it, we may look at metaphor again from another point of view. Some way back, when considering the Renaissance, we found metaphor a limited correspondence, suitable for those in definite worlds. For romantics, however, metaphor, transcending the equation that seems to direct its meaning, may wear another aspect, as we discovered, and, becoming a structure of two objects or a montage of two interacting images, it may produce effects both unforeseen and indefinite. Donne could not have regarded his equation of compasses and lovers in this romantic light, but, putting history aside, we may see his structure as the creative collaboration of Eisenstein's delight. We are on firmer ground with Eliot's conjunction of sunset and patient on table, a romantic product, expanding to the limits of our desire. If, then, we find metaphor montage, as Proust and Dandieu did, we must consider the related terms to find the effectual kinds. Strong similarity links the terms of Proust's metaphor, but the terms of Eliot's simile have less in common. Is the creative power of metaphorical juxtaposition more dependent on the similarity or the dissimilarity of its terms? Is conflict more productive than agreement? When John Cleveland compares a woman's hand to "a jelly gloved," he creates little but amazement and disgust; on the other hand, the terms of a comparison may be so much alike that, leaving us cold, they produce nothing at all. I judge, therefore, that the most productive kind of comparison is one in which similarity is balanced by dissimilarity. That would

212

seem to exclude Sweeney and Agamemnon, but there are exceptions; for art has a way of flirting its tail at our rules as it passes them by. To predict the effect of a conjunction or the most creative distance between its elements may be impossible, and we must judge success by what we feel. I think it safe to say, however, that metaphor, taken as montage of quarreling or collaborating elements, is as symbolic as image or action alone. From our present point of view metaphor is a metaphor for symbol.

Montage of times—to get back to that—is no more provocative than montage of discourse and image or action. I used to be troubled by Lawrence's mixture in *Women in Love* of imagistic splendor with sermons by Birkin, but now I see that the stoning of the moon's reflection in the pool would lack something without Birkin's discursive accompaniment. Though once impatient with those who limited and weakened image by too much talk, I think now, as I implied in an earlier part of this essay, that sometimes the two kinds, working together, may produce something richer than either could. Consider Keats's "Ode on a Grecian Urn." Although some critics have found "Beauty is truth, truth beauty" a discursive intrusion and a flaw, it becomes apparent that the prosaic line is a necessary element. Working with the rich details of that "Attic shape," this line, so unfortunate in appearance, creates the "silent form" that pleases all but those thoughtful critics. Consider Eliot's *Four Quartets*. Plainly successful, this arrangement depends as much upon discourse as image; indeed, it depends upon the two together for its effects. Prosaic abstractions, like the opening section, become creative by contact with images or actions that follow them. What we get from the arrangement of prose and "poetry" is something greater than either could produce alone, something born of their unhappy marriage. Eliot's talk of the need of relieving a long poem by prose or verse of less intensity is nothing. Not relief but the advantages of juxtaposition determined his admirable mixture.

The process might be plainer in a shorter poem, Yeats's "Choice," for example:

> The intellect of man is forced to choose
> Perfection of the life, or of the work,
> And if it take the second must refuse
> A heavenly mansion, raging in the dark.

This thing, one of the greatest Yeats composed, owes drama, mystery, and loveliness to the conjunction of apparently incompatible elements, strict prose on the one hand and infernal action on the other. "Raging in the dark," a phrase no other poet could have put there, combines with the reasonable syntax of what precedes it to present the complexities of Yeats's life and, in their degree, our own.

It is to Wallace Stevens, however, that we must turn for the most elaborate exploitation of this structure. The third poem of "Notes Toward a Supreme Fiction" begins with a more or less abstract discourse on poetry: "The poem refreshes life so that we share. . . ." Refreshing it, the poem brings us back to some immaculate and candid first principle. This lecture comes to a violent end in the fifth stanza; for there is an Arabian in the room "with his damned hoobla-hoobla-hoobla-how." There is a wood dove too with his "hoobla-hoo," and farther off the ocean "howls hoo and rises and howls hoo and falls." "Life's nonsense," the poet concludes, "pierces us with strange relation." Of the relations here several are strange. That among "hoobla-hoobla-hoobla-how," "hoobla-hoo," and simple "hoo" is less of kind than of degree. All three are nonsense, to be sure, but it descends from that of the Arabian mathematician to those of bird and inanimate sea. The strangest relation, however, is that between the first part of the poem and the second. Alike in being parts of life's nonsense, they differ in method, the first discursive and the second nondiscursive. As their juxtaposition creates a feeling of the fundamentals discussed in the lecture and exemplified in hoos or hows, the world of ideas and the world of things become a single vision. As Stevens says in another poem of the same suite, the dependence of opposites on one another, man on woman, day on night, or the imagined on the real, is "the origin of change," but it is also the condition of montage.

"Oh beau caboose," one of Stevens's briefer triumphs in this kind, may serve to introduce and commend our last example. "So-and-So Reclining on Her Couch" proceeds discursively to the last stanza. "My dame," Stevens might have said here as he did elsewhere, "sing for this person accurate songs." So-and-So, an anonymous fact, poses for painters or philosophers on her couch, inviting interpretation. Finding her an abstraction or "the thing as idea" may be called Projection A. Projection B or "idea as thing" is improving her by imagination. Projection C, a compromise between A and B, floats her in their contention. It occurs to the projectors now that nature may be more acceptable than any of their arts:

> Good-bye,
> Mrs. Pappadopoulos, and thanks.

This shocking intrusion of fact upon imagination, of name upon anonymity, of the concrete upon the abstract is the second element of the montage, a thing of opposite nature on which the first depends. So-and-So, variously projected, contends with Mrs. Pappadopoulos to create thoughts and feelings of the nature of things. Structure and consequence are not unlike those of Shaw's *Man and Superman,* in

215

which Tanner's enormous discourse is brought to a sudden end and made creative partner by the curtain line: "Go on talking," says Ann. Joining his eloquence, her remark reveals the nature of man and woman, intellect and fact, and the nature of discourse. Stevens's discourse, odder than Tanner's, is odder by far than customary discourse. Though bare enough, it is not simple or easy to understand; for the plain façade is dramatically interrupted by the florid, the serious by the frivolous and strange. Baudelaire, who anticipated Stevens's taste for the baroque, once said, "Le beau est toujours bizarre." Beautiful and bizarre, the prose of Stevens, a dandy's prose, is nevertheless prosaic enough in such poems as "So-and-So" to contend with the major incursions upon it. Dandyism, also recommended by Baudelaire, expresses Stevens's ironic reservations, his feeling of apartness from the world he accepts, his comment on it, his Baudelairian fondness for artifice, and man's protest against things, compared to which his most prosaic prose is immaculate. "The final elegance," he says, is "plainly to propound."

One propounds by making propositions, which, although prosaic, share with poetic devices a capacity for setting things forth or projecting them. A proposition is something either true or false offered in the guise of statement for our acceptance or rejection. That such structures, however at ease they seem in the logician's alcove, are forms of feeling as well is affirmed by Whitehead in *Process and Reality*. "A propositional feeling," he observes in "Propositions and Feelings," the fourth chapter of the third part, "is a feeling whose objective datum is a proposition." Neither an actual entity nor an eternal object nor a feeling, a proposition is a tale "that might be told about particular actualities." It enters experience "as the entity forming the datum of a complex feeling derived from the integration of a physical feeling with a conceptual feeling." In other words, perhaps, a proposition, no less than an image or an action, may embody and present feeling. In a poem, what looks like leanest prose—"Beauty is truth, truth beauty"—may depart from the rational regions to which it seems committed and stir our hearts. The cause of this departure is context or, in the case of "So-and-So," montage, which owes its drama here to appearances alone; for what we have in "So-and-So" is not a conflict of logic with feeling but a creative contention between two forms of feeling and idea.

Some of my students, failing to understand these things, object to Stevens's propositional method. Enamored of images or, at least, accustomed to them, they clamor for something like Eliot's early poems. Enamored of consistency and decorum, they detest baroque mixtures of image and discourse, treatment and tone. It is vain for me, attempting an analogy of wines, to tell them that the driest wines have the sweetness of dryness; for they have no understanding of wines. It is equally vain, however, to attempt the moral approach and reprove intolerance of the unfamiliar, which, of course, should be familiar enough. The long debates of Settembrini and Naphta in *The Magic Mountain,* the sermons in *A Portrait of the Artist,* and the essay at the end of *War and Peace* may propound idea but, working with narrative and image, these propositional structures are less informative than affective. In a work of art, as Susanne Langer observes, discourse becomes nondiscursive and elemental, and, as Stevens says, prose will "wear a poem's guise at last." The sermon near the end of *The Sound and the Fury* is the plainest example of that.

My third way of joining, while presenting, things is leitmotiv or thematic elaboration. Made known by Wagner's usage, the recurrent image or pattern has become increasingly familiar in literature, from which maybe Wagner got it, until it seems almost a mark of better

217

fiction in our time—though by no means peculiar to it. The device has become so common that Wellek and Warren find all symbols dependent upon repetition, but I find it only one of many symbolic devices. "O Nature, and O soul of man!" exclaims Ahab, "how far beyond all utterance are your linked analogies!" The captain was thinking of correspondences between nature and mind, of course, but "linked analogies," taken from context, are an apt description of the elaborated image. The great authorities on that are E. M. Forster and E. K. Brown, the great practitioners Mann, Proust, and Joyce.

An admirer of *Moby Dick,* Forster says in *Aspects of the Novel* that "if one god must be invoked specially, let us call upon Hermes." I am not sure that he had correspondences in mind at that moment, but he was generally attentive to linked analogies; indeed, "Pattern and Rhythm," a chapter of *Aspects of the Novel,* is the first systematic account of the device as writers use it. Pattern, a word borrowed from painting, and rhythm, a word borrowed from music, are structural. Pattern or what causes us to apprehend "the shape as a whole" is not our immediate concern, but rhythm is. For Forster it has two meanings, the first of which is the relationship between large movements as in a symphony. No example of such massive relationship in literature occurs to Forster, who modestly forgets the three movements of *A Passage to India* and prefers to ignore *Ulysses; To the Lighthouse* came too late, of course, to recall by internal relationship of parts his own work, to which it is indebted. The second sense of rhythm, however, is what we want; for rhythm of this kind is recurrent theme, and his example is Vinteuil's "little phrase" in Proust.

This pioneer analysis of the phrase, though incomplete since Forster wrote before the publication of Proust's last volumes, is excellent nevertheless. Serving to "stitch" the book together from within, that phrase, he says, does more than anything else in the otherwise "chaotic" book to make us "feel we are in a homogeneous world." By cumulative recurrence and development, gradually acquiring new meanings from this context or that, associated now with Vinteuil's horrible daughter, with Swann, with Marcel, and their three loves, the phrase, while stitching all together, comes to mean everything to the reader as well as to those heroes. Not always present, as pattern is, rhythm fills us with surprise by a waxing and waning unlike the contrived, mechanical recurrence of Meredith's cherry tree and Galsworthy's spaniel. Forster doubts that rhythm or "repetition plus variation" and "expansion" can be achieved by those who work things consciously out beforehand.

Without the final volumes at hand, Forster failed to see not only the structure of the book but the difference between Swann's interpretation of the phrase and Marcel's. For Swann the "indefinite" and "ineffable" phrase captures and makes apparent by "harmonious, fleeting form" his love for Odette. When Marcel in his turn hears the sonata, the recurring motif, which reminds him of Wagner, evokes memories of Combray and corresponds to his love for Albertine, but when it recurs for a moment in the septet, where it is transfigured, the little phrase, still bringing Albertine to mind, now seems to embody that created world, beyond analysis, which corresponds to spiritual or interior reality. No longer a symbol of love or no longer that alone, the phrase, "a profound equivalent" now to the privileged moment, is a symbol of art which, while tying the book together, presents the central theme.

Forster's modest reluctance to mention works of his own detained E. K. Brown, who, devoting *Rhythm in the Novel* to them, traces Forster's large rhythm in *A Passage to India* and his small rhythm with its variation and recurrence in *Howards End,* a work which preceded that of Proust by several years. Brown pays particular attention to the image of hay, which occurs at the beginning of *Howards End,* expands or interweaves throughout, and recurs with all its accumulated riches at the end to include the substance of the novel. I had been tumbling in that hay before I read Brown's excellent monograph, and I confess myself not a little disappointed that instead of disclosing tumblings of my own I must applaud another's.

Thomas Mann's use of thematic recurrence preceded Forster's as his preceded Proust's. Forster may have ignored Mann because he planned things out and tells about them. His introduction to *Stories of Three Decades,* for example, and his essay on *The Magic Mountain* in the *Atlantic Monthly* (January, 1953) prove awareness of "rhythm" or leitmotiv by elaborate commentary on his practice. Whatever the extent of this awareness, it is less, he confesses, than that of his critics, who often show him what he has done.

Mann says that, feeling a deep affinity for music, "the shaping influence" upon him, he took the leitmotiv from Wagner and applied the device to literature. "To me the novel was always like a symphony, a work in counterpoint, a thematic fabric; the idea of the musical motif plays a great role in it." This magical formula, "which works both ways, and links the past with the future, the future with the past," establishes the "abiding presentness of the whole at each moment." *The Magic Mountain* may be his most nearly musical triumph, but, he says, his original experiment in the kind was *Tonio Kröger*. Planning that long story, he first conceived of a work in prose "as a weaving of themes, as a musical complex of associations." The results of his experiments proved so difficult that *The Magic Mountain* or even *Tonio Kröger* must be read more than once. Only

220

after the second reading of such a composition "can one really penetrate and enjoy its musical association of ideas. The first time, the reader learns the thematic material; he is then in a position to read the symbolic and allusive formulas both forwards and backwards." Since taking a hint from music does not make music of literature, Mann's success with leitmotiv remains brilliantly literary. Not only carrying feeling and idea, leitmotiv assures the unity and coherence of his structures.

Pencil and Kirghiz eyes are among the motifs of *The Magic Mountain*. Though its thematic structure, like that of *Ulysses* or *Remembrance of Things Past,* is too vast and intricate for compendious analysis, *Tonio Kröger,* a portrait of the artist as a young and middle-aged man, is conveniently short and simple. Like Stephen Dedalus, Tonio is articulate about his difficult position in our society, and, like Joyce, he is torn between loyalties to the bourgeois world from which he has attempted escape and to the world of art he has chosen. Aesthetic Stephen finally becomes one with bourgeois Mr. Bloom, but Tonio, however aesthetic, always remains a *"bourgeois manqué."* Not a matter of montage, his articulateness, like that of Stephen, fails to diminish a feeling carried better by elaborated images than by all his discourse.

As the "winter sun" of the first sentence implies, Tonio Kröger, whose name is equally suggestive of opposites, is an uneasy mixture of north and south, of respectable father and exotic mother. This discrepancy is established and confirmed by repeated images of blond extrovert and brunet introvert. Blue-eyed Hans and Ingeborg, for whom he yearns, and all the satisfactions of the commonplace are balanced by the disreputable pleasures of Italy and Munich and the companionship of artistic Slavs. Tonio's situation is concentrated

221

for us at two dances, the first at the dancing school in his Baltic town, the second, a parody of the first, at a Danish resort. Representing the acceptable rhythm of life, these dances prove Tonio an awkward outsider looking in. The blond ones of his desire, good at dancing, laugh at him, and the only girl who seems to understand falls down. These images of dumb *savoir faire* and knowing ineptitude, joining images of blond and dark, are anticipated by the contrast of Schiller and photography and by the tiger and polar bear, caged in the hold of the ship Tonio takes for Denmark, his refuge from Italy and Munich. Recurrent allusions to Hamlet prepare us for this excursion while suggesting internal conflict. Tonio's interrogation by the police of his native town echoes the case of the convict-banker who reads and writes. "After all," says bohemian Tonio, "we are not gipsies living in a green wagon; we're respectable people." Such phrases and situations, parodying one another as they recur, not only present his conflict while he talks about it, but, tying his career together, make it massive, ironic, and moving. Repetition with variation is plainly the agent of these effects, but neither the expansion nor the development that Forster desires is apparent. For these we must consult Mann's later works or else the works of Joyce.

Though another portrait of the artist, *Death in Venice* is more elaborate than *Tonio Kröger;* and Gustave Aschenbach, the hero, though also torn between the bourgeois and the bohemian, is a larger figure than Tonio and more suggestive. The conflict between social and aesthetic discipline on the one hand and moral abandonment on the other that uses the soul of Aschenbach for theater is projected by many devices—dream and unassigned images among them —but chiefly by themes which, working together and expanding, combine their acquisitions at last in the persons of Tadzio and Aschenbach. Alike yet various, these incremental reappearances are so delicately involved with one another and with the rest of their setting that even after a third reading or a fourth one despairs of disentangling them for inspection.

Four men—or better, four varieties of a man—comprise the most apparent of these motifs. The first man, encountered on the porch of the mortuary chapel in Munich, gives Aschenbach the idea of a journey; the second, an elderly and repulsive dandy, confronts the voyager on the wharf at Pola; the third is the gondolier who takes reluctant Aschenbach to the Lido; and the fourth is the vulgar entertainer at the hotel. These impressive figures, all foreigners and alike in respect of conspicuous teeth, loose lips, and snub noses, also agree, despite obvious vitality, in suggesting death. The gondolier, for example, propels a floating black coffin that invites perpetual rest; and the entertainer, whatever his clamor, smells of carbolic. All four of them, while promising death, seem aspects and predictions of Aschenbach's development. He too is to become a moribund, rouged dandy; and he too, as an artist, is an outcast entertainer in a bourgeois garden.

The traveler in a mackintosh on the porch of the mortuary chapel, significantly Byzantine, inspires a vision of tropical swamps that constitutes the second motif. This monstrous, lush, and steaming landscape, in which tigers pounce, is ambivalent, suggesting both life and death. Recurring in Venice, which suffers a disease from such a swamp, it becomes the image of that place of outward beauty and hidden corruption. Aschenbach's recurrent thoughts of form, adding to this complex of city and swamp, make it plain that art is no less ambivalent. Though a result of order and the image of divine beauty, aesthetic form leads to contempt of morality and to excess. Venice, the triumph of form and the place of mephitic canals, becomes the image of Aschenbach's ideal and all his troubles. Socrates, telling

223

young Phaedrus of a beauty at once worldly and divine, is a fitting parallel, recurrent in Aschenbach's thought.

Tadzio, the object of senile passion, is the final embodiment of what the other elements have implied. The concentrate of an artist's desire, Tadzio has beauty; but like that of Venice, the swamp, and art, that beauty hides disease and death, which, although implicit in all these images, hold promise of life, as the references to Narcissus and Hyacinthus and the final gesture of the boy suggest. Wading in the waters, a "pale and lovely Summoner," he points outward toward an "immensity of richest expectation." Greater than the interweaving motifs that grow and deposit their accumulations in his person, Tadzio includes the ambivalent meanings of the story: the condition of art and of the artist, the decay of beautiful Europe, and the condition of man, compelled by Eros and Thanatos, abandonment and discipline.

Anticipating *Death in Venice,* "The Dead" illustrates not only the "structural rhythm" Stephen talks about in the Circe episode of *Ulysses* but incremental variation. *Dubliners,* of which "The Dead" is the last and best story, concerns the paralysis and death of Joyce's country and moments of self-realization on the part of his moribund or immature heroes. The book finds its climax during the course of this story in the party given by Aunts Kate and Jane Morkan. As we soon discover, their party is an embodiment of death and all the people there are living dead, though each has some connection with life and at least the possibility of living if not much opportunity for it. The image of snow in connection with this party and these guests gradually accumulates the principal meanings, and as it acquires them gives them back to context. The expansion of this thematic image is exemplary.

224

The time is Christmas, season of birth and of the year's death. As Gabriel Conroy, the principal figure, enters the house, his aunts observe that he must be "perished alive" from cold. "A light fringe of snow lay like a cape on the shoulders of his overcoat and like toecaps on the toes of his goloshes." Outside the air is cold yet fragrant in contrast with the deathly festivities within as Mary Jane plays her academy piece on the piano and aunts "toddle" about. Later, after his encounter with Miss Ivors, who leaves the party, almost successfully repudiating death, Gabriel thinks: " How pleasant it would be to walk out alone, first along by the river and then through the park. The snow would be lying on the branches of the trees and forming a bright cap on the top of the Wellington Monument. How much more pleasant it would be there than at the supper-table." About to commence a speech commending the past, Gabriel thinks again of the snow and the pure air out there in the park: "The Wellington Monument wore a gleaming cap of snow that flashed westward." The recurrence of snow and of the Wellington Monument begins to claim our attention. As the guests leave with more goodnights than realism would require, Mary Jane observes that snow is "general all over Ireland"; even the statue of Dan O'Connell, the liberator, has patches of snow on it. Safe at last in the Gresham Hotel, Gabriel and Gretta, his wife, go to bed, but, wakeful and shattered by a sudden awareness of himself, he sees and hears the falling snow: "His soul swooned as he heard the snow falling faintly through the universe and faintly falling, like the descent of their last end, upon all the living and the dead."

This recurrent image, taking what it carries from context and tradition, sometimes supports the meaning of the party and sometimes all that seems its opposite. Since snow is a form of water, a tradi-

225

tional image of life, it holds the possibility of thawing. Ambivalent, therefore, it may hold suggestions of life as well as the death to which its coldness and whiteness appear to confine it.

Of the peripheral images which help to determine these relationships, Gabriel's "goloshes" are important. Designed for keeping out water and snow, these articles point to his character. He even insists that his wife wear them although she prefers to walk unprotected in the slush: "The next thing he'll buy me," she says, "will be a diving suit." Like the macintosh carried by Lenehan in "Two Gallants," an earlier story, or the brown macintosh that becomes a motif of *Ulysses,* Gabriel's goloshes, fixing his hostility to water and snow, prove snow's connection with life, which, as we have seen, attracts him now and again. Another of these peripheral images is the cold in the head: "Everybody has colds," says Aunt Kate. Going home in the snow, Gretta caught one the year before; and this year Bartell D'Arcy, the tenor, is too hoarse to sing. "Mr. D'Arcy doesn't like the snow," says Aunt Kate; but since he is one of the least deathly people at that party, his dislike, emphasizing the deathliness of snow, strengthens that aspect of the ambivalent image.

By its whiteness snow is connected with Lily, the caretaker's daughter, whose name is the first word in the story. That this is not accidental is shown by the flower's traditional connections. Not only for funerals, the lily is for Easter as well. When Lily brings Gabriel three potatoes (roots, seeds, and images of Ireland), she offers life to his deadness. By its whiteness snow offers contrast to Mr. Browne, who, as he says, is "all brown," and who, as Aunt Kate observes, seems "everywhere." Since Joyce has associated brown with decay and death throughout the book, Mr. Browne, issuing out into the cold to fetch a cab, lends snow a kind of vitality. As it lies fresh, white, and cold in Phoenix Park and by the river, obvious signs of resurrection and life, Gabriel carves a "fat brown goose" indoors. That this object, which collects and carries all the meanings of the party, is opposite to the "wild geese" who fled Ireland for foreign parts is suggested by the lady who, when offered a wing by carving Gabriel, refuses it.

In spite of all those goloshes and colds in the head, therefore, snow takes on the color of life and reflects it upon the ambiguous narrative. Gretta's lover, fearless of rain, may have caught his death of cold from melted snow in that garden long ago; but although dead, he is more nearly alive at the end of the story than Gabriel, confronting his own inadequacy. His tremendous final vision of the falling snow, which seems at first glance his union with all the dead, seems to prove on closer inspection an acceptance of death as part of life. Like Thomas Mann's Hans Castorp, who also has his vision in the snow, Gabriel, losing his old identity, may emerge mature from his shattering experience. Leaving goloshes behind, he may go for a walk next morning in Phoenix Park where the Wellington Monument, at once phallic and funereal, may remind him of the nature of things as he passes by. The image of snow carries these meanings to us as well. The last of a recurrent series, which has gradually gathered contradictory meanings, the final image, having received and united them, offers them to our sensibilities for penetration. In traditional fiction, narrative and characters assume the weight of meanings, and images, if there at all, are there to embellish it. But in Joyce's symbolist story, images by a grand "consult" among themselves and with action and character carry the heavier burden. If, attending to action and character alone, we ignore these images, we miss the vision entirely—as those did who used to think Joyce a naturalist.

It is plain that structure, which is partly determined by narrative line and the development of character, is served no less by thematic elaboration of images, which by bringing part together with part

227

and by uniting them at last helps bring them into such harmony that the whole, as Joyce would say, has radiance. Not all particulars of "The Dead" are centered by the snow. Some of them, like the story of the hospitable monks in their coffins, agree with the general idea of death rather than with death's ambivalent image. But sometimes even such unlikely materials as Gabriel's story of his grandfather's horse, who, fascinated by King Billy's statue, walks round and round it, are brought under the command of the recurrent image. This story, which suggests Ireland's political condition, takes its place in the expanding system by relationship with Miss Ivors, the statue of Dan O'Connell, the Wellington Monument, and, by indirection, the snow. Acting his story out, Gabriel "paced in a circle round the hall in his goloshes."

We are familiar with the thematic structure of *A Portrait of the Artist,* which, though more elaborate, is of this kind; and we may recall some of the recurring materials that help make *Ulysses* coherent: the interwoven themes of tea, hat, and water and the parallel of Moses. I think it safe to say that most great novels of our time depend for unity and shape upon such rhythms. Like the works of Mann, *The Sound and the Fury* must be read twice or else, though moved, we may miss the devices that move us and create unity of effect from materials that might seem loosely joined. On second reading we find part linked to part by elaborated themes of tree, mirror, watch, water, and flower—to mention only a few. Benjy's jimson weed develops into Quentin's honeysuckle and into the broken narcissus at last. For Quentin at Harvard the mixed odors of rain and honeysuckle "came to symbolize night and unrest" as the odor of verbena, in the story of that name, comes to hold for young Sartoris the ambiguous message of the South. Developing themes in

The Sound and the Fury help to assure the symphonic relationship of the four parts, which, taken together, are another example of the great rhythm Forster could not find.

Poets too have used recurrent imagery. In Eliot's "Prufrock," room, street, evening, sea, hair, window, small animals, and many other things musically recur. In Stevens's "Sea Surface Full of Clouds," effects are established and structure affirmed by the variants of an image of chocolate, now rosy, now musky, and by a changing refrain in French. Yeats's archetypal tower, joining poem to poem, acquires meanings as it reappears in new contexts until Yeats could say, "I declare this tower is my symbol." While retaining earlier meanings, each poem has added something new to the capacious image, and when the tower appears for the last time in "The Black Tower," the garrison of that refuge defends all that Yeats esteemed. An effect of this expanding recurrence is to make great separate poems seem parts of a greater whole.

As symbol can serve structure, so structure can serve as symbol. To be sure, there is no necessary connection between the structure of a symbol and that of what it symbolizes, but structures as well as images or actions can embody thought and feeling. By structure I mean important framework or contributing shape. Although this may bring significant form to mind, I mean another thing entirely. Form is all the parts together, and its significance, different from their sum, is their creation; whereas structure is but the most considerable of parts. Metaphor: if literary form is a house, words are bricks, images are windows and doors, themes are corridors, and the steel framework is structure, which E. M. Forster calls pattern or "what causes us to see the book as a whole." Emerging from plot or theme, pattern, he continues, is an agent of meaning, unity, and enduring beauty. James's *Ambassadors* or "pattern triumphant" has the shape of an hourglass with Paris at the slender waist and with Chad and Strether shifting sands at the larger extremities.

Before coming to such large expressive frames, I pause awhile at component structures, which, though smaller than Forster's hourglass, are none the less meaningful. Among these I include rhythms, fragments, ambiguities, tricks of grammar or syntax, and the like.

Whether taken as recurrence of theme, arrangement of words in a sentence, or repetitive pattern, rhythm is plainly significant. Mrs. Dalloway, sitting and sewing, embodies death—as we learn from the allusion to *Cymbeline*—but the rhythm of Virginia Woolf's prose, more difficult to define yet felt more immediately, supports that allusion by feeling and corroborates the images of barking dog, "far away barking and barking," and the waves. When in his *Journal* Gerard Hopkins says, "I noticed from the cliff how the sea foots or toes the shore . . . now with a push and flow, now slacking, returning to stress and pulling back," he suggests by the movement of his prose what he is talking about. Of larger rhythmical patterns Dylan Thomas's "force that through the green fuse drives the flower" is a fine example. This poem of life and death suggests their process not only by ambiguities of "quicksand," of "sheet" (which includes winding sheet, bed sheet, the sail of Theseus, and writing paper), and of "crooked worm" (which, although phallic, includes tomb and writing finger), but also by rhythm. The third line of each stanza, shorter than the rest, implies fall as the other lines imply the rise that must precede it:

> The force that through the green fuse drives the flower
> Drives my green age; that blasts the roots of trees
> Is my destroyer.

230

Harmonious with sense, this rhythm alone presents all Thomas had to say: that life is rising and falling, and that, as the tone implies, we might make the best of it. The rhythm is not the poem, but of all its elements rhythm is the most important and nearest to the composite effect in effect.

Such rhythm is important shape at its plainest. Shapelessness, however, can be no less eloquent, as the ends of *The Waste Land* and *A Portrait of the Artist* prove. That this novel suddenly declines from the triumph its course predicts and, avoiding bangs, ends feebly in whimpers from a diary is the most astonishing thing about it. Asking the reason of that, we must conclude, I think, that the confusion of this diary, as carefully planned as the order of the rest, is there to create feelings and ideas for which no shape but shapelessness would do. By terminal chaos Joyce suggests that Stephen's triumph, less than we have been led to expect, is negative, that desire for art is an imperfect substitute for capacity. Centered in himself, as the form of a diary also suggests, Stephen lacks an effectual center for composing things. Fragments of diary, embodying and presenting his condition, predict the disappointment that the first chapter of *Ulysses* confirms. It is not until his meeting with Mr. Bloom that Stephen finds use for his elaborate aesthetic and fulfills his promise. That Eliot's promise, fulfilled in *Ash Wednesday* and *Four Quartets,* is still prevented in *The Waste Land* is shown by an ending not altogether dissimilar to that of the *Portrait.* A mess of quotations from Dante, *Pervigilium Veneris,* Gérard de Nerval, Thomas Kyd, and the Upanishads serves the purpose of Stephen's diary. These "fragments" not only shore up the ruins of fishing Tiresias with memories of culture but present his spiritual failure. Perhaps the most discouraging thing about the poem is its shapeless ending.

As revealing as fragments, ambiguities may present inner contra-

231

dictions for which the rest of the form is inadequate. Hopkins provides the best examples of these in his terrible sonnets. "Ware of a world" in "Spelt from Sibyl's Leaves" may mean aware of a world, beware of a world, or else, becoming a noun, the wares of a world of black and white, right or wrong that has "pashed" all dapple. Since that world is moral rather than beautiful or else not this one but the next, his conflicts appear by the aid of the ambiguity not only aesthetic and neural but theological as well. "Carrion Comfort" owes part of its terror to systematic ambiguities involving "(my God!) my God." The questions with which Yeats liked to end his poems are equally ambivalent. Seeming statements bringing assurance and resolving conflicts, they acquire uncertainty when questioned at the end. "Among School Children" becomes less final than we thought before feeling its punctuation.

Ups and downs, the business of ironists, carry Eliot's comment on J. Alfred Prufrock, whose inflation by the moment of his greatness is followed by the snicker of the eternal footman. Stephen Dedalus was such another as the inflations and deflations of the *Portrait* make plain. As he approaches the beach of his epiphany, his soul soars in ecstasy: "An ecstasy of flight made radiant his eyes and wild his breath and tremulous and wild and radiant his windswept limbs," a levitation that precedes Icarian descent: "O, Cripes, I'm drownded!" His rapture of light and roses after the experience of the wading girl is followed by watery tea and yellow dripping in the ignominious kitchen. Such ascents and descents project Joyce's ironic contemplation of an earlier self.

That distortions of syntax can be as expressive as those of line or mass in the painting of Picasso or the sculpture of Moore is demonstrated so abundantly in the poems of Mallarmé and Hopkins that examples seem unnecessary. The latter's triumphs of grammar,

232

though less conspicuous, are more fascinating; for at times his poetry almost seems its grammar, which, carrying the principal load, becomes a form for feeling and idea. "No worst," the opening phrase of a terrible sonnet, is the grimmest thing in a poem that seems at first to depend upon grim images. Despairing of a superlative, Hopkins is condemned by this phrase to perpetual comparatives, worse following worse without the assurance that the worst provides. His "cliffs of fall . . . no-man-fathomed" are more frightful and more persuasively unfathomable by the deliberateness of their grammatical anticipation.

A passionate grammarian, impatient with the limits of existing forms, Hopkins invented a tense to supply and express his need. "Have fair fallen," the opening of his sonnet on Henry Purcell, is at once novel, exact, and suggestive. This future perfect imperative, a form unknown to Allen and Greenough, is suitable for last judgments, especially on the invincibly ignorant, and for the poet's reservations, hopes, and charity for one who, though English and musical, was Protestant—like those lovely British boys of the lost *Eurydice*. Using the same tense and mood for them, Hopkins prays that God "have heard" prayers at that "awful overtaking."

To pass from tense to interjection is less of a descent than it may appear. We know that words are symbols, but "ah!" is improved beyond all normal possibilities by place and usage in "God's Grandeur," one of the least terrible of Hopkins's sonnets. Brooding over the world "with warm breast and with ah! bright wings," the dove is raised above custom not only by chiasmatic alliteration but by this sublime interruption. Directly expressive of ecstasy, "ah!" is also a symbol of the inexpressible, and, by deferring for a moment the construction's end, it makes bright wings brighter than we can imagine, brighter if possible than the "inexplicable splendour" of

233

Eliot's church. The feeling of the sonnet, concentrated in this charged word suddenly flames out—as if from the Leyden jar of the opening lines. Apprehending what it stores and discharges is a test of sensibility.

Tone, dependent on diction, syntax, and connotation, is the clearest embodiment of feeling and intention. Yeats's "maybe" in "Adam's Curse," the first poem of his renewal, marks his discovery of common speech or what he was to call "natural words in natural order" as noble mask. Such "nonchalance of hand," associated with great artists or aristocrats, is separated from commonness by a suitable distance and by mixture with "all that high breeding of poetical style, where there is nothing ostentatious, nothing crude, no breath of parvenu or journalist." Charged with "a nobility, a passionate austerity," this composite speech had for him the "lofty and severe quality" of his new desire, and its tone, his greatest construction, carries all that is alien to those attics where doors are shut on nonchalance and obscurity, embodying the profound, becomes its symbol.

Frameworks or central structures are elements so large that, like central images, they sometimes approximate the forms they support. For that reason it is convenient to defer skeletal structures of the more intricate kind to the next chapter, where, while considering form, I shall notice the structure of *Absalom, Absalom!* Here we shall have to be contented with two smaller, though no less important, examples, both poems, one by Stevens, the other by Yeats.

"Earthy Anecdote," the first poem of *Harmonium,* is about bucks and a firecat in Oklahoma. Every time the bucks clatter over that remote landscape, the firecat stands bristling in the way, until bucks and cat, tired at last, sleep. Their action brings many things to mind, Blake's Tiger, the life force, or Freud. If Oklahoma is the country of dreams, bucks are male, cats female; if the prevention of one by the other is what the reality principle offers, the poem celebrates things as they are. This interpretation of action and image is confirmed by a structure which embodies the same idea and all its attendant feelings. An introductory passage states the theme, which is illustrated by two actions: the first of bucks swerving to the right, then to the left because of the firecat. Then these actions and frustrations recur more swiftly than before, until the firecat closes his bright eyes and the bucks, though we are not told of their response, are free to clatter in straight lines or to rest. Exotic creatures, lack of reason, and strangeness of place add quality to a design of tensions and release which is that of daily living and no less mysterious.

The pattern of Yeats's "Who Goes With Fergus?" is equally symbolic. This early poem teases our curiosity as it quiets our anxieties by finality of shape in strange union with indeterminateness of sense; but the mystery is not so deep as William Empson in *Seven Types of Ambiguity* supposed. If we take the poem in the large context of what Yeats was obsessed with at this period, it becomes apparent that the opening question, which may seem invitation or warning, is invitation with implicit reservation maybe. Voyages of retreat from the cares of life to some island are a constant theme of Yeats's early poetry, "an old day-dream of my own." The poem before us seems another dream of exchanging the troubles of reality for insulation, and the trouble that invites it is love with all its hopes, fears, and moody brooding; for Yeats had known Maud Gonne a year or two by this time. In the peace of this island, the Land of Youth no doubt, adult responsibilities such as Fergus shirked will be replaced by dancing, games of war, poetry, and magic. The atmosphere, clearly maternal, except for paternal brazen cars, suggests regression, but our immediate concern is the structure of this poem. It begins with a question, the more effective for its uncertainty, and a question, as we have seen, is the embodiment of a feeling and attitude. This question is followed by a double chiasmus or crossing of separated elements, prepared for by the adjective "woven." The third line of the second stanza is hard and triumphant. After that by sound, rhythm, and sense the poem declines softly into a peace which, however, is not entirely without hint of disorder. If "white breast" and "dim sea," spondees, interrupt the relapse it is only to call attention to the comforts of mother. We have, then, the following structure: a question, expressive of uncertainty, an integrating chiasmus, a triumph, a decline, and an all but perfect peace, most passions put aside. Because we have known something like this pattern or find it possible, we respond. While our minds are occupied by the particulars of Yeats's problem, our feelings, more sensitive to such things than our minds, accept the structure these particulars compose or the shape and quality of an experience. Since, conditioned by what it gets from sense, tone, and rhythm, this shape alone corresponds to that experience, there is no other way of presenting it.

The Fur-lined Cup

*T*HAT form or the work itself is a symbol, though not agreed upon by all, is affirmed by respectable authority. Edmund Spenser's Archimago—surely a significant name—is an enchanter, who, assuming shapes and forms, causes visions; but more recent and less enigmatic approaches to what seems symbolic form might be more satisfactory, though not more pleasing. Clive Bell's "significant form" and Roger Fry's "expressive design," whereby "the spirit communicates its most secret and indefinable impulses," are supported, as we have observed, by Susanne K. Langer's "forms symbolic of human feeling." But the words of poets may seem more relevant. During the 1890s André Gide, a disciple of Mallarmé at the time, said that "a well-composed work is necessarily symbolic," and Yeats, proclaiming the poem "an intricate analogy," found "all forms," but those especially in which elements are musically related, "evoke indefinable and yet precise emotions." Hopkins had called poetry speech for inscape's sake and the poem a "shape" for contemplation.

This shape, like Keats's "Attic shape," is a "silent form" to tease us out of thought—and, in spite of Mrs. Langer—back into it. There it is, an object filled with potential meaning, to be interpreted by the reader, who, working by his lights, is also limited by the nature of the object, its sense and quality, for example, and by the internal relationships of such parts. Theme, structure, image, and rhythm, offering possibilities, help to limit his interpretation, and some of these elements may be so important that they all but determine it. Contributory meanings are not the poem, however; for that thing, a result of relationships, is its meaning. A significant form like a painting or a concerto, the poem presents what it is, aiming, as Thomas Mann observes, "always and consistently *to be* that of which it speaks."

The trouble with finding form symbolic, we already know, is that it seems to lack the context to which images and other parts owe their meaning or some of it. How a thing without such surroundings can be like a thing within them, in kind if not degree, is a question that reflecting a little should answer; for nothing is free from context. It may be that the context of a constituent part of the work is more literary than that of the form it helps to create, but, however unliterary the context of the work and however autonomous its appearance, it has surroundings that assist or limit our interpretation. What we know of the period in which it was composed, of the literary tradition to which it belongs, and of the author's habits or aims may function for the work as the work for its images. Our approach to a poem by Donne is necessarily different from that to a poem by Shelley. Each may be a document confronting us with its particulars, but each, like Comus with his rout, conducts a retinue of time, place, person, and fashion which, whatever our protests, we do not ignore. This inevitable accompaniment, moreover, is not only Donne's or

Shelley's but our own; for the faction we support projects its shadow round the text, and those protesting most, projecting more, are working in their shades. The miserable condition of humanity, bound to one law and to another born, was never more apparent.

A poem written in a symbolist period by one we know to be a symbolist carries these circumstances with it to mix, like the tide up a river, with our current and to create the troubled medium in which the poem swims as we observe it. My attitude toward Eliot is part of the context that enlarges and limits my reading of the ode to Harvard. But the context of a work is of less importance than that of a constituent image; for in a sense the work, as autonomous as it seems, owes more of its meaning and the better part to those relationships of part and part that we must make of what we can. Whatever its context, the work is also a text, and to interpret a thing that exists not only in time and place but by the internal stresses of its own arrangement we need the cooperation of history, self-awareness, sensibility, and analysis—knowledge of what we bring and what is there.

The account of symbolic form that I most applaud is the aesthetic theory of Stephen Dedalus in *A Portrait of the Artist* and *Stephen Hero*. Functioning in the narrative as a necessary part of a young aesthete's progress, this theory is an element in Joyce's design, but whether it was his own aesthetic or at least his own when young is not our present concern. What we want is light upon work as symbol, which Stephen's theory, abstracted from its place and abstracted again for convenience, may afford; for Stephen, starting from the artist's image of himself, shows how this "vital," personal matter becomes impersonal object, a composite of relationships, and a symbol.

Of the three kinds of art that Stephen arranges in a scale ascending from the personal to the impersonal, the last alone detains us.

239

Lyric art, the form by which the artist presents his image in relation to himself, is the lowest kind, a cry, "the simplest verbal vesture of an instant of emotion." Epic art, which presents the artist's image at an equal distance from himself and others, is a step toward the splendid detachment of dramatic art, in which the artist's personality has been refined out of existence. No longer around, the artist presents his image now in immediate relation to others, and of the three elements of the aesthetic transaction, the artist, the image, and the audience, only the latter two remain. "The esthetic image in the dramatic form," says Stephen, "is life purified in and reprojected from the human imagination." The surviving relationship between image, which has become what Eliot was to call the objective correlative, and audience is the theater of symbolism and our business. Free from the desire or loathing of "kinetic" art, the "static" object, facing its audience, invites contemplation.

That contemplative company proceeds to enjoy wholeness, harmony, and radiance, the three qualities of the dramatic object which correspond to the three stages of aesthetic apprehension. Confronted with beauty and careless of all else, the enchanted audience immediately sees the object as "selfbounded and selfcontained" against "the immeasurable background of space or time which is not it." The "simple sudden synthesis" by which wholeness is perceived precedes apprehension of harmony or "symmetry," as the young man has it in *Stephen Hero*. "In other words," he proceeds in the *Portrait;* "the synthesis of immediate perception is followed by the analysis of apprehension," as, passing "from point to point, led by its formal lines, you apprehend it as balanced part against part within its limits; you feel the rhythm of its structure. . . . Having first felt that it is *one* thing you feel now that it is a *thing*. You apprehend it as complex, multiple, divisible, separable, made up of its

240

parts, the result of its parts and their sum, harmonious." Or, as Stephen says in *Stephen Hero*: "The mind considers the object in whole and in part, in relation to itself and to other objects, examines the balance of its parts, contemplates the form of the object, traverses every cranny of the structure. So the mind receives the impression of the symmetry of the object," which is not only a closed system of interrelated parts but a thing related to other things. Composed of parts, which analysis reveals, the harmonious object is at once their "result" and their "sum." Since we have been persuaded that the whole is greater than the sum of its parts, his last observation may seem dangerously unorthodox; but Stephen is a logician as well as an aesthete and his whole, aesthetically greater than its parts as the word "result" allows, is also their logical sum.

The result of harmony or symmetry, however fearful, is radiance, the third and highest quality offered to our apprehension. Though radiance or what the articulated form presents seems symbolic suggestion, Stephen is at pains to distinguish between radiance and symbolism. The *claritas* of Saint Thomas, translated as radiance, "would lead you to believe that he had in mind symbolism or idealism," says Stephen, "the supreme quality of beauty being a light from some other world, the idea of which the matter was but the symbol." It is plain, however, that, while limiting symbol to Platonic transcendentalism, which, having rejected otherworldly beauty, he rejects, Stephen is far from rejecting the result of shape and relationship or the significance of form that we call symbolic. A passage in *Stephen Hero* makes this apparent:

After the analysis which discovers the second quality the mind makes the only logically possible synthesis and discovers the third quality. This is the moment which I call epiphany. First we recognise that the object is *one* integral thing, then we recognise that it is an organised composite

241

structure, a *thing* in fact: finally, when the relation of the parts is exquisite, when the parts are adjusted to the special point, we recognise that it is *that* thing which it is. Its soul, its whatness, leaps to us from the vestment of its appearance. The soul of the commonest object, the structure of which is so adjusted, seems to us radiant. The object achieves its epiphany.

Radiance is epiphany, which, in spite of worldly beauty, remained a more congenial term than symbol for Jesuistical Dedalus. It is not for want of other music that the procession of saints, martyrs, and Christian Brothers in *Ulysses,* showing forth praise to the Lord, chants "the introit in *Epiphania Domini* which beginneth *Surge, illuminare,*" from the Mass for January 6, the feast of the Epiphany. Arising and shining are what our symbols do.

Stephen's radiance or showing-forth is not unlike the "inscape" of Gerard Manley Hopkins, which may be defined as the essence or individuality of a thing that shines out from it; but whereas Stephen's radiance is Thomistic *quidditas* or whatness, Hopkins's inscape resembles the *haecceitas* or thisness of Duns Scotus. Though Thomas proceeds from principle to manifestation and Duns from manifestation to principle, their ends are the same. Thisness and whatness, whether proving God's grandeur or that of an artist, are alike in centering upon the object, which reveals what it is. A thing doing that is a symbol, and God and the artist are alike in having created it. The end of Stephen's aesthetic, as we know, is an image of the artist as a god who remains within, behind, beyond, or above his handiwork, "invisible, refined out of existence."

If the artist is a god, his works are worlds, and Stephen's "radiant body," however "ellipsoidal," becomes the "mundball" of *Finnegans Wake.* We admired Virginia Woolf's "globed compacted thing" during the pursuit of Hermes, but almost every author of our time em-

242

ploys that accurate metaphor or another like it. To achieve "the effect of a solid," Proust resolves in the last volume not only to build his book like a church but to "create it like a world, without over-looking those mysteries whose explanation is probably to be found only in other worlds." To E. M. Forster, Dostoyevsky's work seems a translucent globe; and James's *Ambassadors,* no longer an hour-glass, coheres "like a planet," swinging through the skies. Finding his zodiac changed to a sphere in "A Woman Young and Old," Yeats implies change from time to eternity and the work that causes it. In his *Essays* he had praised the "world" of imagination that "must grow consistent with itself, emotion . . . related to emotion by a system of ordered images" until it becomes "solid underfoot." According to "The Blood of the Walsungs," Mann finds a book "a little, all-embracing universe, into which one plunges and submerges oneself in order to draw nourishment out of every syllable." However mixed the metaphor, a world of sorts survives—though without the dryness, austerity, and solitude of Roger Fry's, in which "the mind is held in delighted equilibrium by the contemplation of the in-evitable relations of all parts of the whole, so that no need exists to make reference to what is outside the unity." The pursuit of art for art's sake made Fry more exclusive than Proust, who takes account of worlds besides his own, and far more exclusive than the metaphor allows; for a world, however self-subsistent it seems and however impressive its internal arrangements, is part of a solar system, of a galaxy, of a cluster of galaxies, and so on till space curves round again.

"It is the *mundo* of the imagination," says Wallace Stevens, in whose "Primitive Like an Orb" the "central poem" of his desire becomes the world, and the world that poem. Commonly, however, the poem is the "supreme fiction" toward which he makes his elegant notes, and since the root of fiction, like that of fact, is creating or giving shape, fiction is as good a figure as world for the wholeness of radiant form.

The immediate apprehension of wholeness that Stephen speaks of is confirmed not only by poets's metaphors but by the propositions of Gestalt psychologists, who cannot see parts for the wholes of which experience consists. At once process and product, a Gestalt, according to Wolfgang Köhler, an authority, is "a concrete individual and characteristic entity, existing as something detached and having a shape or form as one of its attributes." It is an organization which, though made of parts, is seen as a shape from which the parts gain virtue and lacking which they are nothing; for it is the figure, immediately perceived, that carries meaning and not its elements. Without its ground or context, however, the shape would neither stand out nor show forth. "Our reality," says Kurt Koffka, another authority, "is not a mere collection of elemental facts, but consists of units in which no part exists by itself, where each part points beyond itself and implies a larger whole."

Facts and significance cease to be two concepts belonging to different realms, since a fact is always a fact in an intrinsically coherent whole. We could solve no problem of organization by solving it for each point separately, one after the other; the solution had to come for the whole. Thus we see how the problem of significance is closely bound up with the problem of the relation between the whole and its parts. It has been said: The whole is more than the sum of its parts. It is more correct to say that the whole is something else than the sum of its parts, because summing is a meaningless procedure, whereas the whole-part relationship is meaningful.

What he says provides an easy transition from wholeness to harmony and the analysis Stephen applauds for this stage of apprehension.

244

The apprehension of wholeness, assuring worth and the possibility of meaning, calls for analysis to justify our impression of organic coherence, and to fit this summons we may change the metaphor of world for that of little world or organism, a body that invites dissection. Our analytic knife, uncovering liver, lights, bag, and tube, may disclose their relationship, development, and function, or what is wrong with them, and these, of course, are the objects of critical search. For that reason this metaphor seems better for those who, following Stephen's attractive process, as we are doing, seek not Gestalten alone but the causes of experience. Such formidable analysts as New Critics see poems as organisms; and the metaphor is central in *Process and Reality*, a "philosophy of organism." Although acclaiming feeling and concrescence, however, Whitehead finds analysis inadequate. Each ultimate unit of reality may be a "cell-complex," as his metaphor demands, but those cells are "not analysable into components"; for "when we analyse the novel thing, we find nothing but the concrescence." While critics of the analytic school, finding organisms aggregates of parts and eminently dissectable, take them into theaters for brilliant anatomies, Whitehead, remaining out of doors, prefers whole and lively bodies, whose excellence, identical with shape, is not referable to parts. T. E. Hulme, another philosopher of development and of those "vital complexities" that the romantic movement commended, also rejects analysis at the end of the famous essay on romanticism and classicism:

Now the characteristic of the intellect is that it can only represent complexities of the mechanical kind. It can only make diagrams, and diagrams are essentially things whose parts are separate one from another. The intellect always analyses—when there is a synthesis it is baffled. That is why the artist's work seems mysterious. The intellect can't represent it. This is a necessary consequence of the particular nature of the intellect

245

and the purposes for which it is formed. It doesn't mean that your synthesis is ineffable, simply that it can't be definitely stated.

Now this is all worked out in Bergson, the central feature of his whole philosophy. It is all based on the clear conception of these vital complexities which he calls "intensive" as opposed to the other kind which he calls "extensive," and the recognition of the fact that the intellect can only deal with the extensive multiplicity. To deal with the intensive you must use intuition.

Who will go follow Stephen now in view of these objections? For explicators that is an awkward question, but the case is not so desperate as it seems; for, not only centering our minds upon the text, analysis, occupying a place between immediate apprehensions, improves them. Placing analysis where he did in his process shows Stephen's estimate of an approach that goes hand in hand with feeling, a little behind it now and now a little ahead. Guided by feeling or leading it along, analysis calls attention to parts that might escape us and to relationships among them. That such parts move us unawares is proved by our initial response, but the awareness given by analysis may make our second response wider, deeper, and richer than the first. It may be true, as Koffka, Whitehead, and Hulme maintain, that analysis is inadequate, suited only to noting parts and summing them up, and that there seems a gap between sum and whole; but as Saint Thomas, it is said, having reached the limits of rational inquiry, resorted at last to mystical intuition for its meaning, so the critic, after his enlightening exercise must call upon intuition of a more secular variety. His job, not only to indicate what might be passed over, to explore the relations of masses, to bring memory to bear upon a thing in its surroundings, is to call upon experience and taste in order to salute the radiance analysis cannot accost.

From one point of view radiance is the feeling and idea we get

246

from form, and from the other—and this is more important—it is what the object presents. If we get less than that, we are inadequate, and if we get more, irrelevant or too ingenious. Not more nor less than what the object is but only that must be the critic's end, however vain his hope of reaching it. Of the three stages of his apprehension, harmony with its analysis demands the greatest space; for we talk of what we can. Our necessity and its common disappointment are illustrated by Susanne Langer's descent in *Feeling and Form* from formal principles to the analysis of a poem by Goldsmith. After such celebrations of form one might expect more than the discovery of theme, an element among many that compose the form.

Goldsmith brings "Sailing to Byzantium" to mind as a suitable test of Stephen's equipment. That this poem, one of the greatest lyrics, has the virtue of wholeness is plain at first reading, but the harmony of parts that creates this effect, though apparent enough, awaits analysis for disclosure of much a casual reading passes by. Useful, discursive, and extensive, analysis is but another way of saying close reading, which any man, in or out of schools, may practice if moderately bright and willing to take the trouble; so let us explicate the text.

"That," the first and maybe the most significant word of the poem, sets tone, attitude, and situation while opening the drama. A distancing demonstrative, it is charged with the ideal of "Ille" and his mask; a gesture in the grand manner, it implies not only separation from the contemptible but the impersonality of an artist's desire, and, combining these uneasy opposites of contempt and choice with triumphant finality of tone, introducing while embodying ambivalence, it seems no more beginning than end—as we know upon returning from the end of the poem, with our load, to begin again. Since poems are made of words, as Mallarmé observed, attention to one of them is good for you, but if you attend to each, there is neither space enough nor time; for analysis, defined as extensive, extends too far for convenience, and it becomes necessary to neglect and choose. So choosing, we observe a disparity between old men and youthful lovers, whether crowding mackerel or singing birds, which seems to center in a conflict of "fish, flesh, or fowl" with the word "commend" that follows this commonplace trinity and, by inappropriate grandeur and distance, makes the triteness of those beasts instructive. Their summer song, both sensual and passing, is alien to unaging, intellectual monuments. At once ironic and grand, those monuments, suggesting the monolithic character of the poem, anticipate other permanent things: mosaics, golden artifacts, and heaven, which, though out of time, are also its memorials. The dissonance of "young" and "song," of "seas" and "dies," relieved by the terminal rhyme, echoes the conflicts of substance and the promise of relief. Restless phrasing, conspiring with sound and sense, troubles the rhythm until the last couplet calms us by its sweep.

The aged man of the second stanza, producer of unaging monuments, is their opposite, like his scarecrowed stick. His singing, unlike the sensual singing of mackerel, is that of soul or unaging intellect; but singing schools and their meager monuments, implying schools of poets or critics, complicate soul and the impersonality of song by ego or mutual admiration. These bitter thoughts, made nastier by the monumental dissonance of "magnificence," lead to the great finalities of "therefore," the important word of this stanza, and of the rhymed couplet in which it stands. He has left that place of lovers, age, and minor poets for a monumental town, and as we rise again at the end of a process, his voyage means success.

Dead and parts of a mosaic, sages in purgatorial fire, reminding us of old men and unaging intellect, are asked to abandon their

248

provisional eternities for perning in gyres or, as Yeats's system of
the moon explains, reentering time. That these gyring masters, at
once in time and out of it, can instruct souls in song and, consuming
desire by form, bring us to art or another kind of eternity is no
more than monuments have suggested; and that Yeats, having
achieved such eternity, is still sick with desire, implies arrival at a
porch or lobby and not the place itself. Plainly not there as yet, he
may dream of what the last stanza discloses.

Once free from a situation that is neither here nor there, the poet
hopes for peace in "forms" that combine eternity with time, such
forms as goldsmiths make of changeless metal, having purged it in
their fires and hammered it. No longer a person but a form which,
though resembling no natural thing, recalls objects of an old man's
sick desire, the creature sings still another song. The golden bough
on which it sits, made from Frazer's book and Turner's picture, is
a passport to the Elysian Fields and all fertility as the sitting form,
though singing of past, present, and future, presents timelessness.
That it sings to lords and ladies suggests all that is foreign to the
time from which it comes and something of the personality it has
otherwise escaped. No dissonance mars its pleasure; nor does shadow
diminish the fullness of a moon now at its fifteenth night, as gold
and artifice imply. Byzantium, the meeting place of East and West,
becomes the concord of all opposites.

In this organization part is linked to part by stanzaic structure,
logical progress, recurrence of theme, and conflict. Parallel to the
others in rhythmic design, each stanza rises from anxieties to a little
triumph at the end, a design of downs and ups that, recurring on a
grander scale, proves structure for a whole in which three troubled
stanzas are followed by a triumphant fourth. A logical progression
which, occupying the mind and pleasing it, creates feelings of unity,

249

ties each stanza to the next until, concluding what feels like a syllogism, we cry "Q.E.D." Reappearing themes, not only that of song, which, as we have noticed, appears with variation in each of the parts, but those of bird and artifact, improve our impression of coherence and massiveness. Establishing another pattern, conflicts of life and death, sense and soul, youth and age, the personal and the objective, time and eternity, nature and art, flux and permanence compose a drama in which even such quarrels as that of stanza with tone play a part, less obvious perhaps than the great quarrel of Eros and Thanatos, but not less affective. Byronic ottava rima, the stanza of Yeats's choice, assumes an unaccustomed grandeur in his hands while preserving memories of a comic past. Diction, ranging from the grand to the commonplace, and tones, ranging from irony and bitterness to nobility and equanimity, add their tensions to the great design of incompatibles.

But the conflicts, great and small, that compose this drama are settled at the end by agreement of image, rhythm, and tone, and we are left in what Yeats once called "measured quietude," the sweeter for the troubles that precede it. The golden bird, bringing artifact together with the natural bird of the first stanza, ends all conflicts of nature and art, sense and soul, life and death, while its song unites eternity with time. Such fusions of idea, however, are surpassed by those great assurances of rhythm, sound, and tone which, although less logical than technical, compose our feelings at the end.

However autonomous this tight organization seems, it depends for part of its success upon things outside it. "Perne in a gyre" is private and meaningless unless we know *A Vision* or some commentary. Knowledge of Yeats's life and all his habits, hates, and preferences improves our understanding of the text, and if we are historians, so do our knowledge of the mechanical bird maintained in Byzantium by the emperor Theophilus and our awareness of the literary tradition in which the poem takes its place. Baudelaire's artificial paradise and Eliot's Chinese jar, moving in its stillness, though parallel, are less important here than Marvell's "Garden," Keats's "Ode to a Nightingale," and closest of all, his "Ode on a Grecian Urn." Providing a closer setting, Yeats's other poems cannot be ignored; for without "Byzantium," a later expansion, "The Lake Isle of Innisfree," an earlier and less mature attempt, and the dancer, at once dead and alive, in "The Double Vision of Michael Robartes" both holy city and golden bird would lack something of the richness the literate find in them.

Emerging from these elements and references, the theme, apparent at last, is a union of dying and hope of heaven with an aesthetic parallel, the making of song. Analysis, which brings us to this point, cannot go beyond it, and my attempt, as good as most, has all the inadequacies that Hulme and Whitehead foretold. Though plainly incomplete and failing to exhaust its matter or to prevent other analyses, whether better or worse, mine may call attention to some of the parts and their relationships and account in part for our first impression of wholeness, but it fails to explain the poem's glory. The exercise of wits is pleasing, but we must know the radiance of form.

For that, rising like Saint Thomas, we call upon intuition or, now instructed to a point, upon impression again. It is evident that radiance or the composite of idea and feeling that the poem as a whole shows forth has some connection with life and death. Far from being a sanctuary for extinct birds, Byzantium is as vital as a place can be, and though presenting golden death, the poem glows with brighter fires than goldsmiths use or sages come from. The pattern of living, dying, and creating—the vital process of conflict and reconciliation—not there for its own sake, is there to serve a vision of art.

251

An example of the work of art, the poem, concentrating the feeling and idea of art's nature, is its symbol. Although many poems nowadays are about poems or poets at work, "Sailing to Byzantium," differing from most, is not only about art but a revelation of timelessness in time or art's essential.

Revealing that, the poem must also create what Yeats calls the semblance of peace if he and many other poets are right about the effect of poems. Speaking of logic, natural law, and art, three ways of knowing, Yeats finds peace the end of art; Dylan Thomas refers to "that momentary peace which is a poem"; and Wallace Stevens's form is a "transparence" bringing peace. Aristotle's catharsis, Milton's "all passions spent," and I. A. Richards's fancy of ordering impulses that quarreled once among themselves support this idea of art's effect. The stasis of Stephen Dedalus and his "enchantment of the heart" seem other ways of putting it; and Eliot, speaking of that Chinese jar in *Four Quartets,* must have had something like this in mind as he discursively pursues discourse beyond itself to image and form:

> Words, after speech, reach
> Into the silence. Only by the form, the pattern,
> Can words or music reach
> The stillness, as a Chinese jar still
> Moves perpetually in its stillness.

These excellent words, which could introduce "Sailing to Byzantium," refer to something like the purged images of "Byzantium," whether dome, mosaics of dancing floor, or golden bird, that, uniting "furies of complexity," make us forget for a moment the tormented seas around us.

My apprehension of what "Sailing to Byzantium" radiates, although supported by parallel and authority, seems no less inadequate than the analysis of harmony that preceded it. It may be that I lack wits for this enterprise or else the system of steps that Stephen commends is better adapted to the apprehension of form than of a form. The works of Susanne Langer, too, almost persuade me that it is easier to talk about forms in general than poems in particular. My admiration of these aestheticians remains undiminished, but I conclude that Stephen's system, however close to art, is not a method; for practice, unable to follow in his steps, must combine intuitions of radiance with analysis at each stage of apprehension in the hope of escaping the meagerness of each alone. Maybe the "organic rhythms" or forms—"the embodiment of the imagination, that neither desires nor hates, because it has done with time, and only wishes to gaze upon some reality" that Yeats, no mean critic, refers to in his "Symbolism of Poetry"—are beyond analysis though not altogether beyond impression. "Although you can expound an opinion," he says, "or describe a thing . . . you cannot give a body to something that moves beyond the senses. . . . The form of sincere poetry . . . must have perfections that escape analysis." That some synthesis of analysis and impression, however, may approximate the effect of the sincerest poetry or, like a metaphor, correspond to it, must remain a hope else critics, discouraged by their tools, can shut up shop.

They may order these things better in France; so let us consider one of those *explications de texte* for which the French are famous to see how they attend to form and radiance. The "demonstration" of Paul Valéry's "Cimetière Marin" by Gustave Cohen for his course in method at the Sorbonne should prove exemplary. Although his "hypothesis" about design and substance seems less hypothetical than assured, his approach, admirably systematic, is excellently clear. "A sonorous frame surrounding floating images," the great poem belongs in method, he says, to the tradition of Baudelaire and Mallarmé, owing "correspondences" to one and "hermetism" or linked suggestions to the other. Consequent obscurity is increased by a condensation peculiar to Valéry; for the twenty years of thought that produced this poem "charged" it with meanings.

The images that veil yet reveal this philosophical experience—veil for common readers but reveal to explicators in their chairs—are the Midi, its sun at noon, the cemetery at Sète, and the scintillating sea that dominates the place. Elaborated like "leitmotivs," these images are enriched by contributory similes, such as that of fruit melting in the mouth, and by significant adjectives, such as *pur,* which means the absolute. Neglecting Mallarméian suggestiveness, Professor Cohen, a specialist in mediaeval literature, assigns definite meanings to these images. Midi and the sun, representing the *pur,* are static, eternal, and inhuman; whereas the sea, representing being in opposition to the nonbeing of South and sun, is movement, change, and time. The meditator's monologue concerns a choice between these opposites, and his consciousness becomes the theater of a metaphysical drama in four acts. Tempted for awhile to unite with motionless nonbeing in a kind of mystical abandonment, the speaker discovers the mobility of being and all its attractiveness, already suggested to us by certain adjectives and verbs of the first and second stanzas. Debate among the tombs weighs the charms of motionless dead and moving worm, until, choosing movement, life, and creation, and emerging, like Valéry, from ten years of silence, the thinker, rejecting the Midi, becomes one with glittering sea, that profound fluid which, with its dovelike or marauding sails, occupies the first stanza and the last.

Historical at times, Professor Cohen brings Valéry's life, ideas, and other poems to bear upon the text, compares the thoughts of famous philosophers with those of Valéry's thinker, and places the poem not

254

only in the symbolist tradition but in the graveyard school; yet his main concern is the text with all its nouns, verbs, and adjectives. Proceeding through the stanzas one by one, he explains all but what selection prevents. His interests seem more rational than aesthetic, however; for though he admits that a poem is not a discourse, that it reports no more than the "frisson" and rhythm of twenty years of thought, he does his best to make an essay of his poem. Elucidating what Richards would call the prose sense or, like Urban, expanding the symbol, Cohen abstracts an element of the poem for display, and the structure he notices is that of a philosophical process. His analysis of that may clear up much that might have remained obscure, but, revealing the limitations of analysis, it does nothing to show poem as poem, as Valéry's comments, published as an introduction to Cohen's commentary, hint.

The poet, who was present at this academic exercise, is pleased, he says, at having work of his exposed among classics before a blackboard, but, however tolerant of hypothesis and however polite, he insists, as his italics show, that for him *"il n'y a pas de vrai sens d'un texte."* Neither critic nor author turned explicator can have the final word. Thinking of what he intended, the author allows his intention to hide what he has made, which, independent now, is another thing entirely; yet to Cohen's admirable attempt he may as well append his own. When he wrote the poem, he was obsessed with a craftsman's ideal of perfection; and for him the poem, a victory over reluctant syntax, harmony, and idea, was a "world of reciprocal relations," opposite to the world of prose which loses itself in its ideas. The poetic world, established "by the number, or rather, by the density of images, figures, consonances, dissonances, by the linking of rhythms and turns," cannot be reduced to prose without diminishing it. "Poetic necessity is inseparable from sensible form; and

255

thoughts, announced or suggested by the text of a poem, are not at all the sole or important object of the discourse—but *means* which, working together *on an equal footing* with sounds, cadences, rhythm, and ornament, provoke and sustain a certain tension or exaltation, creating a *world* in us—or a *state of being* that is altogether harmonious." When asked what he intended to say in a poem, he answers that he did not wish to say but to make.

"Le Cimetière Marin," which came to him as a decasyllabic pattern of six verses, demanding certain contrasts and correspondences and, later, a subject to fill the pattern out, is a creation of something from nothing, like that of God in Genesis. Once established in his mind, this form "permitted me to distribute in my work what it ought to contain of the sensible, the affective, and the abstract in order to suggest, when transported into the poetic universe, the meditation of a certain *self*." Since the ideas with which this self or speaker is concerned do not play the same rôle or have values of the same kind as ideas in prose, the introduction of Zeno, for example, was not to present the ideas of that philosopher but to establish the speaker as an "amateur of abstractions," to provide necessary contrast with the sepulchral meditation of the previous stanzas, and to draw upon philosophy for a little of its color. What Valéry thinks he created is an "apparatus" that each, including its creator, may use as he can. It is plain, therefore, that the philosophical process upon which Cohen concentrated is but matter for a form to Valéry, for a form that means what it is and radiates itself. If the maker of this radiator had been able to define it or its radiance, he would not have had to make it.

"A world of reciprocal relations," as Valéry describes it, his poem is self-contained, rounded by the meeting of the last stanza and the first, made solid by the balance of masses and firm by internal stresses, connected by recurring themes. As massive and tense as "Sailing to Byzantium," it also brings its conflicts to an end in peace. That such constructions, which hold before us all the peace our time can know, are not the only kind of art and not the only kind that pleases us is apparent from many poems which, by no means visions of unity, peace, and better worlds than ours, present our condition by their form. Not final or static but endlessly dynamic, inharmonious, and restless, these forms are less like worlds than inconclusive wars or, to change the metaphor, less like well-wrought urns than fur-lined cups.

That however inharmonious and unresolved, these uneasy structures of incompatibles are aesthetically satisfying and no less radiant than the harmonious worlds we have considered is proved by the terrible sonnets of Hopkins and, less obviously, by "Easter 1916," a vision of becoming, not of being. Easter, a suitable time for rising, for renewing a vision of a "romantic Ireland," once thought "dead and gone," leaves Yeats torn between conservative leanings and heroic ideals. A quarrel between contempt and acceptance or between what he used to think and what he is now almost compelled to think determines a structure true to internal conflict or sitting on the fence. On one hand is his habit of "polite meaningless words" and daily encounters in the street with people he had reason to dislike, one of whom, annihilated by a phrase, "rode our wingèd horse," and another of whom, a "lout," married Maud Gonne, and on the other hand is astonishment at their transformation. More appropriate than real, his acceptance of their heroism fails to quiet fears that "excess" may have bewildered those heroes to the point of doubting England's possible honor. Dissonance and dramatic surprise keep new beauty

257

from being more than "terrible," and we are left with a cup from which our lips seem kept by a lining not unlike the white fur Hopkins thought growing on his lungs, or worse.

Not a container of ashes as the image of the well-wrought urn suggests, such a poem is a cup that, containing living water, pours it out and into us; but our satisfaction, in spite of all that fur, is a problem. Speaking of opposites, Coleridge, as we know, holds that their aesthetic effect is not from balance or neutralization but from creating a third thing in our minds; Baudelaire, inclining to dynamic art, finds beauty "always double, though the impression it produces is one"; and Nicholas of Cusa, whose world was composed of contraries, found them reconciled in God, as, extending his idea to aesthetics, we may find them reconciled in the mind of the beholder. Whether contraries, contradictions, or incompatibles, the warring elements of such a work, evoke a third thing that, like Stevens's So-and-So, "floats in their contention." Depending upon our apprehension of this floating thing, the work is restless and incomplete, like the elements of montage, until the interaction of three elements, one here and two there, produces unity akin to peace; yet the two original elements of this all but harmonious triad, retaining something of their incongruity, allow the form to hint the world we live in.

Both "Easter 1916" and "Le Cimetière Marin," however different in lining or shape, radiate visions of being and process that are not altogether dissimilar. The first with its unconciliated quarrels is no less a form for presenting a daily experience than the second with quarrels settled by a choice from contending opposites. What both these forms produce appears to be the experience of choosing or the idea and feeling of thinking. That such radiance is not uncommon is affirmed by many poems, those in particular of Wallace Stevens, whose "So-and-So" is a good example, but whose "Man With the

Blue Guitar," being more elaborate, is a better. The guitarist's tune, "beyond us, yet ourselves," includes the kinds of poetry.

This sequence of thirty-three short poems, partly the player's meditation and partly the demands of his audience, concerns the claims of imagination and fact. Should tunes upon the blue guitar present things as they are or things transformed as in the mind of Stevens's Lady Lowzen, who thought "what is was other things?" Is art, represented by the guitar and its blueness, a mixture of imagination and green reality as the recurring rhyme of "guitar" and "are" suggests, or is it more of one than the other? Such questions, which have preoccupied Stevens for thirty years or more and have drawn him from his desk in Hartford, are asked and variously answered in these poems, each of which is a way of looking at the problem, holding it up to different lights, or just approaching it. The variety of lights and tones provides dramatic interest as the speakers examine not only the relationships of imagination with fact but those with politics, society, religion, and the artist's personality. As for the central figure of the guitarist, which suggests Picasso's arrangement in blue, now in Chicago, Stevens has neither seen it nor heard of it, or so he told me one day in my parlor.

One is tempted, as many critics have been, to take Stevens's images as signs and his discourse as discourse alone. If we are persuaded that Stevens is writing essays on imagination and reality, we can take this sequence as a treatise, and very intelligent too; but if we do that, finding it saying no more than his other poems say, we have reduced his blues and greens to that "universal hue" he calls "the basic slate." This monotony, which comes of turning poems into prose, is what we might expect; for he is not a composer of monographs on aesthetics or metaphysics but a poet, and his thoughts, pretty much the same from one poem to another, are only their materials. Compelled like Valéry to fill his structure out, Stevens also chose what moved him, but neither his excitement nor its cause is the point of what he made. Not thought but "poetry," as his guitarist observes, "is the subject of the poem," and what he ambiguously calls "the thinking of art" is not thinking about it but the significance of form. If the poem is a "supreme fiction," or something shaped and formed, the matter of his poetry consists of notes toward it.

The form of "The Man With the Blue Guitar" shows tracts of serious bareness and economy along with intrusions by the frivolous, the grotesque, and the bizarre. Repetition and confusion, ironic asides, hesitations followed by momentary assurances and those in turn by unanswerable queries, composing no systematic process, are the shape of thinking things out on the street perhaps or between interruptions in the office. Not to propound a theory of art but to suggest the process of trying to frame one and to embody the experience of trying to know any difficult thing seem the end of this complex design, which, in poem XXV, becomes a world twirled upon the creator's nose:

> His robes and symbols, ai-yi-yi—
> And that-a-way he twirled the thing.

But the noser and the nosed and all their intercourse find a place in a larger world that, although not brought "quite round" in its creator's opinion, is round enough to shape the experience of creating it. The radiance of this imperfect form, like that of "Easter 1916" or the form more like a world of "Le Cimetière Marin," I repeat, appears to be the idea and feeling of thinking, and differences among them or their effects come from varieties of shape, substance, and agreement.

My apprehension of what these poems radiate, though preceded

260

by analysis that I do not display, is not the result of a rational endeavor but rather the more or less sudden result of long acquaintance, improved by analysis. Although what these three poems radiate seems much the same to me, and although I am persuaded that all poems are centered in some fundamental process or state, it is not my opinion that the effects of all are either identical or similar. These three poems may project aspects or qualities of thinking, but other poems project other no less vital states that impression, preceded by analysis, may approach.

The poems of Dylan Thomas, for example, hardly ever approach the feeling of thought or the idea of it. Celebrating the fundamentals of experience, preferably embryonic at first and then both adolescent and mature, these poems embody feelings of considerable variety. Analysis of "Fern Hill," one of the great lyrics of our time, will lay bare the rhythm, diction, and imagery that affect us: the recurrence of "Time" and of "green" and "gold," the confusion of seasons, and the reference to Adam and Eve in their garden. The rhythm, a somewhat "sprung" extension of ballad meter, improves the sense of timeless freedom and freedom from utility while the intrusion of maturity at the end adds distance and pathos to the opening vision and suggests Eden's end. These are parts, of which theme may be the determining element, but it is the Gestalt that moves us first and last. What it gives me is the feeling and idea of being young or rather, because of the last stanza, the more poignant feeling and idea of having been. Echoes of fairy tales, the holiness of dingle and rosy wood, and fears of the Thief in the night conspire to make "In Country Sleep" an embodiment of how it is to be a father. When in a bar one afternoon I told Thomas of these impressions, he was much affected and cried a little, though whether from pain, drink, or agreement I cannot tell.

261

Finnegans Wake, midway between the conditions of poetry and prose, is at once simple and unfathomable, like the letter found by hen in dump. We seem as unable as the interpreters of that letter, whether historians, psychologists, or sociologists, to find what the simple thing is all about, try as we may. The third chapter, which concerns Earwicker's sin in the park, is a case in point. Parallel to that of Adam, Earwicker's sin appears to involve two girls and three soldiers, but whether guilty Earwicker sinned at all or, if so, how, we never know although the matter is subjected to analysis by lawyers, journalists, gossips, and professors, who introduce analogies of the most suggestive kind. The notes that explain the simple action of the tenth chapter, explaining nothing, increase our confusion.

That these confusions are no less functional than the occasional certainties is plain enough. By a circular pattern of monotonous recurrence and endless variety Joyce outlines a world at once clear and obscure. Going on day after day, things repeat themselves, but however great our understanding, their ultimate meaning escapes us. Such certainties and obscurities compose a form which by a concert of elements presents something obvious and mysterious, commonplace and exciting, amusing and tiresome, or life itself and its very sensation. Our complaints about obscurity are vain; for if we could fathom the book entirely, it would lose an effect which depends on partial discovery, increasingly greater as we descend from meaning to meaning, and residual frustration. For Joyce's purpose parts must yield their meaning at once, other parts must yield to effort, and some must baffle us. Our joy at discovering an echo, a relationship, or a complex of meanings belongs no more to the intended effect than the despair of deeper and deeper penetration without arriving at some end. What *Finnegans Wake* seems designed to present is not only the rhythm, texture, and density of life but the experience of trying to understand it. "O life!" says Stephen at the end of the *Portrait*, "I go to encounter for the millionth time the reality of experience." *Finnegans Wake* with its rewards, difficulties, and frustrations, seems the symbol of that endeavor.

As Joyce's brother Stanislaus says of *Ulysses,* and what he says is also true of *Finnegans Wake,* "The whole is one vast symbolic figure." Such figures, however, are so vast that we find it impossible to apprehend them at a glance as we may a plastic object. Equally temporal, the lyric is there on its page, but the novel as a whole is never before us for contemplation as a painting is, and we are forced to contemplate the current part. If wholes are more important than their parts, that is a great disadvantage, greater in the case of symbolist novels than of a simpler kind; for whereas the common novel depends largely upon narrative to carry its meaning and narrative is suitably temporal, the symbolist novel depends less upon sequence of events than upon reflexive relationships among its elements.

These difficulties are the basis of "Spatial Form in Modern Literature," an essay by Joseph Frank, who tries to solve them by translating time into space. The reader of a modern reflexive work, he says, is not only "intended" to apprehend it spatially rather than as a sequence but is compelled to. If this is right, we should be able to apply the attractive idea to music, a form as temporal and reflexive as the symbolist novel, but few would want to. Never making music space, I leave it where it belongs—in time, where, preferring not to confuse the arts, I leave the novel. Extension in time, although a disadvantage of literature perhaps, need not prevent the apprehension it makes difficult. It is true that reflexive relationships would be plainer if displayed in a space that is not too large for apprehension in time, but since they are not, we must rely upon rereading and taking notes for a sense of relationships and of the whole. Although

263

Mr. Frank has put a finger on a difficulty of symbolist fiction, his "spatial form" appears to be a metaphor for an effect of memory, which, spreading all the little it retains before us, seems to make time stop and take shape. To make our memories plain we may draw our metaphors from space.

Notes, memories, and metaphors seem inadequate for a work as large and complex as *Absalom, Absalom!* Faulkner's great novel concerns Quentin's effort to understand the career of Sutpen, the nature of the South, and, beyond these, to realize himself. In his cold room at Cambridge, he tells Shreve what others have told him and he recalls; and those roommates, calling upon imagination, create what must have been. Seeming at first the center of the story, Sutpen finally seems material for fictions as Kurtz serves Marlow in *Heart of Darkness* or as Great Gatsby serves his Carraway. Like Marlow, Quentin is the center, and his mind is both our theater and our factory. More than materials, Sutpen and the South are Quentin or his greater part.

The elements from which Quentin composes his fiction are as familiar as the allusions to *Macbeth, Hamlet, Faust,* and the myths of Greece that help to make it deeper and more general. Sutpen's house, the central image, is intended by that symbolic hero to surpass the mansion in Virginia where he suffered his childish trauma. Designed to shelter a great family, constructed in fury, almost attaining magnificence, the great house falls into decay at last and final destruction. At once dream and façade to Sutpen, to Quentin this house is a symbol of a South that the houses of Sartoris and Snopes do not suggest, and to us, bringing parts together and aligning feelings, it presents the troubles of Quentin and Rosa. There are other recurrent images: the horseman, the tombstone, black and white, and enclosures (dusty office and attic, perfumed boudoir, and dormitory room), but of such images we need consider only one.

Memories of wistaria, serving to connect Rosa, Quentin's father, and the South's brief summer, carry much of the burden of Quentin's nostalgia and despair. Shreve, in his overcoat, looking out at northern snow, may be cynical about wistaria, but to Rosa, Quentin, and the reader the flower becomes what Rosa calls a "globed concentrate."

Her metaphorical extravagance, recurring metaphors of fever and swamp, ponderous sentences without definite shape, actions in slow motion—all these are expressive devices that help create the feeling of nightmare. That thick atmosphere, giving the vision its quality, is one of the principal elements of the form. It may be that dream, logically considered, is a way of showing that Sutpen, Rosa, and the South lived a dream that Quentin is redreaming, that "too much, too long remembering" is nightmare. We can be certain, however, that Rosa's incubus oppresses us as it obsesses Quentin and that reading the book is our nightmare. As in the worst of fever dreams, we are compelled to endure a thing again and again.

The structure—if I may take my metaphor from space—is circular. Like Conrad's idiot boy in *The Secret Agent,* the book describes "circles, circles, circles: innumerable circles, concentric, eccentric; a coruscating whirl of circles that by their tangled multitude of repeated curves, uniformity of form, and confusion of intersecting lines suggested a rendering of cosmic chaos, the symbolism of a mad art attempting the inconceivable." Around Quentin as center, Rosa's story of Sutpen describes the inner circle. Next, describing a larger circle around that center, comes the version of Quentin's grandfather and beyond it that of his father. Then comes Shreve's hypothetical construction and finally that of Quentin himself. These concentric circles, however, are less circles than segments; for none is complete and each at another radius repeats segments of the others.

"Maybe nothing ever happens once and is finished," says Quentin. "Maybe happen is never once but like ripples maybe on water after the pebble sinks, the ripples moving on, spreading . . . across its surface . . . to the old ineradicable rhythm." This two-dimensional image, which suggests the structure and its effect, is less exact than Rosa's three-dimensional "globy and complete instant" that "repeats (repeats? creates, reduces to a fragile evanescent iridescent sphere) all of space and time and massy earth." With all it carries of character, image, feeling, attitude, and tone, this globy structure approximates the form.

Being from Vermont or some other place, we may have little concern with the South or with the troubles of a Southerner; but such indifference is no real loss, for, as Tonio Kröger says, "what an artist talks about is never the main point; it is the raw material in and for itself indifferent, out of which with bland and serene mastery, he creates the work of art." Raised to generality, Faulkner's local matters, far from being the point of the book, become all memory and guilt. Another nightmare of circling history, *Absalom, Absalom!* is a form for presenting not only a sense of times and place but, it seems to me, the horrors of obsession.

My way of approaching such forms and their radiance, a cooperation of analysis and impression, must displease partisans of either method, but, while lacking the assurance of logic or faction, my way seems suitable enough for something at once articulated and indeterminate. The analyses in this chapter, displaying some of the parts that most affect my impression of the whole, are necessarily selective; for to be nearly complete, the analysis of a form as complex as *Absalom, Absalom!* would have to be longer than that novel; and at the end of a dissection so immoderate the whole would disappear among its parts. Impression alone, on the other hand, would stray without the restraint of parts that only analysis can disclose. There-fore, impression based upon a text made apparent and familiar by moderate analysis appears a decent compromise.

If forms are symbols and symbols, though definite, are indefinite in effect, I cannot be positive about meanings; if forms are intricate analogies for something unexpressed, my impression of their radiance can be no more than an attempt at telling what forms are like. My inconclusive conclusions, no more than reports of possibility, may be challenged by those who are either more or less familiar with the text than I or more or less sensitive to its shape and quality. When I say that the radiance of "Sailing to Byzantium" is an experience of timelessness in time, that *Finnegans Wake* is a vision of trying to understand, or that *Absalom, Absalom!* is a form for all obsession, I am more tentative than I may seem since by brief, convenient *is* in those places I mean *suggests to me* after some acquaintance with the object and some reflection. Such conclusions, neither exhaustive nor exclusive, are not attempts to reduce the nondiscursive to dis-course or to define the indefinable but to report an apprehension that may yield to another tomorrow.

A friend of mine who attended a lecture at the Sorbonne came away with the conviction that all the professor had to say was "de ce point de vue-ci" and "de ce point de vue-là." Amazed among my *buts, howevers,* and *maybes,* I see myself in that professor, and all I can be sure of is what Valéry, leaving the Sorbonne, proclaimed: *"Il n'y a pas de vrai sens d'un texte"*—a symbolist work has no certain meaning.

DEDICATED
TO SAINT GREGORY THAUMATURGUS

Index

271

Hersey, John, *The Marmot Drive,* 100 f.
"Hollow Men, The" (Eliot), 4, 132
Hopkins, Gerard Manley, 237; sonnet on spring, 116; *re* landscape, 130; use of ambiguities, 232; distortions of syntax, 232 f.; "terrible sonnets," 232 ff., 257; invention of a tense, 233; "inscape," 242
— "The Blessed Virgin Compared to the Air We Breathe," 61; "Carrion Comfort," 232; "God's Grandeur," 233; "Spelt from Sibyl's Leaves," 194, 232; "Wreck of the Deutschland," 114
Hulme, T. E., "vital complexities," 245 f.; "Notes on Language and Style," 102

Ibsen, Henrik, *The Master Builder,* 133 f.; *The Wild Duck,* 124 f.
Idea of a Theater, The (Fergusson), 145
Idea of Nature (Collingwood), 33
Illuminations (Rimbaud), 54
"In Country Sleep" (Thomas), 261
Inferno (Dante), 197
Integration of Personality (Jung), 129 f.
Interpretation of Dreams, The (Freud), 64 ff., 168 ff., 185
"In the White Giant's Thigh" (Thomas), 208
Intruder in the Dust (Faulkner), 165
"Invitation au Voyage, L'" (Baudelaire), 135
Isis Unveiled (Blavatsky), 57
It Isn't This Time of Year at All! (Gogarty), 182

James, Henry, 12; *The Ambassadors,* 230, 243
Johnson, Samuel, *re* Donne's metaphor, 35
Joyce, James, and Hermes, 56 f.; influence of Flaubert, 76; portrayal of symbolic cuckold, 111 f.; desert as symbol, 133; use of dream as symbol, 170 f.; use of parallels, 185 f.; use of the pun, 206 f.;

use of recurrent theme, 224-29; theory of symbolic form, 239 ff.
— *Chamber Music,* 76; "Clay," 128; "The Dead," 224 ff.; *Dubliners,* 224; "An Encounter," 15; *Finnegans Wake,* 59, 206 f., 262 f.; *A Portrait of the Artist as a Young Man,* 57 ff., 76 ff., 91, 170, 207, 217, 231, 239 ff.; *Stephen Hero,* 76; *Ulysses,* 57 f., 149 f., 170 f., 195-202
Judgment of Paris (Vidal), 187
Jung, Carl G., *re* symbols, 16, 66; *Integration of Personality,* 129 f.

Kafka, Franz, *The Castle,* 139-41; *The Metamorphosis,* 63 f.; *The Trial,* 174 f.
Keats, John, 20; "Ode on a Grecian Urn," 213, 251
Kirkegaard, Soren, 131
Klein, A. M., 171
Koffka, Kurt, 244
Köhler, Wolfgang, 244

Lady Chatterley's Lover (Lawrence), 112
"Lake Isle of Innisfree, The" (Yeats), 251
Langer, Susanne K., 217, 237; *Feeling and Form,* 7 f., 247
Language and Myth (Cassirer), 8 f., 177
Language and Reality (Urban), 11
"Last Looks at the Lilacs" (Stevens), 63
Lawrence, D. H., *re* his own symbolism, 14; *re* fruit as symbol, 127
— *Birds, Beasts, and Flowers,* 127; *Lady Chatterley's Lover,* 112; *The Man Who Died,* 180; *The Plumed Serpent,* 189; *Studies in Classic American Literature,* 22
Laxdale Hall (Linklater), 187
Lévi, Eliphas, *Le Dogme de la Haute Magie,* 54
Lewis, C. S., *The Allegory of Love,* 31 ff.
Light in August (Faulkner), 166
Linklater, Eric, *Laxdale Hall,* 187

277